Hamps'

www.ha.

O

SOUTH
DIVISION
FAREHAM
282715

05. MAR 09.

SdA
(TWM)

TOT

02

JUL 02

08. JAN 03.

08. MAY 03.

07. JUL 03

942.037092

GREEN

This book is due for return on or before the last date shown above: it may, subject to the book not being reserved by another reader, be renewed by personal application, post, or telephone, quoting this date and details of the book.

**HAMPSHIRE COUNTY COUNCIL**
**County Library**

100% recycled paper

DIV.
Account   12/01

*In a sense, this book is about fathers;*
*their successes, failures, their influence and their legacies.*
*This is dedicated, for all they have given me, to Alec Green,*
*Stan Burr, Peter Coventry, John Tweedy Smith (and, of course, to my Mum)*

# THE BLACK PRINCE

## DAVID GREEN

TEMPUS

First published 2001

PUBLISHED IN THE UNITED KINGDOM BY:

Tempus Publishing Ltd
The Mill, Brimscombe Port
Stroud, Gloucestershire GL5 2QG
www.tempus-publishing.com

PUBLISHED IN THE UNITED STATES OF AMERICA BY:

Tempus Publishing Inc.
2 Cumberland Street
Charleston, SC 29401
1-888-313-2665
www.arcadiapublishing.com

Tempus books are available in France and Germany
from the following addresses:

Tempus Publishing Group
21 Avenue de la République
37300 Joué-lès-Tours
FRANCE

Tempus Publishing Group
Gustav-Adolf-Straße 3
99084 Erfurt
GERMANY

British Library Cataloguing in Publication Data.
A catalogue record for this book is available from the British Library.

ISBN 0 7524 1989 7

Typesetting and origination by Tempus Publishing.
PRINTED AND BOUND IN GREAT BRITAIN

# CONTENTS

# LIST OF ILLUSTRATIONS

# ACKNOWLEDGEMENTS

I should like to thank Michael Jones who first introduced me to Edward of Woodstock, and Alison McHardy and Tony Goodman who suggested how I might get to know him better. Tony put me in touch with Jonathan Reeve of Tempus to whom I am very grateful for his enthusiasm and support.

Claire Taylor and Simon Constantine have read parts of the typescript, improved many aspects of it and shaped more than they know — thanks poppets.

I am particularly grateful to Andrew Midgely for his help and professional expertise with many of the photographs and his remarkable willingness to head off to far-flung parts of the country in search of 'BP-related' sites.

My thanks to the past, present and future students of the History Department of the University of Nottingham and most especially to the very splendid Jeannie Alderdice, Paul Bracken, Simon Constantine, Mike Evans, Paul Evans, Jon Porter, Kevin Sorrentino and Claire Taylor for their friendship, support, and thirst that made it all worthwhile.

To Tweed and Ray (my fellow 'ghosts in the library') who've taught me what's important, usually with glass in hand, my thanks although by now I don't suppose it should be necessary, and love to my sisters, Kate Green and Caroline Hamilton.

I'm indebted to all those who have shared the Black Prince with me, especially those whose lectures and seminars may have focused rather more on Edward of Woodstock than they should have and who have often made me reassess my opinions or forced me to look at aspects of his life and career in different ways. In particular thanks are due to my Hundred Years War special subject group at the University of Birmingham.

# PREFACE

The need for a new biography of Edward, prince of Wales and Aquitaine may not be self-evident. What more can or needs to be said about this figure whose reputation and character is so well known but has been so shaped and shrouded by chivalric myth, who has been seen as a brutal but no less shadowy representation of the worst and at the same time most praiseworthy characteristics of the late medieval period? In part, it may be enough to say that it is over 20 years since the last biography of the Black Prince was published, concluding a flurry of interest in Edward of Woodstock that was on a scale which had not been seen since the end of the previous century when his qualities were valued more highly.[1] Much of the commentary in the intervening years has been negative. The impression, although not one often given by his biographers, has tended to be of a violent, grasping, profligate and arrogant man. That the prince could be all these things is not in doubt, but there was much more to the man that won his spurs in the vanguard at Crécy aged 16, who married for love and not for politics at 31 years (an extraordinary age for the heir-apparent), and who formed a vibrant court, the envy of Europe, at Bordeaux. For a man who was so much a product of his own time, he has been judged to a great degree by the standards of a later age. The success of a late medieval prince was determined in no small way by military talent, his ability to secure adequate finances from his estates, the successful distribution of those revenues in the form of patronage and as a demonstration of power, and pride in his lineage and achievements. That such priorities might be seen to descend into violence, avarice, profligacy and arrogance, is to some extent merely a matter of vocabulary. The intention of this book is not to provide a post-revisionist picture of the Black Prince, but to place him in context, to place him in the milieu in which he was, until the last years, almost effortlessly comfortable.

Recent years have seen the publication of a considerable body of scholarship concerning the late medieval period in general, notably the Hundred Years War and the fourteenth century in particular. The rekindling of interest in medieval military history in conjunction with extensive work on the chivalric ethic has refocused interest on Edward the Black Prince. A central concern of this book will be the campaigns and expeditions which he undertook in 1346, 1355-6, 1359-60 and 1367, and the contemporaneous developments in matters such as strategy, tactics and recruitment; in essence the 'professionalisation' of the English (or Anglo-Welsh/Anglo-Gascon) armies. The Black Prince did not fight in a strategic or tactical vacuum, nor were his methods of recruitment, funding and equipping his soldiers conducted in an environment outside the experiences of his father, his commanders and the structures of local and national government. Indeed, it was those structures and the experiences of many of those that comprised the force which was victorious at Crécy that provided the platform for future success and established the English and the heir-apparent among the finest soldiers in Europe.

Of additional and particular interest is the period of the principality of Aquitaine (1362-71), which has been greatly under-represented in English works on the war. This and the reopening of hostilities in 1369 is too important an event to cast aside as simply the consequence of the overbearing pride of the spoiled heir-apparent.

This book has developed partly as a consequence of my doctoral thesis on 'The Household and Military Retinue of Edward the Black Prince', and if what follows seems not always to be as much a biography of Edward himself but of those that surrounded him, then it can be attributed to that research and also to a deliberate attempt to highlight the collective and individual importance of that exceptional company.

# 1 THREE EDWARDS

Edward, prince of Wales and Aquitaine, duke of Cornwall, earl of Chester, founder knight of the Order of the Garter, hero of Crécy, victor at Poitiers, the Black Prince, died on 8 June 1376, Trinity Sunday, the feast day for which he had particular reverence. It was recorded that the news was received in England and across the Channel with great sadness and mourning and not only for the sake of form. His life and death exemplified many of the incongruities of the political milieu in which he lived and his career mirrored the triumphs and disasters of the nation that he represented. Much of his brief life was characterised by war and as the term 'Hundred Years War', the conflict to which the prince dedicated himself, has been misapplied to a punctuated confrontation that lasted at least 116 years,[1] so likewise the name by which Edward of Woodstock is most commonly known is uncertain in origin and in meaning. It was in common usage by the end of the sixteenth century. Leland named him as such in his *Itinerary* and Holinshed used the term in his *Chronicles*, which may have been a source used by Shakespeare.[2] The idea that the name derived from a penchant for black armour remains unsubstantiated, as does the theory that the name was of French origin, brought on by the brutal raids and his victories in battle. Nonetheless, the prince's reputation in France was certainly 'black' and is, for example, apparent in the Apocalypse tapestries of Louis of Anjou commissioned in 1373 and which are said to depict Edward III as a demon followed by his five sons. In a subsequent panel, the primary horseman is said to represent the Black Prince. In this series of images, the war perpetrated by the prince and his father 'is rendered monstrous, a virulent plague sent by the heavens to punish mankind',[3] with the Plantagenets, a dark instrument of divine (or diabolical) judgement. Considerably later, King Charles VI says, according to Shakespeare, prior to Agincourt, that they must fear Henry V because:

> he is bred out of that bloody strain That haunted us in our familiar paths:
> Witness our too much memorable shame
> When Cressy battle fatally was struck,
> And all our princes captiv'd by the hand
> Of that black name, Edward, Black Prince of Wales;
> While that his mountain sire, on mountain standing,
> Up in the air, crown'd with the golden sun,
> Saw his heroical seed, and smiled to see him,
> Mangle the work of nature and deface
> The patterns that by God and by French fathers
> Had twenty years been made.[4]

Such comments, made over 200 years after the death of the prince, may be seen as a mark of the impact made by both Edward III and his eldest son on the collective memory and imagination of the country. Politically and in terms of 'national' reputation, although such a concept was probably alien to the prince, the years from 1346-67 were unquestionably triumphant, and by contrast with the collapse of English power in France and the fractures of the Wars of the Roses in the fifteenth century, there was undoubtedly an Edwardian 'Golden Age' to which those in the sixteenth century could look back.

His reputation, contradictory still, was set by the sixteenth century if not earlier, or indeed before his death. That reputation was indicative of the troubled times through which the prince lived and the stark contrasts between his triumphs at the battles of Crécy, Poitiers and Nájera, and the debacle of the failure of the principality of Aquitaine and loss after 1368/9 of nearly all that the English had gained in the years since the war had begun. The contrast was intrinsic also in the prince's health and character, and furthermore was evident in the changing nature of the chivalric ethic with which the prince was associated from a very young age and of which he had become an exemplar by the time of his death. The England of 1376 was not so very different from the England of 1330, but her star had risen and fallen a very long way in the intervening years. She had suffered the ravages of the Black Death, been subjected to heavy financial and military burdens and many of her southern coastal towns had been raided. She also lost the man who had seemed certain to be her future king.

Edward was born at Woodstock on 15 June 1330, the eldest child of Edward III and Philippa of Hainault. There is no reason to believe that the future Black Prince had a troubled childhood, but the country was certainly suffering the consequences of the reign of Edward II. The story of the deposition (often with grisly embellishment) is well known and the shadow of the event stretched over the English monarchy and, significantly, marked the career of Richard II, the prince's son, who became the second English king to suffer the fate in the fourteenth century.

When Edward III came to the throne in 1327, the country had been wracked by civil strife and war with Scotland. The rule of Edward II, characterised by the overbearing influence of the king's favourites, Piers Gaveston and later the Despensers, and the rebellion of Thomas of Lancaster, paved the way for opposition from an unlikely quarter. For much of her reign, her husband and his courtiers treated Queen Isabella abominably. As a French princess, she lived under constant suspicion of treason, her lands were seized and servants dismissed. Only when the opportunity for making a peace treaty arose did her position as sister of the king of France make her useful. The agreement that resulted from her negotiations stipulated that, as had his father and grandfather, the king should do homage and fealty for the duchy of Gascony, the main area of contention in Anglo-French relations. Edward refused but sent his son, the future Edward III, in his place. Once out of the direct influence of the king and his supporters and with control of the heir, Isabella refused to return to England until and unless the Despensers were removed from power. Isabella was not the only person the king had offended and she sought allies among the English exiles abroad. Of these, Roger Mortimer was the most notable but they also included the earls of Richmond and Kent and the bishops of Hereford, Winchester and Norwich. Additional support was gained by marrying the future king to Philippa, daughter of the count of Hainault, in exchange for a small band of soldiers who accompanied the rebels on their return to England. Once Isabella landed, support for the king dissolved, most significantly in London. Edward II was abandoned by most of his officials and household, he fled to Wales with the younger Despenser and was captured in Glamorgan by Henry of Lancaster. Despenser was executed after a trial at Hereford in which he was convicted of being a heretic and sodomite; his genitals were hacked off and burned in front of him.

The king was summoned to parliament in January 1327, but refused to attend. Opposition grew further and feeling hardened against him. The Archbishop of Canterbury declared that as the magnates, clergy and people no longer regarded Edward as such, he was no longer king. Edward, greatly distressed, received the news at Kenilworth where he resigned the throne in favour of his son. The question remains as to whether he was deposed or abdicated.

The last days of Edward at Berkeley Castle have been told many times since the story and manner of his murder originated with the chronicler, Geoffrey Le Baker. Perhaps more interesting is the tale told by a Genoese priest, Manuel Fieschi, who claimed to have met Edward after his supposed death and heard his confession. According to Fieschi, a papal notary, Edward had escaped from Berkeley castle, travelled to Ireland, France, Cologne and then to Italy, where he became a hermit. In 1338, whilst in Cologne himself, Edward III met a man calling himself William le Galeys who claimed to be his father. The claim was not taken seriously, but Edward's reaction to his father's 'murderers' was muted, and many of them and their families found favour in the 1330s and '40s. Perhaps the king needed to use such resources as he had in terms of manpower and influence in the localities, and had witnessed the folly of losing the support of his nobles. Perhaps he had not cared for his father, or perhaps there was no need to victimise those who were guilty of no crime since his father was still alive.

Edward III was fourteen when he was crowned, and as a result of his minority, a regency council was established initially centred around Henry of Lancaster. However, it was not long before the king's mother and Roger Mortimer made their influence felt. Mortimer was created earl of March with the estates of the elder Despenser and the earl of Arundel, and in his arrogance and avarice outdid Edward II's former favourites. The new administration was not a success either at home or abroad. The 1327 campaign against the Scots was a disaster and resulted in the 'Shameful Peace' of Northampton. Opposition against Mortimer and Isabella grew, first under the leadership of Lancaster, the earls of Kent and Norfolk, but it was quickly and brutally stamped out. The blind earl of Lancaster was forced to come to terms and Kent, after abandoning his former allies, was executed for his pains. In the event, just as opposition to the former king had come from within the palace, so too did the most significant challenge to Mortimer and Isabella.

In October 1330, the Council was summoned to Nottingham. It was there that the young king decided to make his move. His conspirators, including William Montague and Robert Ufford, made their way up through the labyrinth of tunnels that led into the castle, seized 'gentle' Mortimer despite the protestations of Isabella, and with that, the coup was effectively over. Mortimer was taken to London, tried for treason and executed in a

1    *Edward III and his family. Left to right: Thomas of Woodstock, duke of Gloucester; Edward III; Philippa of Hainault; Edward the Black Prince. This drawing was traced from fresco paintings accidentally discovered in 1800 behind a coating of wood panelling at St Stephen's Chapel, Westminster and which were walled up again immediately after copies and tracings had been taken from them. The date of the frescoes is about 1356, before the battle of Poitiers, as indicated by the presence of the King's youngest son. The paintings were lost in the fire that consumed both Houses of Parliament in 1834*

manner not unlike that accorded the younger Despenser. Isabella retired from private life and Edward III began to rule in fact as well as name.[5]

The Black Prince was, of course, unaware of all this but it may be that his birth on 15 June 1330, combined with Mortimer's increasingly antagonistic and threatening attitude, encouraged the Nottingham coup and thereby brought an element of security to the realm that had been lacking since the death of Edward I. In addition to the domestic upheavals of the reign of Edward II and the disruption of the minority of Edward III, conflict with Scotland and France presaged the hostilities that would shape the prince's life and career. Those conflicts prepared the English for the war in France. The long shadow of the defeat at Bannockburn exacerbated trends that had been evident since Edward I's wars in Wales and Scotland and led to an increasingly professional army recruited to implement a range of particular strategic and tactical plans. Such plans would be further developed and the army tempered for the French wars when Edward III sought to undo the indignity of the treaty of Northampton in the early years of his personal rule.

Anglo-French hostilities had been endemic from at least the reign of Henry II. The relative positions and the disparity in feudal authority between the king of England,

2 *Chester, Dee bridge. The original bridge was rebuilt in stone by the prince's administration*

who happened also to be duke of Gascony, and the king of France were unclear, and the subject of protracted legal wrangling after matters were formalised, if only theoretically, by Louis IX and Henry III in 1259 at the treaty of Paris. In the intervening years the duchy was confiscated by the king of France on several occasions, military action had broken out more than once, most notably in the War of St Sardos (1325-5), and relations were barely cordial at the best of times. In this context, the war that erupted in 1337 was merely part of a broader conflict that began much earlier and certainly did not conclude with the fall of Bordeaux in 1453. However, there were differences and distinctions in the nature of the hostilities that involved Edward III and his son from those that had transpired earlier. The most significant of these followed from the death of the last Capetian king, Charles IV, in 1328. Edward III and Charles of Navarre both had better claims to the French throne than Philip VI who became first Valois king of France, but Edward's was transmitted through his mother and was thus invalidated by Salic law, or at least prevented by Salic law as it was formulated by French lawyers in the years after 1328. Whether Edward seriously expected to sit on the French throne is open to question; it may be that he used the claim to the crown of France as a bargaining tool to re-establish sovereign rule over Gascony. In any case, the English claim to the French throne, although not made formally until 1340, changed the nature of the conflict and moved it onto a level where peace or at least the absence of war was more difficult to maintain.

This was the environment in which the prince was raised: a legacy of domestic strife, a deposed and possibly murdered grandfather and a king and father seeking to regain authority and military prestige for the throne after years of disgrace and disruption. The reconstruction of the prince's career must be set before such a contradictory background and perhaps appropriately such a reconstruction is dependent on a variety of not always complementary sources.

Such sources are numerous although often problematic. It has long been held that the evidence of chivalric and other chronicles is unreliable if not deliberately mendacious and more recent studies have relied rightly on governmental and administrative documentation as the basis for their conclusions. Nonetheless, the Black Prince's

*3   Chester cathedral*

reputation was shaped by contemporary literary sources and those written soon after his death and the popular conception of his character remains bound up with them.[6] Such chivalric characteristics and qualities as the prince was believed to have exemplified were considered worthy and laudable up until at least the end of the nineteenth century, resulting in a plethora of biographies, plays and other tributes. One of the most striking of these being an equestrian bronze unveiled in 1903. It was commissioned for Leeds in 1894, a year after the acquisition of city status. Thomas Brock designed and cast the statue. He was a noted sculptor who made the statue of Queen Victoria outside Buckingham Palace and designed the queen's head on the coins of the realm. The Black Prince was chosen as he was thought to represent a range of admirable virtues including chivalry, courage, democracy and good governance [see fig. **5**].

Edward was therefore destined to become a chivalric icon because the main sources for his character, if not his career, are the chronicles of Jean Froissart and the biography composed by Chandos Herald.[7] That these portraits were flattering, if not encomia, is not in doubt. Nor can it be questioned that this was the milieu in which the nobility and aristocracy wished to be seen to exist, and in some cases did so. According to Froissart, and the anonymous herald of Sir John Chandos, the prince's days both on and away from the battlefield exemplified chivalric virtues, and he was the cynosure of knightly skills in hunting, feasting, jousting and 'courtly love'. As such, they were deliberately selective in their choice of information. Chandos Herald makes no mention of Roger Clarendon and John de Galeis, the former who was and the latter who may have been the prince's illegitimate sons, or the colourful past of Edward's wife, Joan the 'Fair Maid' of Kent.[8] Neither does he discuss the siege (or sack) of Limoges, although by contrast Froissart paints a vivid portrait. Rather, the Black Prince was described as:

> This noble Prince [who] . . . from the day of his birth cherished no thought but loyalty, nobleness, valour and goodness, and was imbued with prowess. Of such nobleness was the Prince that he wished all the days of his life to set his whole intent on maintaining justice and right.[9]

These were the traits of an ideal prince, an ideal knight and entirely in keeping with those values expressed by such as the author of the probably contemporary tale of *Sir Gawain and the Green Knight*. The Arthurian ideal there described was one that found favour in the court and was developed by Edward III in his putative military organisation, the Round Table, and later found form in the Order of the Garter. This chivalric/Arthurian atmosphere coincided with the revival of alliterative poetry, such as *Sir Gawain*, and many such works may have been created in the Lancashire/Cheshire region. The palatinate of Cheshire was the first major estate granted to the prince and links with the earldom were evident in the composition of the prince's household and military retinue. In several campaigns, the bulk of his expeditionary forces were recruited from the area and some of his most high-ranking officials and military associates lived in the region or held land there. It thus provided an audience and milieu for chivalrous writing and it has been argued that the works of alliterative revival could have been encouraged by or written for 'expatriate' careerists from Cheshire, such as the professional soldiers Hugh Calveley (see fig. **4** for tomb in Bunbury church), Robert Knolles and Sir Thomas Wetenhale, seneschal of the Rouergue, when they lived and fought with the prince in Gascony and elsewhere.[10]

Other literary sources may also provide other references to the prince and to his followers. It has been suggested that the anonymous poem *Wynnere and Wastoure* could refer to the Black Prince. According to one interpretation, it is concerned with the economic problems of the day and involves representations of Edward III and the Black Prince along with allegories of the papacy and the mendicant orders (Wynnere), and the nobility and the soldiery (Wastoure). It may have influenced William Langland. Lines 72-5 may be a description of the prince's funeral achievements.

> With ane helme one his hede, ane hatte appon lofte,
> And one heghe one the hatte ane hattfull beste,
> A lighte lebarde and a longe, lokande full kene,
> Yarked alle of yalowe golde in full yape wyse.[11]

4    *Tomb of Hugh Calveley, Bunbury church, Cheshire. The Cheshire* routier, *probably the cousin of Robert Knolles whom he often fought alongside, served Jean de Montfort in Brittany and in Spain with and against Enrique of Trastamara and became something of an expert in Iberian affairs. He fought at Poitiers and by the time of the prince's death had been granted an annuity of 200 marks. He died in 1394 and Froissart described his life as 'the happy triumph of prowess over lineage'*

Mention of the prince's arms of peace, the three ostrich feathers, has also brought some to the conclusion that the poem must refer to Edward of Woodstock. However, it might also refer to any number of the sons of Edward III or indeed Richard II, Roger Clarendon or Henry Bolingbroke; many members of the royalty and aristocracy of Europe used the ostrich feather device. Intriguingly, it has also been suggested that the second knight may be one of the members of the Wingfield or de la Pole families, both of whom were closely linked to the Black Prince [see figs **18, 21, 22, 24**]. The poet also rails against Sir William Shareshull, chief justice of the realm and close associate of the prince of Wales.[12]

At the age of sixteen, Edward, who was to become the Black Prince (although not in his lifetime), set sail for France and was knighted on landing there. The campaign that followed will be discussed below, as will the battle that concluded the *chevauchée*, the wide-scale, destructive, fast moving raid that characterised English military strategy in France in this period. The victory at Crécy in 1346 established the prince as a chivalric exemplar and the glory of that success, much increased by the triumph at Poitiers ten years later, drew men to his service in large numbers. The territorial settlement of the treaty of Brétigny (1360) provided Edward with a principality comprising nearly a third of France and real status on the European stage. The result of such military success and chivalric glamour has left us with a picture of the man probably far removed from reality, being little more than a blueprint of the ideal knight.

The picture that such evidence paints shows that the foundation of chivalric achievement was military ability, and consequently there is little to choose between the image of the Black Prince as a chivalrous knight and the Black Prince as a victorious general. This was not a static period however, in terms of an appreciation either of chivalry or military virtue. The very character of the chivalric ethic was in a state of flux as both the structure of the aristocracy altered, and more prosaically but no less significantly, the means by which armies were recruited, organised and fought. Such a fluid state was compounded and encouraged by a range of social, economic and political forces that shaped and distorted late medieval society.

Of these, plague was one of the most significant. The emergence and impact of the Black Death has long been held to have changed the conditions in which people lived, both noble and peasant, and their conception of the world about them. That it also acted as a catalyst to a variety of existing trends is also widely accepted. Of these, for example, the collapse of the feudal/manorial system had been evident for some time, but the scale of mortality in the plague years after 1348 broke many of the few remaining bonds that tied men to the soil. That the government in England tried repeatedly to re-establish these bonds is probably indicative of the ineffectiveness of such legislation as the Statute of Labourers. The introduction of sumptuary and game laws later in the century may be indicative of similar forces at work attempting to shore up the borders of a social system that if not destroyed was almost fatally wounded by the Black Death. The breakdown of the land-service nexus also had implications for the army. Again this was not a new phenomenon, but it is significant that the Crécy-Calais campaign of 1346-7 was the last major expedition recruited with a substantial 'feudal' element. In its place developed a paid, although not standing, army. Mercenaries also were, of course, nothing new, but after 1347 in England all members of the army received at least nominal payment for military service. The distinction between a

5   *Leeds statue, Leeds city square*

mercenary and a professional soldier could sometimes be vague and the 'mercenary' aspect of the chivalric classes was very apparent in the Black Prince's retinue; professional soldiers were, for example, a core component of the army that he led to Spain in 1367. To provide a literary comparison, there may be analogies to draw with the character of Geoffrey Chaucer's knight, as some have interpreted him as a *routier*, a cynical mercenary, rather than a 'parfait gentil knight'.[13] Whether or not this is an accurate assessment of *the Knight*, it is certainly the case that the aristocracy and the institution of knighthood were increasingly the targets of literary and physical attack both in England and France throughout the later years of the fourteenth century. Outbreaks of social unrest proceeded from the Black Death to the *Jacquerie*, to the Peasants' Revolt and combined in later years with English failures in the French campaign. The motivation behind these events was very different and should not in all cases be seen as part of some growing class consciousness (although the Peasants' Revolt had decidedly revolutionary overtones). Nor should the association with the Black Death be seen as a direct link or indeed reason for rebellion. The plague may have created the conditions whereby *a* Peasants' Revolt was more likely, or indeed could take place at all, but it did not create the revolt. By contrast, in France, opposition to the knightly aristocracy was not simply the result of 'feudal' oppression but a reaction to the defeats at Crécy and, particularly, at Poitiers, which were attributed to the failure of the chivalry of France to fulfil adequately their traditional martial role.[14]

The role of chivalry in the person and retinue of the Black Prince mirrors the part that it played more generally in the fourteenth century phases of the Hundred Years War. The prince's retinue encompassed the aristocracy at its greatest extent in terms of military and chivalric ranks and titles. This 'community', noble and otherwise, was bound together by a variety of ties in Edward III's campaigns and chivalry was not the least of these. The clearest manifestation of the combination of chivalry and royal policy was in the foundation of the Order of the Garter in 1348. The prince and a number of the members of his retinue were important members of that Order.

Chivalry, at root a combination of Christian and warrior ideals, had strong religious connotations and was a guiding ethos among the members of the prince's retinue and within his household. However, in order to examine the nature and character of that ethos one is required to use sources that are by no means reliable. Nonetheless, they convey an image that the aristocracy wished for itself and which, to an extent, governed their behaviour. Chivalry provided the Black Prince, his household and retinue with a collective identity within that greater bond of international knighthood, which, although weakening, still had a part to play in continental relations.

The chivalry of the fourteenth century was not chivalry as it is commonly viewed, through a Victorian filter, just as many of the buildings and stylised details of the Gothic Revival have little to do with the practicalities and underlying philosophy and theology of medieval Perpendicular architecture. Many, if not all, of the military aristocracy (in its widest sense and including the broad body of 'professional' soldiery), considered themselves chivalrous, but it was not a chivalry that would sit easily on the canvas of a Pre-Raphaelite painting. This was a 'Chivalrous Society' only in a highly restricted class sense. Chivalry was founded on caste solidarity and mutual self-interest and was self-sustaining because it justified the primacy of the ruling order and conveyed real benefits to those who

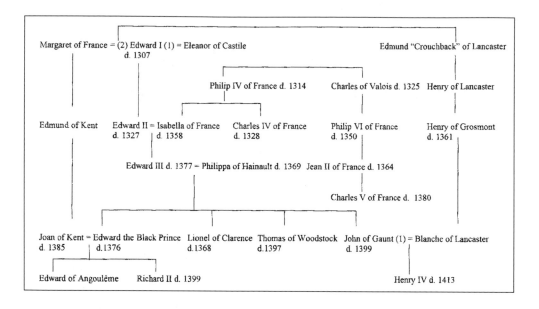

Margaret of France = (2) Edward I (1) = Eleanor of Castile        Edmund "Crouchback" of Lancaster
d. 1307

Philip IV of France d. 1314     Charles of Valois d. 1325   Henry of Lancaster

Edmund of Kent    Edward II = Isabella of France    Charles IV of France    Philip VI of France    Henry of Grosmont
d. 1327   d. 1358       d. 1328       d. 1350       d. 1361

Edward III d. 1377 = Philippa of Hainault d. 1369   Jean II of France d. 1364

Charles V of France d. 1380

Joan of Kent = Edward the Black Prince   Lionel of Clarence   Thomas of Woodstock   John of Gaunt (1) = Blanche of Lancaster
d. 1385    d.1376       d.1368       d.1397       d. 1399

Edward of Angoulême      Richard II d. 1399                   Henry IV d. 1413

*6    Plantagenet and Valois family trees*

practised it. Consequently, for much of the prince's lifetime, anti-French propaganda had little effect on the aristocracy since the chivalric elite was an international order, membership of which transcended national boundaries. In addition, for many on both sides of the Channel, there had been shared military experiences, perhaps in the crusades in Prussia, and there were kinship ties between a great number of families. In the context of the Hundred Years War, one reason that this war occurred was due to such ties between the families of Plantagenet and Valois.[15]

# 2 FORMATIVE YEARS
## SEA BATTLES AND SIEGES (1330-45)

The prince's infancy has not left a surfeit of records, and information concerning his childhood is relatively sketchy. We do know that news of the prince's birth at Woodstock on 16 June 1330 so delighted Edward III that he rewarded the yeoman who told him of it with a pension of 40 marks a year.[1] The prince's first biographer, Chandos Herald, tells us nothing about his early years and merely lists the virtues that he acquired in childhood.[2] The *Register* that provides such a wealth of detail about Edward's career until 1365 only begins with the preparations for the campaign of 1346. It was concerned with matters such as estate administration, orders to officials, demands for troops, rewards for service and many others, and was divided geographically into sections dealing with Cheshire, Cornwall, and the English estates. There are only very fragmentary remains of the north Wales register and most unfortunately, the Gascon register, if such a volume existed, does so no longer. The records of the daily business of government and administration necessarily increased as estates were bestowed upon the prince: the earldom of Cheshire in 1333, the duchy of Cornwall in 1337 (on its creation), and on only the second occasion that the title had been granted, the principality of Wales in 1343. The prince also held the office of *custos angliae* (keeper of the realm) when his father was campaigning abroad in 1338, 1340 and 1342-3. It was a mainly ceremonial office, but not an unimportant one. As keeper he was 'advised' by a number of peers, Ralph Neville, the earls of Arundel, Lancaster, Huntingdon and principally John Stratford, the archbishop of Canterbury.[3]

The prince's childhood was spent, for the most part, in the household of Queen Philippa, with his sisters Isabella (b. 1332) and Joanna (b. 1333). His estates, as they accrued, were also administered through his mother's household until he, and they, outgrew it. The first of these estates was granted on 18 March 1333 and thereafter the foundations of the prince's household and administration were laid alongside the government of the earldom of Cheshire. Many of the officials appointed to his service in these early years would become long-standing associates and have distinguished careers, but few of them at this point were high ranking or men of great standing in their own right. A number would later achieve episcopal rank, including William Spridlington (bishop of St Asaph, 1376-82), John Harewell (bishop of Bath and Wells, 1366-86), John Fordham (bishop of Durham, 1382-8, of Ely, 1388-1425) and Robert Stretton (bishop of Lichfield, 1360-85),[4] but at this time the only figures of national significance were the masters of the household, Sir Nicholas de la Beche and Sir Bartholomew Burghersh, senior. Among the episcopacy, the prince was also close to Henry Burghersh, bishop of

Lincoln (his godfather) and William Edington, bishop of Winchester. Edington would have links to the order of the Garter and shared interests of religious patronage through the houses of Bonhommes at Ashridge and Edington.

Among the officials of the prince's household in these early years Guillaume St Omer and his wife, Elizabeth, from the queen's homeland of Hainault, were steward and mistress and guardian of the young earl respectively. Joan Oxenford was the young prince's nurse as she would be to Edmund of Langley.[5] It may be that the prince had, as his tutor, the renowned scholar, Walter Burley, but this is conjectural, as the tradition first emerged in the sixteenth century.[6] John Brunham was treasurer, and by 1334, William Stratton was employed as tailor foreshadowing Edward's later interest in and considerable expenditure on clothing.[7] Financial concerns, income, or rather the lack of it, would become an acute problem for the prince and it was an issue for his father and administrators from an early stage. Despite its limited size and range of functions, the prince's household could rarely 'live of its own'. The crown made occasional additional payments, but it was not until 1336 that a partial solution presented itself with the reversion to the crown of the earldom of Cornwall following the unfortunate death of John of Eltham, the king's brother.

Cornish wealth lay mainly in tin and the stannary towns that served the industry. Yet this could not all be used to allay the prince's financial concerns, since 1,000 marks were already assigned to the king's companion and the future earl of Salisbury, William Montague, and a further £100 to one Thomas West, so additional revenues were attached to Cornwall and granted to the prince from Exeter, Mere, and most importantly, Wallingford. On 9 February 1337, Cornwall and its attendant 'foreign manors' (estates held outside the county) passed to the king's eldest son. With the acquisition of the duchy, as with Cheshire, four years earlier, the prince acquired further servants and officials and a central organisation developed to co-ordinate the activities of local government. Again, a number of those who soon found employment in Cornwall would become of importance elsewhere in the prince's demesne.[8] Of these, the most significant was Peter Gildesburgh who came to the prince's notice through service to the king and the Burghersh family and in 1340 became controller of the Cornish stannaries and keeper of the prince's wardrobe in the following year. He later became receiver of Cheshire and, in 1349, he was the prince's envoy to the Pope in Avignon.[9]

Significantly, in view of the increasingly hostile relations with France about to develop into open war, Edward III chose at this time to further reward some of those that had supported him in the 1330 coup and in his reign up to that point. He aimed to secure and establish a significant section of the nobility to aid him in the military action that lay ahead. His son, not yet seven years of age, would in time be the mainstay of that effort, and the king wished to distinguish him from others within the peerage, thus the earldom of Cornwall became a duchy. At the same time, six other titles were granted to the upper echelons of the aristocracy. Henry of Grosmont became earl of Derby, William Montague received the earldom of Salisbury, William Clinton that of Huntingdon, Robert Ufford, Suffolk, William Bohun, Northampton, and Hugh Audeley, Gloucester. Such men were to be intimately involved with the war effort and a number were closely acquainted with the prince as well as his father.

*7, 8  Kenilworth Castle, Warwickshire. A later Norman foundation converted by John of Gaunt into a palace, adding, in particular, the Great Hall. John's daughter, Joan, married Ralph Neville and their grandchild, Richard Neville, became 'the Kingmaker'*

9   *Flint Castle, one of Edward I's great fortresses built to subdue the Welsh. The Black Prince granted the custody of Flint to his servant, Ralph Davenport*

By this time, the die in the Anglo-French 'game' had been cast and the significant issue lay not in Gascony, but in Scotland. The king had begun campaigning there soon after the birth of his first son. On 12 August 1332, he was victorious at Dupplin Moor, thereby establishing Edward Balliol as king, who acknowledged Edward III as his liege. Balliol's deposition by David Bruce resulted in a second expedition in which the king defeated the Scots at Halidon Hill on 19 July 1333. He went on to take Berwick, and by 1336 he had established control over much of the lowlands including the fortresses of Roxburgh, Edinburgh, Perth and Stirling. As a result of this, in 1334, David Bruce had arrived as an exile in France and thereafter, Philip VI declared that Scotland had to be included in any Gascon settlement. Just as the duchy was a thorn in the flesh of the French monarchy, so was Scotland in England's, and the questionable feudal relationship that had existed since 1259 was put under greater pressure than it could stand with French interference in the domestic affairs of the king of England.

The confiscation of Gascony had happened on several occasions since the treaty of Paris, but the conditions were such in 1337 that the outcome was not a relatively brief fracas but a conflict that would continue for at least 116 years. The reason for this 'final straw' was the banishment of Robert of Artois and his harbouring in the English court. To shelter an outlaw such as Robert breached Edward's duty as a vassal of the French king. On 24 May 1337, Gascony and Ponthieu were ordered to be seized, and although military action did not break out until 1339, England and France were at war.

The English approach to the conflict took a familiar pattern, based in Flanders (after the Francophile Louis of Nevers was all but replaced by Jacob van Artevelde in 1337-8) and using large numbers of foreign mercenaries. An alliance, negotiated by the earls of

Salisbury and Huntingdon and Henry Burghersh, bishop of Lincoln, was formed with Louis of Bavaria, the king's brother-in-law, but even the ambassadors were not convinced of the wisdom of such a course, fearing that 'the king would not be able to bear the expense of the conditions which they demanded'.[10] Additional treaties were made with William of Avesnes, count of Hainault and a number of other princes of the Low Countries including the count of Guelders, the marquis of Juliers and the duke of Brabant. Edward III set sail on 16 July 1338, landing at Antwerp six days later. The intention was to recover the castles of the Cambrésis, but the relationship between the allies was not easy from the outset. The princes were unwilling to commit their forces until they had been paid in full, and with their inactivity, the wage bill rose. That bill was additional to the initial fees, which in total exceeded £160,000. To cover such expenses, Edward borrowed £70,000 from the Italian bankers, the Bardi and Peruzzi, mortgaged his crown as well as gold and jewellery, and acquired loans from the wool merchant William de la Pole and others, some at rates of 50% interest. The pressure on England in the form of taxation and purveyance grew as the autumn turned into winter, with nothing to show for the expenditure.[11]

While Edward's allies were prevaricating, Philip of Valois took the opportunity to launch a number of sea-bourn raids on English territories in the Channel Islands and military pressure increased on Gascony with the loss of Blaye and Bourg in April 1339. In England, parliamentary discontent grew from February and there was further concern as a result of French and Genoese raids, initially on the south-west of England and into the Bristol Channel, and then towards Plymouth and the Isle of Wight. They were repelled when trying to land at Dover and Folkestone, but burned Hastings. Coastal defences were a further expense and the king was completely incapable of honouring his payments to Louis of Bavaria and his other allies. Edward seems not to have been aware of the gravity of the situation, or rather he attributed it to corruption and mismanagement within his own government.

Edward eventually cajoled his allies into an expedition and left Brussels early in September 1339. The attack on Cambrai began sometime after 20 September, but Philip VI made no attempt to try to relieve the city and the assault failed. The domestic political repercussions were considerable and marked, for the first time, a parliamentary grant that was conditional upon certain reforms, including the establishment of a committee to control government expenditure. This was hardly surprising, as the campaign of 1339-40 cost some £386,465.[12]

It is extremely significant that although hostilities between England and France began formally in 1337, Edward did not claim the throne of France until 1340. The motivation, at this point, seems clear:

> Finally, having considered and thought over everything, and weighed the good against the bad, he [Edward III] did take the arms of France, quartered with those of England, and from then on he styled himself King of France and England, and did everything that the Flemings asked of him, and as King of France, quit them of any obligation they had to the King of France; and from this point the Flemings continued to aid him during the rule of Jacques van Artevelde.[13]

10   *Launceston Castle, Cornwall. Located in one of the chief stannary towns and controlling the road into Cornwall, the original Norman castle was rebuilt in the mid-thirteenth century and further repaired by the Black Prince after 1341*

Thus, Edward's claim to the French throne, at least in the opinion of Jean Le Bel, the chronicler from Hainault and precursor of Froissart, was to secure the support of the Flemish.

The quartering of the French with the English arms and the arrogation of the *fleur de lys* was one of the most powerful demonstrations of Edward's claim to the throne of France. Initially, the arms were quartered with the English device foremost, but this was altered in line with Edward's dynastic pretensions in 1340, placing the *fleurs* in the paternal position. By 1348, coins were minted using solely the French arms, and despite informally giving up his claim in 1360, Edward retained the arms.[14]

The first notable English success in the war with France was at sea, in a battle fought at the mouth of the river Zwyn. The Black Prince was only ten years of age on 24 June 1340, so took no part in the battle of Sluys, yet it was significant in the development of his military career and marked one of few early successes for the English in the Hundred Years War. Several of those who would become part of his household and military retinue did fight, and it was in the context of this encounter that Nigel Loryng, who was to become one of the prince's closest advisors and valued servants, was knighted. Indeed, it was at Sluys that the experiences of the Scottish campaigns, of the victories at Dupplin Moor and Halidon Hill, were put to good use in the war with France.[15] Despite it being a naval battle, the characteristics of the victory would become familiar; a larger French force

*11   Warwick Castle, showing the east front of the castle icluding the gatehouse and Guy's tower,
built 1394*

was defeated by superior tactics and a more effective use of the conditions. The victories at Crécy and Poitiers would be based on such experience.

The victory at Sluys prevented a potential French invasion of England but was not supported or followed by effective military action on land. Edward's inability to pay his allies resulted in their abandonment of him, and he was forced to come to terms with the French, signing a truce at Espléchin, near Tournai, on 25 September 1340.

Edward III, unable to take advantage of the situation in France, took revenge for his failure at home. John Stratford, the archbishop of Canterbury, in particular was held responsible for the lack of funds that had prevented success in the campaign in Flanders. But the king realised that he could not buy allies, at least not with money; future campaigns would rely primarily on Anglo-Welsh and Gascon troops, and political support would be sought from those that had something personal to gain from siding with England in the Hundred Years War.

As Scotland, Flanders and Gascony had encouraged and catalysed the Hundred Years War, other conflicts in other areas would continue to fan the flames. The outbreak of civil war in Brittany between Charles de Blois and Jean de Montfort brought that struggle within the Plantagenet-Valois war. The English supported Montfort and close links were to develop between the prince and Jean, particularly after 1362. Montfort accompanied the prince on his *tournée d'hommages* of the new principality of Aquitaine, and this may have brought Jean into contact with John Chandos who became the leader of Montfort's forces at the battle of Auray in 1364. The prince had attempted to resolve the succession crisis bringing the parties together on two occasions at Poitiers in 1363-4, when this failed direct military assistance was offered to Montfort. Chandos was not the only member of the prince's retinue to fight alongside Montfort at Auray and elsewhere. Links were further strengthened by the marriage of Joan Holland, the prince's stepdaughter to Jean on 26 March 1366.[16] The association is vividly apparent in the seemingly unlikely setting of St Margaret's church, King's Lynn, where the arms of the Black Prince and those of Montfort flank a stylised image of a face, presumably Edward III on a misericord. Both the prince and later Montfort had associations with the Norfolk port through rights to the tollbooth and the nearby estate at Castle Rising. The county and surrounding area was a surprisingly rich recruitment area for the prince despite his limited tenurial interests there (see figs **12**, **13**, **18**, **21**, **22**, **26** for examples of other East Anglians among the prince's entourage). A number of the East Anglian knightly community would become retainers on the occasion of the prince's military baptism in 1346 and thereafter. Throughout his career, the prince's retinue was in a constant state of flux and evolution and this began at an early stage. The grant of the principality of Wales in 1343 further galvanised Edward's administration and the development of his household. A wardrobe account of 1344-5 reveals a number of significant retainers who would rise to high office within the retinue, and in some cases the nation. Amongst these were John Dabernon (from 1347 keeper of the prince's fees in Devon and Cornwall), Ivo Glinton (keeper of the great seal), Nicholas Pinnock (auditor), Peter Gildesburgh, Robert Stretton, William Shareshull, and Richard Stafford (member of the prince's council from 1343, knight bachelor of the household).[17] Alongside the governing officials, Wales was to provide the bulk of the troops for the prince's first military campaign and his personal retinue began to take shape in the preparations for the 1346 expedition when the prince took his first role on the international stage.

# 3 War, Plague and Chivalry (1346-54)

## 'Let the boy win his spurs', Crécy and Calais

The reign of Edward III has often and continues to be described in glowing terms (if only until 1369), but before 1346 he had achieved little, at least in France. The policy of alliances had brought England to the verge of bankruptcy, and the king had only narrowly avoided a major political crisis in 1340-1. The campaign of 1346 was, in some respects, a 'last throw of the dice'; the victory at Crécy was needed to preserve Edward's continental ambitions, reputation and the support of the country, particularly in parliament.

The failure of the 1344 peace talks at Avignon resulted in a hardening of both French and English positions regarding Gascony. King Philip appointed the dauphin, Jean, as duke of Guienne, and at about the same time, Henry of Grosmont and the earl of Arundel were despatched to the duchy as Edward III's lieutenants. Grosmont returned in 1345 with an army and as sole lieutenant. Further forces were sent to Brittany under the command of Northampton, and the king and the Black Prince set sail for Flanders. Certain key members of the prince's household accompanied him, including Edmund Wauncy (household steward and bachelor, member of the council), Richard de la Bere, Roland Daneys and Guillaume St Omer. The intention was to reopen hostilities from Flanders, but this was scuppered by the assassination of Jacob van Artevelde. The king returned and plans were afoot for an expedition to France by 29 September when commissions of array of Welsh troops were ordered.[1]

In the development of the plan for the 1346 Normandy operation, the role of Godfrey d'Harcourt was central.[2] Harcourt had been knighted in 1326 and became lord of Saint-Sauveur-le-Victomte in the Cotentin four years later. This was one of the strongest fortresses in western Normandy. He came into conflict with another Norman noble, Guillaume Bertran, concerning the marriage of Jeanette Bacon, one of the wealthiest heiresses in the province. Open hostilities broke out and the king and *parlement* sided with Bertran and condemned Harcourt who sought refuge in London, and as Robert of Artois had done in 1336, gave homage to Edward III.[3]

The war had not been a success thus far; a different approach was needed to stave off political opposition at home and to secure a victory abroad, one secured at a cost that parliament would accept. The failure at Tournai (1340) and the subsequent truce of Espléchin necessitated a change of English strategy that was both political and military. The crushing expense of the foreign alliances were set aside in favour of predominantly

12  *Original brass of Hugh Hastings, Elsing church, Norfolk — 'the most elaborate military monumental brass of the fourteenth century'. The side-shafts, some now lost, depicted Hastings' companions-in-arms: Edward III, the earls of Lancaster, Warwick, Stafford, Pembroke, John Grey, Almaric St Amand and Edward Despenser. An East Anglian manuscript tradition may have influenced the curving style of the brass. William Eltham married Hastings' daughter, Elizabeth, and his brother-in-law was John Wingfield*

English and Welsh troops, and the king sought to implement the strategy that had seen so much success in Scotland. In the course of the previous campaign, he 'had found himself helpless against an enemy who concentrated on defensive tactics and refused to be brought to battle'. The target for this new assault was greatly influenced by Harcourt, whose own interests led him to encourage Edward to attack Normandy, which also had the advantage of being the closest landfall to Portsmouth and was virtually undefended. There were further advantages that the Norman emphasised, such as the wealth of the region and the advantage that could be gained through the use of his personal knowledge of the area.

There were strict attempts to maintain secrecy prior to and during the operation of 1346, but the scale of preparations was such that the timetable became almost common knowledge. However, the French did not know, at least until very late in the day, the destination of the fleet, which was altered on a number of occasions and probably not revealed to any but the king's closest confidants. Adverse winds may also have altered the intended destination; consequently, French defensive preparations were inadequate. The Flemish alliance and a commission given to Sir Hugh Hastings [see figs **12**, **13**] in June shows that a landing in northern France had already been considered as an option if only to divert French forces from the duchy. On 20 June, Hastings, who had recently returned from Gascony, was appointed the king's lieutenant and commander in Flanders and Brittany. Hastings, John Moleyns, John Mautravers and perhaps John Montgommery led a force of 230 archers and a few men-at-arms while several Flemish towns provided additional troops.[4]

In 1346, the prince had his first real taste of the military life and he was suitably prepared and equipped for the experience. His personal retinue included 11 bannerets, 102 knights bachelor, 264 men-at-arms/esquires, 384 horsed archers and 582 on foot, a total of 1,343 soldiers. However, some of these may have been drafted in for the subsequent siege of Calais, the loss of the pay accounts for the expedition makes the reconstruction of the army problematic.[5] The primary recruiting area for the bulk of the army was Wales, which was to provide some 7,000 soldiers, half from the principality and half from the Marches, and a further 100 archers were to be brought from Cheshire.

There were fears that in the course of the expedition, a reciprocal invasion might be launched and so, on 26 July, watches were ordered to be set in Flint and north Wales for French and, remarkably, Turkish ships. The Turkish 'threat' may have simply been another element in the king's propaganda campaign, emphasising the danger of invasion in order to demonstrate the defensive nature of the war and to propose that there was an alliance between the French and the heathen Turks. It is quite an extraordinary statement considering that the 'Sarazins' did not acquire a European base until 1354.[6] However, the fear of a French invasion was not unfounded as plans found at Caen proved, suggesting that a force of 4,000 men-at-arms, 5,000 foot and 5,000 crossbowmen would be mustered for an attack on England. It was in the king's interest to exaggerate the threat of invasion in order to ensure continuing revenue from taxation, which in theory, would be provided only for a war fought in self-defence.[7]

The main attack was preceded by small incursions in other regions. In addition to Hastings' expedition, Thomas Dagworth rode against the French-allied claimant to

Brittany and defeated Charles de Blois on 9 June 1346 near Saint-Pol de Leon. Richard Totesham, with the garrison from La Roche-Derrien, raided and sacked Lannion.[8] At Aiguillon, small groups of English and Gascon troops commanded by Lancaster managed to infiltrate and seize the town. Lancaster's deputy was Walter Manny and the troops included Ralph Stafford, then the keeper of the prince's estates, as well as Nigel Loryng and perhaps Richard Stafford. They were then themselves besieged. This may have been the event, compounded by the influence of Godfrey d'Harcourt, which decided Edward on invading the Cotentin peninsula.[9] Harcourt's involvement indicates that the original plan may have been to attempt some sort of occupation of Normandy and perhaps what began as a campaign of conquest became a *chevauchée*.[10]

The army landed at La Hogue on 12 July 1346. Disembarkation was an extended process lengthened by the necessity to rest the horses after the long crossing. In that time, the king took the opportunity to recoup some of the costs of the campaign and mark its beginning by knighting his eldest son and a number of others. The occasion traditionally allowed a tax to be levied.

Edward's motivation in the course of the campaign and indeed in this general period of the war remains an area of contention and is very much open to question. Clifford Rogers has argued strongly against traditional opinion and the fabian military advice of Vegetius, that Edward III intended to bring his opponent to battle, as he had singly failed to do in earlier expeditions and 'to win his rights by force of arms'.[11]

La Hogue and Barfleur were attacked on 13 and 14 July respectively. There was continuing support from the fleet which burnt and laid waste the whole seacoast from Barfleur as far as the Fosse de Colleville near Caen, and likewise burnt the town of Cherbourg and the ships of la Havre, so that 'one hundred or more great ships and other vessels of the enemy' were burnt.[12] Alongside the policy of devastation, attempts were made to incite rebellion against the Valois monarchy. There was certainly support for Edward, but whether this was gained through intimidation or political sympathy is not clear. In any case, ransom payments made to the English and resistance in the Cotentin was very limited.[13]

The army was divided into three 'battles' or divisions. The vanguard under the nominal command of the prince included the earls of Northampton and Warwick, the constable and marshal respectively. The king was in the main body while the earls of Suffolk, Arundel and Huntingdon led the rearguard. The three divisions allowed the army to march on a wide front to maximise the destruction. The vanguard reached Pont Hébert on 21 July where the bridge, broken by the retreating Robert Bertrand, marshal of France and sire de Bricquebec, was rebuilt. Bertrand had responsibility for the defence of the coast of the Cotentin from Honfleur to Mont-Saint-Michel. This was no easy task, as apart from Cherbourg, there were no notable fortifications.[14] On the following day, believing erroneously that Bertrand intended to give battle, Edward knighted Henry Burghersh, another member of the family that had close links to the royal family. After capturing Saint-Lô and sacking the town with particular viciousness since it had offered token resistance, they burned their way to Caen. Edward III arrived there on 24th while the prince was at Cheux, two miles to the west. The forces in Caen were commanded by Raoul, count of Eu and constable of France, the lord of Tancarville, and the recently

13   *Recreation brass of Hugh Hastings*

arrived Bertrand. The numbers of defenders is very uncertain; estimates vary between 1,000 and a less likely 6,000 men-at-arms, Genoese mercenaries and militia. The prince set up camp to the north, near the deserted Abbaye aux Dames.

Despite orders from the king, the western gate was seized and the earl of Warwick, who had been sent by the king to recall the attackers, joined in with the fighting, and entered the town followed by Northampton and Richard Talbot leading a disordered contingent. The battle spread along the river and overran the defenders, the constable surrendered to Thomas Holland, future earl of Kent, and the chamberlain to the prince's retainer, Thomas Daniel. Captives from Caen were taken to England by the earl of Huntingdon. Those who were not worth ransoming did not fare so well.[15]

Shortly after, on 29 July, Philip VI proclaimed the *arrière-ban*, recalling the duke of Normandy from the siege of Aiguillon and leaving only a small detachment to defend against the expected attack from Flanders as Philip concentrated his defences on the Seine. The abrupt departure of the army from Aiguillon meant that horses, tents and other equipment were left behind and taken by the English. In this, one of the prince's associates and sheriff of Merionneth, 'That arch-spoilator Walter Mauny took the lead.'[16] Lancaster then led his troops in pursuit of the duke northwards. Meanwhile, Philip tried to slow the invaders by breaking the bridges along the river.

At this point the English army formed two columns and slowly marched east toward Rouen. They were repulsed at Pont de l'Arche and moved towards Paris, storming Longueville and killing the garrison, although they failed to take the bridge at Vernon. The prince spent a night at Mounceaux.[17] On 11 August, while near the bridge of Meulan, the earls of Warwick and Northampton and a detachment from the prince's division were sent to investigate the possibility of forcing a crossing but they were taunted into a disorganised assault and driven back.

On 12 August, the army came within 20 miles of Paris causing panic and hastening defensive preparations. Although he had a larger army than Edward (some 8,000 men-at-arms, 6,000 Genoese and a large number of infantrymen), Philip could not defend the city from all sides. The bridge at Poissy was broken, headquarters were established at Saint-Denis and the army was encamped at Saint-Cloud. The English occupied Poissy and Saint-Germain-en-Laye where the prince stayed in the old palace. Despite French attempts, the bridge was rebuilt.[18]

Philip withdrew to the plain between Paris and Saint-Denis on 14 August, and issued a challenge to Edward, which was probably accepted as the French army assembled in battle order near the abbey of Saint Germain on the southern wall of Paris. From there, they marched to what was, presumably, the proposed battleground among the vineyards of Bourg-la-Reine and Antony. This allowed Edward to retreat northwards after burning Poissy and breaking the bridge towards Auteuil. Philip hurried in pursuit. Rogers suggests that although Edward accepted the challenge, he did not accept either the time nor place of battle, which appears unlikely.[19] In a succession of forced marches covering about 25 miles a day, the French raced to beat Edward to the Somme. Part of the reason for the English failure to reach the river with any time to spare, despite their head start, was the indiscipline of the prince's vanguard. A day was wasted attacking the insignificant village of Vessencourt. They were stopped on the point of assaulting Beauvais, but could not be prevented from burning the suburbs and most of the outlying churches while the walls of Poix-en-Beauvais were undermined and assaulted in direct contravention of the king's order. The prince spent the night of the 16 August at Grisy-le-Plâtres and the 18th at Milly. On the following day he reached Grandvilliers and on the 20th Molliens. When they finally reached the River Somme, it was found to be impassable. Warwick failed to force a passage on the 22nd at Hangest, and the French approach forced a retreat towards the coast turning north at Oisemont to the mouth of the river. Shortly after midnight on the 24th, the English army discovered a ford across the river at Blanchetaque.[20] Godemar du Fay (later to become seneschal of Beaucaire and Nîmes)[21] defended it on the opposite shore with 500 men-at-arms and 3,000 infantry. Northampton, Hugh Despenser and Reginald Cobham led 100 men-at-arms and archers of the vanguard across the stream. When they were in range, the archers opened fire, providing cover for the men-at-arms to attack the north bank and establish a bridgehead while the others then crossed behind. Godemar was forced to retreat while Philip, who had pursued the English to Blanchetaque, was beaten by the tide. At about this time (24 August), the Flemings abandoned their campaign after failing to take Béthune. Philip returned to Abbeville then took the Hesdin road to try to cut Edward off from the north. The English army halted near the village of Crécy.

It may have been the numerical superiority of the French army that led to the English withdrawal over the Somme and then to Crécy. Alternatively, rather than fleeing from Philip, the entire campaign strategy may have been an attempt to bring him to battle. Edward had failed to do so at Vironfosse in 1339 and, a year later, Philip had declined to confront him at Tournai. The expense of these failures was such that Edward may have decided that only a major large-scale victory could secure the French throne. Perhaps the devastation wrought during the march from La Hogue was designed, in addition to damaging the tax revenue, to cause baronial discontent and induce pressure to attack. The plan may have been laid out in particular detail since in view of the speed with which he took up position after crossing the Somme, the battlefield must have been reconnoitred in advance and certain defences prepared including pit-traps to hamper the French cavalry. The path taken in the retreat from Paris was convoluted and the time wasted in attacking Oisemont, and in the two days following the Somme crossing could indicate that Edward was hoping to induce a battle. Certainly, Giovanni Villani, the Italian chronicler, noted Edward was looking to select a suitable site for the encounter.[22] The king had faith in his cause, his army, and its commanders. Warwick, Arundel and Suffolk had seen service in Scotland, Flanders and Brittany, and Warwick and Arundel had fought at Sluys in 1340. Northampton had fought in Flanders and Brittany (including at Morlaix in 1342). Edward III had fought in all these theatres and was noted in particular for his victory at Halidon Hill. Morale was good and the army was perfecting a tactical system that had defeated odds of ten to one at Dupplin Moor. Although the English were exhausted after marching over 300 miles in the previous month, they did have time to prepare. Furthermore, the move towards Flanders provided the possibility of reinforcements and an escape route in the event of defeat, and there may have been financial considerations. Parliament had advised the king to seek battle. The 1344 subsidy had been granted on that condition and he had publicly and privately proclaimed this intention. It was in his best financial interests to

14  *Jupon with the arms of Edward the Black Prince from his tomb in Canterbury Cathedral Church 1376*

seek a swift resolution since taxation revenue was all but exhausted.[23] The delay could simply have been due to indiscipline and/or poor geographical awareness, but it may be significant that a similar 'mishap' befell the Black Prince in the days leading up to the battle of Poitiers.

> . . . about midday [26 September] new reports came to King Edward that King Philippe was ready and arrayed his men in three lines of battle. King Edward rejoiced . . . drew up his men and marched to the bridge at Crécy, and about the hour of vespers or a little before he saw the enemy approaching. The English had by now fasted a long time, having stood so as to be ready for the French.[24]

After the French had reconnoitred the strength of the English army and its formation, Philip decided to attack, despite advice to the contrary. The French army was organised in three battalions, one behind the other. In front of these were Genoese mercenaries armed with crossbows commanded by Carlo Grimaldi and Otto Doria. French reinforcements continued to arrive throughout the afternoon. Philip probably commanded 12,000 men-at-arms, 6,000 Genoese and several thousand infantry, creating a force of 20,000-25,000 soldiers.

The English made their stand at the end of an expanse of gently rising ground with their backs to the forest of Crécy-Grange and the sun. The prince led the vanguard with Warwick, Northampton in addition to Kent, Godfrey d'Harcourt, and Chandos. The king commanded the centre and the bishop of Durham with the earls of Arundel and Suffolk led the rearguard.[25] The archers were probably deployed on the wings of each 'battle', but may have begun the encounter in front of the dismounted infantry. There were also a number of cannon, which were used primarily to frighten the French horses. It was one of the first appearances of artillery on a battlefield.

The French attacked in the rain of the late afternoon led by the Genoese. Outranged by the English archers and without their shields, which were yet to arrive, they soon fled for their own lines and were cut down by the furious French cavalry who led by the count of Alençon, then attacked the English vanguard. The archers heavily disrupted the charge but some reached the English lines and a fierce fight ensued. The standard fell and was raised again by the prince's retainer, Thomas Daniel[26] and the prince himself was struck down and rescued by his standard-bearer, Richard FitzSimon.[27] The French cavalry repeatedly wheeled, rallied and charged. It was during one of these attacks that entreaties may have been made to the king to ensure his son's safety. Edward is said to have responded that he should not be sent for

> as long as my son is alive. Give them my command to let the boy win his spurs, for if God has so ordained it, I wish the day to be his.[28]

As the French attacks failed, the horses were brought up from behind the English lines, and as they were to do at Poitiers, the men-at-arms remounted and charged the surviving French troops. At this, the bulk of the army fled leaving Philip with only a handful of companions, his personal bodyguard and some infantry levies from Orléans. After being injured, he was led away by John of Hainault abandoning the *Oriflamme* and the royal standard.[29]

On the following morning 2,000 infantry reserves, still following from Abbeville, arrived, unaware of the battle. They were scattered in a single charge by Northampton, Suffolk and Warwick and perhaps the prince.[30] English casualties from the battle were very low. Only 40 men-at-arms were reported as missing, although presumably there were many more infantry and archers killed. By contrast, French casualties were extreme. This was a result of Edward's orders, before the battle, that there was to be no plundering of the dead and no quarter for the living. This also followed from the French deployment of the *Oriflamme*, which, as at Poitiers, was seen as a sign of 'guerre mortelle'.[31] Reginald Cobham, Michael Northburgh and others counted 1,542 French knights and squires who fell near the prince's lines alone.[32] Amongst them were John, the blind king of Bohemia, and his knights, said by Froissart to have been tethered together so he might strike a blow in the conflict. It may have been from John, possibly slain by the prince himself, that Edward adopted the ostrich feathers as his device as prince of Wales. Another of the fallen was Jean d'Harcourt, Godfrey's brother.

Crécy provided the blueprint for the troop composition of the prince's later expeditions. Although it may not have begun as a *chevauchée*, the complement of the English forces in the 1346 campaign demonstrated the benefits of recruiting a balanced army of men-at-arms and archers who could offer a range of effective and flexible tactical options. In real terms, this meant a combination of dismounted men-at-arms and archers fighting together in a defensive position to repulse a numerically superior opponent. The archers reduced enemy numbers at a distance and disrupted their approach, giving the advantage to men-at-arms fighting in close formation. The combination of dismounted knights and archers was not new; William the Conqueror had used such a blend at Hastings, but it was considered innovative by contemporaries such as Thomas Gray in his description of the battle of Courtrai (1302) and still held good nearly 50 years later.[33]

The traditional view of the battle of Crécy has attributed the English victory to the stout yeomen archers and their longbows, but this was not the only advantage. 'L'armee d'Edouard III etatit remarquable . . . par sa discipline et son esprit combatif.'[34] However, despite these qualities, the French assault failed, at least partly due to a lack of co-ordination. The French army was multinational and this resulted in communication problems. By contrast, the only foreign troops in Edward's army were the Welsh and were organised in small groups with English-speaking commanders. In the past, Philip had successfully avoided battle. This challenge proved too great to evade, and he was forced into combat more by domestic political concerns than military necessity, as Enrique of Trastamara was to be at Nájera over 20 years later. It is uncertain why he felt the need to attack before his troops were all assembled. The destruction of the Genoese crossbowmen might have been averted, or at least mitigated, had they been equipped with their shields (*pavises*), which were *en route* from Abbeville even as the arrows were falling. The lack of tactical direction from Philip, who had proved himself no mean general at Cassel in 1328 — the French victory there was one of the last battles to be won by an opening cavalry charge and may have coloured Philip's actions at Crécy — and the impatience of the French nobles, especially Alençon, contributed much to the defeat. There seems to have been some success in the attack on the vanguard but it proved ultimately indecisive, and was, in any case, no real solution to their tactical problem.[35] The role of the prince himself and his division should not be overlooked either. For all the superiority of the archers, the victory at Crécy depended on the ability of the vanguard to hold against repeated charges of those knights who, before that day, had been numbered among the finest in Christendom. The French cavalry displayed great skill in the battle. Despite the defensive preparations that had been made, the use of cannon to frighten the horses, the lack of central direction and control and the threat of the archers, they managed to repeatedly charge, wheel and reform to attack again. The lack of central co-ordination did not stop the French aristocracy from ably fulfilling its traditional military role, although to no avail.

15 *The younger Hugh Despenser, shown in a stained glass window commissioned by his mother, Eleanor de Clare, in Tewkesbury Abbey*

Perhaps unfairly, blame was heaped upon them by contemporaries for attacking in disorder and allowing themselves to be defeated by dismounted men-at-arms and mere archers, 'gens de nulle value'.[36]

The victorious army, urgently in need of supplies, marched relatively slowly to Calais. The king's decision to lay siege to the town does not appear to have been discussed in advance, and consideration may have been given to assaulting Boulogne, which was certainly attacked by English ships on 4 September. The siege of Calais began the day before and lasted until 4 August 1347, and may have involved up to 32,000 soldiers in the course of the operation. The coastal port may seem a meagre reward after the scale of the victory at Crécy, and in part it was. Certainly, the length of the siege and the consequent cost in money and manpower was excessive. The distinction between the sieges of the 1340s and 1440s and the efficacy of artillery is very apparent. However, Calais was highly significant and provided an extremely valuable base and the launching point for many subsequent campaigns.

*16 The jousting helm of Sir Richard Pembridge, KG, who died in 1375. The 'barrel helm' was made in three parts, the lower cylinder, the cone and the top section which were then welded together. The metal thickens and turns outwards to provide protection for the eyes*

The prince's role in the siege is not clear, but there was extensive administrative activity leading to reinforcements, supplies and assorted provisions being sent from Cheshire, Wales and throughout his demesne to Calais. The loss of the central pay accounts makes the reconstruction of the army at Calais difficult. Ayton has pointed to a number of other documents that appear to be partial transcriptions from the originals and which may show the assembled siege force. He has also emphasised the problems associated with such transcripts, the most famous of which is Wrottesley's *Crécy and Calais*. The siege necessitated a great expansion in the size of the army. Estimates of the numbers of troops involved during the course of the operation range from 26,000 to 32,000.[37]

Cheshire reinforcements for Calais were demanded on 12 September 1346 and were led by Griffith ap Jor'ap Meyler and William Brereton, who may have died during the siege. Thomas Danyers was ordered to bring further reinforcements on 16 March 1347 and Richard Baskerville in May. Orders were also sent to Alexander Wasteneys, William Tabley, Ralph Oldington, Ralph Stathum and Richard del Hogh, sheriff of Flint. Sir Rhys ap Griffith (a trusted knight of Edward II, and one-time justiciar of south Wales) led a contingent of Welsh reinforcements. He returned from France to lead them to Winchelsea. Welsh forces before Calais probably totalled 4,572.[38] A number of the prince's retinue returned to England over the winter, but rejoined the siege in May. These included the younger Burghersh, Richard Stafford, Thomas Daniel and Stephen Cosington (a former member of Lancaster's retinue, and later a member of the prince's council and bodyguard with additional ambassadorial and diplomatic duties).

Philip VI took steps to relieve the siege and began to rally his forces as early as 3 October. There were French attempts to break the naval blockade but this failed and no supplies reached the town until soon after the embargo began. Alternative efforts were made to displace the English. Philip encouraged David Bruce to lead an attack from

Scotland. He encountered an army at Neville's Cross, near Durham, in October 1346 and was captured himself and his army completely defeated. French allies suffered a further loss in June 1347 when Charles de Blois was captured by Thomas Dagworth.

On 27 July 1347, Philip finally rallied his forces and brought an army to relieve the siege. This was offset somewhat by the appearance of Flemish reinforcements for the English. There was some skirmishing between the armies, but little of consequence. Negotiations opened and continued until 31 July, but came to no real resolution, and when Philip struck camp on 2 August, with the last hope for rescue gone, the town surrendered on 4 August.

## THE ORDER OF THE GARTER

The Hundred Years War and the victory at Crécy reintroduced the English aristocratic community to positions of military importance that had diminished somewhat in the latter years of the reign of Edward II. The Edwardian 'military renaissance' had considerable implications for chivalry. Victory reinforced the martial implications of knighthood and strengthened the aristocracy's taste for war. Such attitudes were enshrined in the formation of the Order of the Garter, which served as a perpetual memorial to Edward III's continental aspirations and created a chivalric elite within the ranks of the military aristocracy. The symbol of the order had nothing to do with an embarrassing incident involving the countess of Salisbury losing a garter at a ball (the lady in question was said by some to be Joan of Kent), but was in fact reminiscent of a belt or arming buckle, with the 'knot' symbolizing the ties of loyalty and affection that bound the companionship of the order together. Likewise, the motto, *Honi soit qui mal y pense* or 'Shame on him who thinks ill of it' was a direct reference to those who might doubt the veracity of Edward's claim to the French throne or the manner by which he sought to make good that claim.[39]

The Garter was designed to be a chivalric forum of the highest order, recruitment to the 26 stalls (including the king and the prince of Wales) in St George's chapel, Windsor, was international and membership was, at least theoretically, dependent not on political rank but chivalric achievement. However, those who were seen to have obstructed Edward in the early years of the French campaign did not find inclusion in the order's ranks. The practical benefits of membership of the Garter were very limited, being essentially ceremonial and honorific as were the obligations of the members, but it became the highest achievement of English chivalry. Edward's policy in melding chivalric values with foreign policy was mimicked in France through the creation of the Order of the Star and with much the same motivation. Due to peculiarities of recruitment and particularly because many of the prince's close military associates were also members of the Garter, the battle of Poitiers was, at least among the command ranks, a conflict of these two Orders.

Through propaganda and the example of the king and his eldest son, substance was given to the Arthurian myth, which Edward III had sought to create in the prototype of the Garter, the Round Table (1344).[40] The Garter was formed in 1348 and its membership seems to have been primarily dependent on service to the king in the campaigns leading

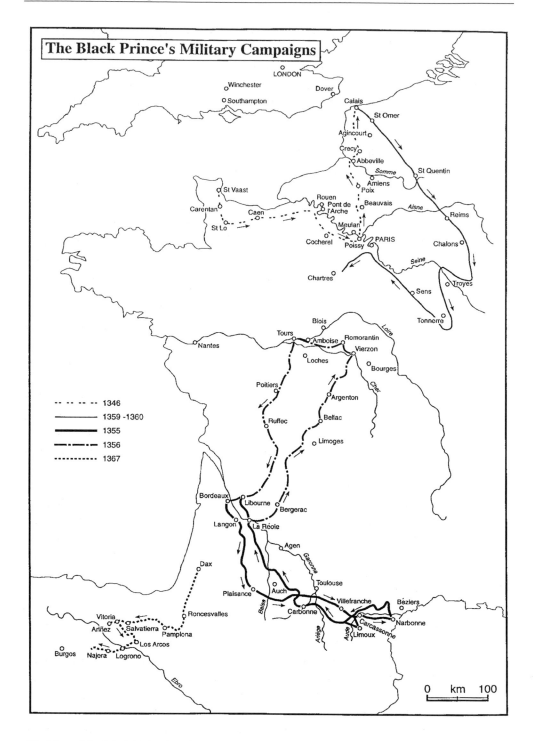

*17  Map of the Black Prince's military campaigns*

up to the battle of Crécy. All but four, or at most six, did not play some part in the battle or in the 1346 campaign. Of these, many of the founder knights had or developed close connections to the prince. All of the founder members that sat on his side in St George's chapel had fought with him in the first division at Crécy. They included Richard FitzSimon, who carried his standard, James Audley (the prince's constant military companion alongside John Chandos), Walter Pavely (household bachelor and annuitant), Henry Eam (bachelor and annuitant), Nigel Loryng (a life retainer of the prince and trusted military and political adviser), Lords Mohun and Wale, the captal de Buch, Bartholomew Burghersh, the younger (steward of Wallingford, justice of Chester), John Lord Grey of Rotherfield and Roger Mortimer, earl of March.[41] As the Order gained status and stature over the years, many more of the prince's followers, and those of his wife, found inclusion in this select group such as Walter Manny and William FitzWaryn. The process continued in Richard's reign. Lewis Clifford joined the order and was also a member of Philippe de Mézières' crusading Order of the Passion. John Burley, Simon's brother, who was retained by the prince in his last years was elected to the Garter in 1381 where he joined Thomas Felton, Nicholas Sarnesfield, John Devereux, Peter Courtenay and John Bourchier, who had also seen service with Richard's father.[42]

The original statutes of the order have been lost and the earliest extant version is based on a seventeenth century transcription. The first regulations may not have been as detailed as those formulated in later years, but it seems very likely that some form of statutes governed the members of the order in the fourteenth century and probably from the outset. The most significant ceremonial occasion fell on St George's Day (23 April). The companions assembled at Windsor the day before, where matters concerning the order were discussed and the members attended vespers. High mass followed the next day and new members might be introduced. A banquet and final service concluded the festivities. A requiem mass was celebrated on 24 April.[43]

Meetings of the Garter were often accompanied by splendid tournaments, many of which were staged in true Arthurian style with knights fighting incognito or wearing fantastic costumes.[44] Both Edward III and the Black Prince are known to have participated wearing disguises or costumes. Such events may have been particularly significant if, as has been suggested, the Garter was comprised of what could be two tourneying teams headed by the king and his son. Tourneying was a regular and important feature of the prince's life. At Windsor, perhaps for a Garter tournament in 1352, he purchased 60 buckles, 60 girdle-tips and 120 bars for 'knights of the prince's companionship'.[45] At Eltham in 1354, he gave Chandos and Audley a pair of plates of armour covered, interestingly enough, with black velvet, unfortunately for those looking for a reason for his pseudonym, he purchased red velvet covered plates for himself. For the Garter tournament of 1358, the prince gave £100 as a gift to the heralds and minstrels at the jousts. At Smithfield in 1359, he purchased 11 ostrich feathers for the jousts and there are several other records of gifts of shields and other arms being 'powdered' with his device.[46] Tournaments were becoming increasingly organised and less dangerous although fatalities were still relatively common. The mêlée as a form was becoming increasingly outmoded and with it the excuse of the tournament as training for military service. It still provided a taste of combat, but was little real preparation for a young knight or esquire. Nonetheless, tournaments certainly played an important part in the courtly life of the prince and further enhanced his military reputation. Cuvelier, the biographer of Bertrand Du Guesclin, attributed the prince's military success to his being surrounded by knights hardened in the tourney.[47]

Arthurian connotations were not only reserved for the tournament and the Garter — they became part of the image and glamour of the royal family. Jean le Bel, on whose account much of the early part of Froissart's chronicle was based, depicted Edward III as the second Arthur. The Black Prince was described similarly by Geoffrey Le Baker as the Boar of Cornwall. In time, literary motifs gave way to prophesy such as that of John Erghome, written to encourage Edward III to continue the war and which ended with the 'reign' of the Black Prince by then firmly established as the king of France.[48] In addition, the prince was said to be in possession of a statue of a golden eagle, which contained a stone flask containing holy oil, presented by the Virgin to St Thomas. The first king to be anointed with it was 'destined' to recover Normandy and Aquitaine without force and be the greatest amongst kings. A priest presented it to Henry of Lancaster who in turn gave it to the Black Prince. The eagle was supposedly placed in the Tower of London in a locked chest but, significantly, it was not there when it was looked for in 1377 for Richard II's coronation.[49]

In the years from 1345-8, the situation for England, Edward III and his son had changed radically. Triumph on the battlefield had been followed by a major acquisition in the form of Calais, a launching area for further assaults and a permanent base in the north of France to complement Gascony in the south. The opportunity for further campaigns and to capitalise on the situation was, however, prevented in a manner that was utterly terrible and completely unforeseen.

## THE BLACK DEATH

The bald statistics are shocking enough; the reality must have been appalling. Throughout Europe and certainly in England and France, between 30% and 50% of the population died in the years from 1347 to 1349. It was a scale of mortality that Europe had never witnessed and never has subsequently.[50] There has been a tendency by later commentators to see a range of mitigating, even beneficial aspects to the plague. It has been viewed as a Malthusian check since the population had outstretched the ability of the soil to sustain it and thus some sort of demographic 'limiter' was necessary. The direct role of the plague itself has also been questioned, as the population was already declining after the Great Famine of 1315-17 and so the plague struck a weakened population. The Black Death and its consequences have been viewed as, to use Sellars and Yeatman's celebrated phrase, 'A Good Thing'.[51] There were great opportunities open to the survivors and socio-economic benefits in land, trade, social mobility and the like; however, such opportunities can have provided little comfort for those that survived this first outbreak of the plague and witnessed the death of one in three or perhaps one in two of their friends, family and loved ones. It coloured and shaped the attitudes of at least a generation and its effects were evident for the remaining half of the century.

*18  Tomb of Michael de la Pole, Wingfield church, Suffolk. He was born c.1330 and was said to have fought with the prince during the Reims campaign. In 1366 he made his first appearance in Parliament and returned to Aquitaine for the resumption of the war. He was present at the siege of Limoges in 1370. He founded the Hull charterhouse in 1378-9. On 6 August 1385 he was created earl of Suffolk. He married Katherine, the daughter and heir of John Wingfield. He fled from the Appellants in 1387 and died two years later on 5 September 1389 in Paris*

The endemic incidents of bubonic, pneumonic and possibly septicaemic plague have received widely differing accounts by historians over a long period of time. Some have discounted the effects of the plague as negligible, whilst others have attributed such diverse events and attitudes as Lollardy, the Peasants' Revolt, the wool trade and nothing less than the end of feudalism to the catastrophic consequences of the death of perhaps half of the population. Neither extreme is true, but it is nonetheless difficult to underestimate the immediate impact and the long-term consequences of the repeated outbreaks of plague that struck Britain and the continent from 1347 until the early years of Henry IV's reign. The socio-economic impact cannot be quantified, except in microcosm, and the psychological effects are even more problematic, especially when the vast majority considered the epidemic to be divine retribution on a sinful people. Despite this, the evidence for 'change', in concrete terms and in the attitudes and outlook of the survivors and their children, is compelling.

One of the most significant areas, given the 'God-given' nature of the epidemic, was religion. As a catalyst, the plague encouraged an increasingly Christocentric form of worship and also strengthened the doctrine of purgatory. The failure of the clergy to foresee or forestall this divine retribution encouraged individuals to seek a more direct and personal link with God and his saints. This took various forms including the foundation of chantries by which benefactors could receive the personal spiritual attention of a number of chaplains, portative altars and licences to hear mass in domestic chapels.

Church architecture and features may also have been influenced. This is most apparent in the form of monumental effigies and tombs. The denigration of the body and the barren values of the material world were demonstrated by tombs showing wracked, twisted and tormented bodies.[52] Alternatively, it has been suggested that there could have been Arthurian connotations to such effigies and that such examples as the tombs of William Kerdeston, one of the prince's Norfolk retainers, and Oliver Ingham, the one-time seneschal of Aquitaine, depicted lying on stones and pebbles, show an image of the questing knight, lost in a mythical forest.

It is particularly interesting in the context of the prince and his retinue that the lead in a range of innovatory forms of religious patronage was taken by militarily active knights. For example, Hugh Calveley and Robert Knolles, two of the most celebrated and hated mercenary captains of the fourteenth century, were among the founders of St Thomas' (Becket) hospice in Rome, as was a certain John Hawkwood. Both men have been described as 'well-known philanthropists' and Knolles 'appears to have been genuinely conscientious in religious matters'.[53]

Support for the Carthusians also became popular, at least partly because of the interest in and respect for the contemplative life. They were one of the few orders to remain free of criticism from such commentators as Langland and Wyclif. Amongst those close to the Black Prince, Walter Manny and Michael de la Pole founded the Charterhouses at London and Hull respectively. Manny's interest in the order may have been prompted by his association with Grosmont and Gaunt, both of whom had dealings with Beauvale priory, Notts, and he was assisted with the foundation costs by the bishop of London, Michael Northburgh.[54] Previously Manny had provided a graveyard for plague-stricken Londoners and founded a college for twelve secular priests to pray for the dead.[55] One of those who requested their prayers in his will was William Lord Latimer. De la Pole's motives for founding the charterhouse in Hull are clear. His father had been the first mayor of the town in 1331-5 and had represented it in parliament. Michael was granted the custody of the town and the manor of Myton in 1366.[56] Peter Veel, the prince's retainer and later MP for Gloucestershire and constable of Gloucester castle, in 1387 granted the advowson of Norton FitzWarren, Somerset, to the London charterhouse. Such gestures may well have had origins in a group mentality.[57] Richard II gave the institution a tun of Gascon wine annually after 1382 and was associated with the foundation of the Coventry charterhouse. The prince himself granted the Selwood charterhouse five marks a year on 6 August 1362. The prior and order of Hinton received ten marks a year in lieu of one tun of wine on 3 March 1362, and the prior of Witham five marks.[58]

Alongside such ideas, although not a consequence of the plague, concepts were being shaped, both akin to and those which would, through the part played by John Wyclif, become Lollardy with its focus on predestination, denial of transubstantiation, attacks on images and pilgrimages, suspicion of sumptuous tombs and elaborate requiems.

The Black Death both shaped English and French society and restricted Edward III's ability to prosecute the war on any scale. However, military activity did not cease entirely.

In 1349, plans were made in France for the recapture of Calais. Geoffrey de Charny tried to bribe Aimery of Pavia, the galley-master of the town and commander of one of the gate towers of the citadel, to allow Charny and his troops to enter secretly at night. Aimery, however, reported the plan to Edward III, who hurried across the Channel at Christmas with a small force including the Black Prince, the earl of March and a number of their retainers and servants.

Charny approached Calais on the night of New Years Day 1350. Before dawn the following morning, he and several of his companions entered, but the drawbridge was closed behind them. Some of those remaining outside and led by Charles de Montorency fled, but the rest held firm until caught between the forces of the king and prince of Wales who both fought incognito under the banner of Walter Manny. Among those captured were Charny himself, Eustace de Ribemont and Oudart de Renti.[59]

Geoffrey de Charny was one of the pre-eminent knights of his, and perhaps any other, generation to be placed alongside Henry of Lancaster, Bertrand Du Guesclin, the Black Prince, Edward III and in later years, Marshal Boucicault. He was the first known owner of the Shroud of Turin and died bearing the *Oriflamme* at Poitiers. He wrote a number of military and chivalric treatises, and his *Livre de Chevalerie* was most likely composed for King Jean's Order of the Star. The raid on Calais was not the jewel in the crown of an otherwise glittering career, but it serves to demonstrate the wide range of skills and abilities required of the military aristocracy and the mutability of the chivalric code by which they lived.

Limited action also continued at sea and the prince's first naval encounter was at Winchelsea in 1350. On 29 August, the English fleet, numbering something over 40, intercepted about 24 much larger Castilian ships led by Charles de la Cerda, who had been raiding in English waters. Despite the Anglo-French truce, the Castilians had continued to raid and attack English shipping, and preparations had been made to counter their threat. Ships were requisitioned and fitted out for action at Sandwich, the commanders of which included the king himself, his eldest son, the duke of Lancaster and the earls of Northampton and Warwick. During the battle, the prince's ship tried to ram another vessel, but was itself holed. The earl of Lancaster boarded the prince's intended target from the other side and pulled the prince and the young John of Gaunt, who was with him, to safety as their ship sank. Losses on both sides were very considerable and the Castilians were able to inflict great damage before they were boarded.[60]

In the main however, these were relatively quiet years for the prince, spent at court and at his numerous residences in and around the capital. The most significant of these were Kennington, Wallingford and Berkhamsted, which was the favoured country retreat. The palace at Kennington, in Lambeth, was located across the river from Westminster and extensive work was undertaken there between 1342 and 1363. The property consisted of a hall standing on an undercroft alongside a large building called the Prince's Chamber, which contained the main living apartments. There was also a separate kitchen. The prince's mason, Nicholas Ailington, carried out early renovations and improvements. The garden walls were built by the celebrated architect, Henry Yevele, who entered the prince's service in *c.*1356 and probably through this came to the king's attention. He worked on the castles of Queenborough and Rochester as well as the Black Prince's chantry in

*19   Lydford Castle, Devon. Built in 1195, the castle served as a court and jail for issues regarding the tin industry*

Canterbury Cathedral and the cloisters and south transept there, as well as the first cell and the cloister of the London Charterhouse. He also designed John of Gaunt's chantry for Old St Paul's and began the rebuilding of the nave of Westminster abbey.[61]

## 'Diplomacy': Home and Abroad

The years from the Black Death until the prince's first independent command in 1355 saw him increasingly involved in matters of state, and also witnessed the development of his household and administration. There is no evidence to show that he was closely involved with the daily business of government, but he was present on a number of significant occasions in court and at parliament. His administration in Cornwall, and particularly in Chester and Wales, began to flex its muscles.

At the end of October 1354, the prince with other dignitaries including the earls of Warwick and Stafford, Bartholomew Burghersh, and John Beauchamp were present at Westminster when the king appointed Lancaster and Arundel as his ambassadors to the Avignon. They were sent to confirm the terms and stipulations that had been made with the French at Guînes. The most significant of these was that Edward III should have in perpetuity and in full and free sovereignty (as an alod), the duchy of Guienne, in recompense for the crown of France. In addition, he was to have the duchy of Normandy and the county of Ponthieu as well as Angers and Anjou, Poitiers and Poitou, Le Mans and

*20   Restormel Castle, Cornwall. The castle overlooks the River Fowey, and was first built c.1100. It is characterised by its huge circular shell keep that encloses the principal apartments of the castle. The prince held court at the castle on several occasions*

Maine, Tours and Touraine, Angoulême and Angoumois, Cahors and Quercy, Limoges and Limousin, and all the other lands, castles and towns acquired in the course of the war. Edward also made it clear that he expected to take possession of any additional lands if they should be found to have been, at any time, part of the demesne of the kings of England. The ambassadors were to complete the process by 1 April.

In the event, the treaty of Guînes was a failure and the unwillingness of the French to ratify its terms provided the springboard for the prince's *grande chevauchée* and the blueprint for subsequent negotiations and agreements, namely the putative treaties of London (1358/9) and Brétigny-Calais (1360).[62]

Far from the capital, the Janus-faced character of the prince's administration was becoming apparent. In Cornwall and elsewhere, very considerable steps were taken to alleviate the worst financial consequences of the plague. However, in Cheshire and Wales the vicarious presence of a prince eager to assert his authority and increase his demesne income brought him into conflict with his tenants and his neighbours.

In 1353, Cheshire was marked by crime and disorder, which occasioned one of the prince's two visits to the earldom. The administration of the palatinate was the responsibility of the justiciar and chamberlain of Chester, at this time offices held by Roger Hopwell (after the death of Sir Thomas Ferrers on or about 10 August) and John Brunham, junior, respectively. The prince's visit was not occasioned by a rebellion but was 'in response to the express grievances of many of the people of Cheshire'. A general eyre was held before the community of the county in the shire hall and a fine of 5,000 marks payable over four years was agreed in return for the prince suspending the eyre for 30 years. However, the prince's justices did hold a great many sessions of trailbaston, probably in excess of 130 cases in about three weeks. Alongside these judicial investigations, there was a major overhaul of government in which the lieutenant-justiciar, the county sheriff, the constable of Chester castle and all the serjeants of the peace lost their offices. It was at this point that John Delves, one of the prince's key officials, came to prominence as the new lieutenant-justice of north Wales and Chester. The 1353 episode was a serious attempt to quell disorder and raise revenue, and it reflected a serious breakdown in relations between the most powerful members of Cheshire society and those beneath them. It was not terribly effective and the prince and his council were called on to return in 1358. It was not a problem that was resolved and led to further problems during Richard II's reign.[63]

Similarly in Wales, the government of the principality had become increasingly efficient throughout the prince's tenure of office. The previous administration had been characterised by absenteeism, pluralism, extortion and economic decline. Changes throughout the mid-fourteenth century to increase revenue and the prince's authority made the administration more productive and competent. These changes resulted in objections from the Marcher lords who, as they had the pretensions of Edward I in the 1290s and the younger Despenser, now closed ranks against the Black Prince. Edward III took steps to separate the factions and made clear the division and independence of the marches and the principality in the 1354 statute, which stated that Marcher lands were held directly of the king.[64]

The prince's activities in the March have been held as indicative of his attitudes and actions elsewhere. His direct involvement is questionable and policy there may have been determined and implemented by his administrators. Certainly, the prince should be held accountable for the actions of those acting in his name, but it may not have been a policy which he was prosecuting deliberately. The relatively new presence of an active and undoubtedly forceful administration in Cheshire, Flintshire and Wales, where previously there had been something of a power vacuum, was bound to come into contact and conflict with a number of vested interests. That the prince might have handled a number of these incidents more diplomatically, for example concerning the lordship of Gower, is not in doubt, whether it can be directly attributable to his avarice and rapacity is more questionable. Nonetheless, given the political atmosphere which was created in the March, it might be said that the king was taking a chance when he gave his son his first independent command in an even more politically sensitive arena, the duchy of Gascony.

# 4  GASCONY (1355-6)

## 1355: THE *GRANDE CHEVAUCHÉE*

As in 1346, it was an appeal for military assistance that led to an English expedition in France. In January 1355, members of the Gascon nobility, including the captal de Buch and the lords of Lesparre and Mussidan, present at the birth of Edward III's son, Thomas, expressed their concern at the attacks of the count of Armagnac whose lands became the principal target of the first raid. Armagnac had been appointed King Jean's lieutenant in Languedoc in November 1352. Two months later he began hostilities with the siege of Saint-Antonin, and by the end of May 1354 Armagnac was only 27 leagues from Bordeaux on the banks of the River Lot.[1] The resumption of Anglo-French hostilities had, in spite of this, become very likely after the failure of the French to ratify the treaty of Guînes and the breakdown of negotiations at Avignon.[2]

The prince and his father signed an indenture specifying his conditions of service and appointment as the king's lieutenant on 10 June 1355, which post-dated many of the preparations for the campaign. These included the purveyance of hurdles (used for separating horses when onboard ship) to be sent to Plymouth, by the sheriff of Devon, from Wales. On 27 May, Thomas Hoggeshawe, lieutenant of John Beauchamp, the admiral of the fleet west of the Thames, was appointed acting admiral of the prince's fleet, and John Deyncourt, sub-admiral of the northern fleet, was also involved. General orders were sent out in April;[3] Henry Keverell was paid for the purchase of gear for the prince's ship, items were delivered to John le Clerk and his fellows, the keepers of the *Christophre*, and on 16 July, ships from Bayonne were 'arrested' in various ports,[4] having been previously used to transport Lancaster's troops to Normandy.[5] Safe conducts were issued to the prince's men between 8 June and 6 September. It seems that preparations were undertaken with the intention that the expeditionary force should arrive in France very soon after the expiration of the truce on 24 June. In the event, contrary winds and perhaps delays in securing sufficient numbers of ships prevented their departure until 9 September. During the delay at Plymouth, the prince stayed at Plympton priory and concerned himself with affairs concerning the duchy of Cornwall. Advance groups were sent over prior to the arrival of the prince and the main fleet. On 1 July 1355, Tiderick van Dale, usher of the prince's chamber, was paid £20 on going abroad with Bartholomew Burghersh, the younger. He received a tun of wine and ten quarters of wheat at Plymouth prior to the muster.[6] Stephen Cosington and William the Chaplain were also sent to prepare the archbishop's palace at Bordeaux for the arrival of the prince who stayed there, whilst not on campaign, until his return to England in 1357. The main fleet sailed on 8/9

21  *Tomb of John Wingfield, Wingfield church, Suffolk. He first came to prominence in the service of the earl of Surrey and then William Montague, earl of Salisbury and served in his retinue at Crécy and Calais. By 1351 he transferred to the employ of the prince of Wales and became a bachelor of his household, steward of his lands, a chief councillor and 'governor of the prince's business'. He was sent to consult with the king over the implementation of the treaty of Brétigny. His daughter and heir, Katherine, married Michael de la Pole, the future earl of Suffolk*

*22   The tomb of John Wingfield*

September and arrived in Bordeaux eight days later at the height of the *vendage*. The earls of Warwick, Suffolk and their retinues embarked and sailed from Southampton. On 21 September, the prince spoke before the citizens of Bordeaux; his appointment as the king's lieutenant in Gascony was pronounced and his father's letters read out before the leading figures of the duchy in the cathedral of St Andrew.[7]

As in 1346, the campaign was preceded by an attempt to divide French forces. Lancaster was again involved, raiding from Gascony as he had in 1345, and on this occasion he attacked Normandy with Charles of Navarre, while the prince rode from Gascony, leading an expeditionary force of 800 men-at-arms and 1,400 archers. Among his commanding officers were the earls of Suffolk, Oxford and Warwick, Sir John Chandos, Sir Reginald Cobham and Sir James Audley. The advance cost of the expedition, war wages and regards was some £19,500, and shipping another £3,300. In the year from September 1355, over £55,000 was spent on the prince's military operation in Gascony.[8]

No attempts at secrecy preceded the attack which the prince led in 1355. Hostilities had already broken out between Armagnac and the Gascons, and the raid from Bordeaux was to be merely one element in a wider operation. French forces would be divided if they tried to deal with the prince, Lancaster and the king simultaneously.

The army left Bordeaux by 5 October, its strength augmented by the forces of the Gascon nobility, at least a further 4,000 men, bringing the total number to between 6,000 and 8,000 troops.[9] It marched south and a little east before heading almost due east on reaching Plaissance, thereafter the raid continued to the Mediterranean coast and Narbonne. The return to Bordeaux followed a not dissimilar path, widening the band of destruction to encompass Limoux, Boulbonne and Gimont.

Near Arouille, following usual practice, the army divided into three columns in order to march on a broad front. Anglo-Gascon casualties were low throughout 1355, John Lord Lisle being a notable exception, falling at Estang. Lisle had first seen service in 1339 and had served in Gascony in the early 1340s in addition to serving with Derby and at Crécy. A founder member of the Order of the Garter, he was also involved at Winchelsea and such service may have aided in his appointment as sheriff of Cambridgeshire and Huntingdonshire and governor of Cambridge castle.[10]

Promotions were a regular feature of the 1355 campaign, although there was no ceremony comparable to that held at La Hogue in 1346. Richard Stafford was made a banneret at Bassoues on 19 October and a number of new knights were dubbed including William Stratton, the prince's tailor, and Tideric van Dale, usher of the prince's chamber, on 12 November. After marching south for a hundred miles, the army swung east, crossed the River Gers, which marked Armagnac's eastern border, and approached the count's headquarters at Toulouse. At this stage, the larger towns tended to be avoided and those less well defended were pillaged and burned. This was not a siege train but a swiftly moving raid of devastation. The army forded the Garonne to the south and then the Ariège. This was a highly audacious move,

> an unthinkable idea to those who knew the area, and one which does not seem to have occurred to Armagnac . . . [who] . . . was confident that the Anglo-Gascons would not be able to penetrate into Languedoc beyond Toulouse.[11]

Armagnac was not drawn out and the army arrived at Carcassonne on 2 November. The city attempted to bribe the prince with 250,000 gold *écus*. It was not accepted and the *bourg* (the outer town) was burned, although no attempt was made on the heavily defended *cité* (the fortified, administrative centre). Narbonne, which they reached on 8 November, provided even less resistance, and although the citadel similarly held out, the town was virtually uninhabited and undefended when the prince arrived. Edward stayed in the Carmelite convent while the rest of the town was looted, albeit while suffering attack and bombardment from the *cité*. They withdrew on 10 November, pursued by furious troops and townsmen.[12]

Two French armies began to converge on the prince at this point from Toulouse and Limoges, led by Armagnac and Jacques de Bourbon respectively. The Marshal de Clermont also brought troops from north of the Dordogne and further support was expected from the Dauphin until he was diverted to Picardy. The prince marched north crossing the Aude at Aubian and when approached, the French fell back. Armagnac's policy was that of Philip VI's before Crécy, and with better reason, because of Crécy. He aimed therefore to defend the principal river crossings, towns and fortified sites. Prior to leaving Narbonne, the prince received letters from the pope who was fearful of the intentions of an army not far from Avignon. The messengers were not received courteously, and after a considerable wait were told to address their concerns to the king.

The march back was determined by the proximity of Armagnac and Bourbon, and the prince's motivation is uncertain. Was he seeking battle or seeking to avoid it? Edward rode towards Béziers before turning east, perhaps in the face of French reinforcements, towards

Armagnac. The prince was certainly expecting a battle even if he was not trying to engineer one, but Armagnac continued to withdraw. The prince followed him as far as Carcassonne and then headed towards the comparative safety of the lands of the count of Foix. The date of the 15 November marked an iconic moment in the raid and indeed the whole *chevauchée* strategy; Edward and his commanders spent the day at the Dominican house at Prouille, it being Sunday, while the rest of the army burned four towns in 12 hours.

The prince met Gaston Fébus, count of Foix, on 17 November at Boulbonne, and some agreement was reached. Gaston's lands were to be spared any attack and some of his troops were involved in the campaign the following year. The route back to Gascony was difficult and treacherous, taken perhaps in an attempt to avoid Armagnac, although if the count tried to engage Edward, it was not until he crossed the Ariège. There was some fierce but limited skirmishing and the army re-entered the duchy on 28 November and reached La Réole on 2 December.[13]

The *chevauchées* of 1355-6, like those that preceded the encounter at Crécy, struck at the military and personal reputation of the French monarch and nobility and seriously affected royal tax revenue. It was deliberately destructive, extremely brutal, yet was methodical and sophisticated. After the conclusion of the first raid, Sir John Wingfield, the prince's business manager, wrote to the bishop of Winchester. His letter, often quoted, shows great concern with determining the exact value to the French crown of the areas that were overrun in 1355 and thus the extent of the economic damage they were causing.[14]

> For the countryside and towns which have been destroyed in this raid produced more revenue for the king of France in aid of his wars than half his kingdom, as I could prove from authentic documents found in various towns in the tax collectors' houses.[15]

The experiences of 1346 were to be highly influential in the campaigns that followed. The 1355 expedition was an archetypal *chevauchée* and proved to be a remarkable tactical and logistical achievement. The prince marched from Bordeaux to the Mediterranean coast and back, fighting only a few minor skirmishes and causing a vast amount of damage. French defensive preparations were generally ineffective and over 500 villages were burned, it was 'une catastrophe sans précédent'.[16] The only exceptions to the destruction were to be religious buildings and the lands of the count of Foix. While officially neutral, Gaston Fébus assisted the prince, 'non seulement il assura son ravitaillement, mais encore il permit aux Béarnais de s'engager dans le corps expeditionnaire.'[17]

Armagnac's failure to react to the prince's army is very peculiar considering the extent of the destruction and the possible prizes should he win a battle. Hewitt argues that 'It is most probable that he had a secret understanding with the English',[18] but there seems to be little evidence to support this view and far more to suggest that he was a loyal Valois subject. In any case, the avoidance of pitched battle was extremely common. The association of the prince with the count of Foix must have given him pause for thought. Furthermore, there are no accurate figures concerning the forces that he had at his disposal and he may have been greatly outnumbered.[19]

During the winter of 1355-6, the troops were billeted along the northern march. Warwick remained at La Réole, Salisbury went to Saint-Foy, Suffolk to Saint-Emilion. The prince, with Chandos and Audley, marched to Libourne. Three weeks passed before any further action was taken.[20]

As with many campaigns during the war, regular communications were sent back to England for purposes of propaganda and public consumption at a variety of levels. Personal letters also exist. The 1355-6 expedition was no different, and such documents are extremely valuable, providing a great deal of information about the period between the *grande chevauchée* and the raid that would lead to a battlefield outside Poitiers.[21] The church tended to be the conduit for news, and prior to departure in 1355 the prince had visited Westminster to pray for success in the forthcoming expedition. Two letters were later written at Bordeaux on 23 and 25 December 1355 to William Edington, bishop of Winchester, from the prince and John Wingfield.[22] Edington was the head of the prince's council in England, and communications were sent initially to the prince's officials and were then more widely circulated. Richard Stafford and William Burton carried them to England. Requests for prayers were regularly made. The Friars Preachers, Friars Minor, Carmelites and Austin friars, the city of London and its bishop, were contacted with this demand. On his return from Poitiers, the prince gave thanks for his victory at Canterbury. Wingfield wrote at Libourne on 22 January, probably to Stafford, who had returned to England for reinforcements and supplies, and related events subsequent to the first raid.[23] Three letters recounted the events of the second raid and the battle of Poitiers. That of 25 June 1356, sent to the bishop of Hereford, was brief and requested prayers and masses. On 20 October, Roger Cotesford, one of the prince's bachelors, took another letter to the bishop of Worcester. The most important missive was carried by Nigel Loryng to the mayor, aldermen and commonality of London and was probably also intended for distribution outside the capital.[24] Other members of the retinue who wrote home also passed information. Bartholomew Burghersh penned communications to John Beauchamp, and Henry Peverel corresponded with the prior of Winchester. The prince also wrote to the prior naming all those killed or captured at Poitiers. News was also passed by papal envoys, via the wine trade, and the sub-admirals Deyncourt and Hoggeshawe who returned with some of the ships that had taken the army to Gascony.[25]

These letters do not, however, provide a great deal of evidence concerning military activity in Gascony during the spring of 1356 after Wingfield's letter of 22 January. The policy was to harass the enemy, possibly whilst waiting for reinforcements, or a further English invasion, or perhaps simply until the weather improved. The prince also had a number of administrative matters to deal with, such as an appeal of the commonality of Bayonne against the count of Albret, and diplomatic contacts had to be maintained with the count of Foix.[26]

The frontiers of Gascony were extended and fortified, a task simplified by the support, won and bought, of a number of Gascon nobles who had not participated in the earlier campaign, including Jean de Galard, Bertrand de Durfort and the lords of Caumont and Chalais. The army was deployed along the frontier and, under the command of some of the key figures in the military retinue, made a number of small-scale raids. The distribution of forces along the borders was a useful defensive measure against counter-

23 *Helm and crest, and gauntlets, from the tomb of Edward the Black Prince in Canterbury Cathedral Church 1376*

attacks, also serving to enlarge the Anglo-Gascon 'Pale', and it may have reduced any tensions that existed within the army. Despite this, the French retook over 30 towns and castles.[27] The difficulties of defending the borders of Gascony would be multiplied many times over when the Black Prince attempted to maintain the political integrity of the much larger principality of Aquitaine.

The raids had begun around Christmas. In Saintonge, the front probably lay along the River Charente, from Rochefort (threatening La Rochelle) to Taillebourg and as far as Cognac, where Burghersh was stationed. From there, he raided northward into Poitou and perhaps beyond. The captal de Buch was particularly successful, recapturing a number of castles in the east of Saintonge before invading Poitou in January and turning south toward Périgeux which he took and handed over to the lord of Mussidan. In the region of the Dordogne, the operational headquarters were at Libourne, with reserves at St Emilion. The earls of Oxford, Salisbury and Suffolk, with Elie de Pommiers and the lord of Mussidan, commanded 1,000 men and raided across the valley of the Dordogne towards Rocamadour. They took Souillac and Beaulieu-sur-Dordogne. The Garonne formed another boundary, although the French had some garrisons west of the river. Warwick probably crossed somewhere near Port Sainte Marie, which was captured by a detachment under the command of Chandos and Audley in January 1356. Warwick then swung northwards along the right-hand bank of the Garonne. Clairac was also taken before he marched on and captured Tonneins. At the time of Wingfield's letter, he was near Marmande. Chandos and Audley were in the Agenais. They took Castelsagrat after crossing the Garonne and raided towards Agen.[28] Baldwin Botetourt (master of the prince's great horses) was based at Brassac. The first six weeks of 1356 was scarcely less damaging to French royal interests in the south than the *grande chevauchée* itself and perhaps in strategic terms were more significant. Territorial gains were modest but important due to their concentration in the north-west march, and the new-found, if unreliable, Plantagenet allies brought further territorial control. Durfort controlled some 30 walled towns, Caumont a further six and Galard and Albret were highly significant landholders. More than this, 'They were the weather-vanes of the south-west',[29] their allegiance marked the ascendancy of the English and the prince; their defection in 1368-9 would similarly mark his decline.

## 1356: POITIERS

The success of the first raid and the support of new allies and the despatch of reinforcements demanded a succeeding campaign. Letters of protection were made out for Edward Despenser (lord Despenser from 1357), William third lord Morley, Edward Courtenay (household bachelor and retainer) and 119 others going to join the retinues of the prince and his captains on 28 March 1356.[30] It was to be fought under different conditions however, as on 12 January, Edward III had given the prince authority to undertake peace negotiations with the French.[31] The 1356 raid was part of a wider strategic programme involving Lancaster and possibly also the king. The intention seems to have been that the prince was to join forces with Lancaster. In retrospect, problems of communication and the pressure and opportunities created by the French defenders meant that if such co-ordination was achieved, it would be more by luck than judgement. Lancaster invaded Normandy in June and was joined by Robert Knolles, Jean de Montfort, Philip of Navarre and Godfrey de Harcourt. They departed on 22 June, re-supplied the Navarrese strongholds of Pont-Audemar and Breteuil, avoided battle and diverted attention from the south. On 8 August, Lancaster was commissioned to begin a campaign in Penthièvre.[32]

Gascony was again not left undefended, particularly as the prince had received intelligence that Armagnac was likely to attack after his departure. John Chivereston, the

*24 Badge of Edward III from MS Vincent 152 at the Heralds' College*

seneschal, Bernard d'Albret and Thomas Roos, mayor of Bordeaux, remained behind in command of the defence. The reason given for the expedition was that the prince wished to face the count of Poitiers, now the king's lieutenant in Languedoc, who was believed to be at Bourges and had been gathering troops since mid-May. Troops assembled there in June and July led by Jean le Clermont, Jean le Maingre, the seneschals of Poitou, Saintonge and Toulouse, and the royal secretary, Pierre de Labatut.[33]

The prince left Bergerac in early August with an army of 6,000-7,000.[34] They marched north along the east of the Massif Central through Périgord, the Limousin and Poitou. The second raid was not characterised, at least by the chroniclers, as being as destructive as that of 1355, but this is not to say that the Agenais, the Limousin and La Marche escaped without harm. After crossing the Vienne, there was some inconclusive skirmishing outside Bourges, which, despite the count of Poitiers not being present, was strongly defended. The force attracted attention almost from the outset, and Jean II raised the siege of Breteuil and rode south. The prince's army headed for the French interior and Edward spent the night at Vierzon, which he burned on leaving. Scouting parties made contact with French forces and Chandos and Audley encountered a French detachment led by

Philip de Chambly. On about 28 August, the prince learned that Jean's army was at Orléans and had not joined the count of Poitiers. The army advanced along the valley of the Cher to Romorantin, which fell on the 30th, although the keep of the castle held out for another three days when Marshal Boucicaut and the sire de Craon were captured. The delay caused by the siege gave the French an opportunity to overtake the prince. As in 1346, relatively small gains were given precedence over the potentially disastrous consequences that could result from the time lost to acquire them.[35]

The raiders marched westwards towards Tours down the bank of the Cher, but were unable to cross the Loire, near Amboise, thereby precluding any meeting with Lancaster. The prince was hoping for support and was 'intending to meet our dear cousin . . . of whom we heard for certain that he was trying to march towards us'.[36] Lacking supplies and ever more aware of the approach of the French army, the prince found himself resting for four days near Tours after a march of 320 miles in 32 days. The French royal army had moved more swiftly but in doing so had become extended over a considerable distance. After reaching Montbazon on 18 September, the prince's scouts found the French army outside Poitiers. Attempts were made by Cardinal Talleyrand de Périgord to make peace and the prince appeared willing to make a number of concessions. However, the French insistence on total surrender was refused and the battle lines were drawn on broken ground on the plains of Maupertuis.[37]

There is some disagreement about whether the English forces were retreating before battle was joined. The delay caused by Talleyrand's attempts to broker a truce may have offered the prince a route of escape and he may have been trying to get away up until the moment of the French attack. On Monday 19 September, following a council held the previous evening, the earl of Warwick led the baggage-train over or towards the River Moisson, probably at Nouaillé. This prompted the French to an immediate attack.[38] The prince wrote:

> Because we were short of supplies and for other reasons, it was agreed that we should retreat in a flanking movement, so that if they wanted to attack or to approach us in a position which was not in any way greatly to our disadvantage we would give battle.[39]

This was written after the event but does not indicate that the prince was looking for a battle at that time, nor did he feel the need to hide the fact that retreat was part of his plan. It is unclear if the prince intended to retreat as early as possible or only if the attack proved to be too strong. It is possible however, that it may have been a ploy to provoke a French attack.[40]

The charge was led by Audrehem and Clermont and was repulsed by the English archers. The Dauphin's 'battle' followed on foot and managed to engage the dismounted Anglo-Gascons, but was similarly driven back. This may have caused the division under the command of the young duke of Orléans to flee towards Chauvigny; 'from the moment this large body of troops turned away from the fight a French victory became almost impossible'.[41] The 'battle' commanded by King Jean may have been separated from the main army. Burne places much emphasis on this for the final French defeat. Its approach was slow and gave the Anglo-Gascons time to recover, although some of the force may have pursued the dauphin and Orléans.

These attacks, poorly co-ordinated and impeded by the terrain, foundered against the English forces, and the prince took the initiative by remounting a number of his men for a counter-attack. The most important aspect of this manoeuvre was the flanking strike of the captal de Buch into the left rear of the French army that crumpled under this attack. Burne gave two reasons for the cavalry charge: firstly that the defensive position occupied by the English was more effective against mounted than dismounted troops, and Jean was attacking on foot; and secondly, since the morale and resolve of the prince's troops was ebbing away, he would rely on the surprise and trust of the old cavalry charge, a frontal assault made in conjunction with a flanking manoeuvre. It was decisive.[42]

The prince's forces in 1355-6 consisted of three types of troops: men-at-arms, horsed archers and footmen. This allowed for an extremely flexible tactical response to a variety of situations. It is uncertain whether a set-piece battle was ever intended. If a meeting with Lancaster had been achieved, then the combined force would have been strengthened to such an extent that a successful battle might have seemed likely. Certainly, Crécy provided a precedent. Had additional forces and resources been available, and the arrival of the Black Death not precluded further military action, then the victory at Crécy might well have yielded far greater spoils than Calais and the ransoms and deaths of many of the French nobility. With the later Reims campaign in mind, it appears that a once-and-for-all victory was considered to be the best way of achieving success.

After the defeat at Crécy, the French had made several attempts to combat the English, particularly through imitating their tactics and dismounting their own men-at-arms. Tout noted the battles of Lunalonge (Poitou, 1349), Taillebourg (near Saintes, 8 April 1351), Ardres (6 June 1351) and Mauron (14 August 1352) as indicative of this. The example of battles such as Courtrai, Morgarten (1315) and Crécy had affected French military thinking and they endeavoured to find a weakness in the infantry-archer formation. In the event, these approaches proved ineffective, or were not put into action at Poitiers.[43] The use of a mounted force to lead the attack was one such innovation[44] but the defeat at Poitiers destroyed the illusion that French military changes could be effective. The contrast between the French response in 1356 with that of 1359 is very clear. It was these defensive tactics that allowed them to turn the tables on the English, firstly by denying Edward the crown in 1359-60 and then by reversing the territorial gains that the English had gained through the treaty of Brétigny. This was only possible when they had an easily assailable military objective, the principality of Aquitaine.

The location of the battle of Poitiers is highly conjectural, and as the terrain played an important part, this is significant. Jean caught the prince south of Poitiers trying to cross the River Moisson. The prince, it appears, was able to draw his force to an area of broken ground uncharacteristic of the plains of the area. Three divisions defended a position protected by natural obstacles, hedges, trees and marshy areas that allowed the French only two routes of attack. The difficult terrain and the volleys of arrows broke the charge led by Clermont and Audrehem.[45]

The formations used are also unclear. The French appear to have had a small advance cavalry force, which tried to attack and disrupt the archers at the opening of the battle.

*25  Warwick Castle — Caesar's tower, built 1360*

Three large divisions led by the dauphin, the duke of Orléans and Jean fought on foot. The English were also arranged in three major 'battles'. The Anglo-Gascon vanguard was led by Warwick, Oxford and the captal de Buch, and the rearguard by Salisbury and Suffolk. The bulk of the prince's retinue was in the centre led by Edward, with Burghersh, Audley, Chandos and Cobham. The archers were stationed on the flanks and possibly at right angles to the enemy. Their positions may have been defended with earthworks. The French divisions attacked in turn, although it appears that Orléans fled before engaging the enemy. The flanking force led by the captal de Buch may have included Gascon crossbowmen. The Anglo-Gascon army was probably composed of 3,000-4,000 men-at-arms, 2,500-3,000 archers and 1,000 other light troops. The French army may have included 8,000 men-at-arms, 2,000 *arbalesters* and numerous other poorly trained and lightly armed troops totalling some 15,000-16,000.[46] Jean could raise fewer men for Poitiers than his father had ten years before, although contemporaries did not attribute defeat to a shortage of manpower. Rather, and particularly by the author of *La complainte sur la bataille de Poitiers*, blame was heaped upon the nobility.[47] Furthermore, the French had few missile weapons with which to retaliate:

> Par son recrutement, et plus encore par sa préparation immédiate, la petite armée du prince de Galles était dans les meilleures conditions pour vaincre.[48]

The victory at Poitiers combined the defensive tactics demonstrated and witnessed by the prince at Crécy with the chivalric traditions of an earlier age. Only the French vanguard, led by the marshals, was mounted. After the failure of the French attacks, the Anglo-Gascon response was the classic heavy cavalry charge. The battle was thus a fine illustration of the use of dismounted troops who, as at Crécy, in concert with archers in a defensible position, broke the French attacks, then remounted and were victorious by the use of a cavalry attack, which was now uncommon, if not anachronistic.[49]

## ARCHERS AND THE LONGBOW

The role of the longbow in the early campaigns of the Hundred Years War is a contentious matter. A number of issues are open to argument and interpretation, ranging from the nature of the weapons themselves, their power and rate of accurate fire, to the disposition of the archers on the battlefield. The archers formed an integral part of the English tactical system, seeking to slow or disrupt an enemy advance. At Crécy, the bowmen were very effective against the French cavalry and at Poitiers against dismounted men-at-arms. These battles showed the superiority of the longbow over the crossbow. At this point, the range of the crossbow was less than the longbow and its speed of fire considerably slower, and at Crécy this may have been further reduced by rain and weather damage. The success of the archers in 1346 altered the structure of future English armies both proportionally and tactically.[50] In 1357 and 1369 the export of bows and arrows was forbidden and in 1365 archers were forbidden to leave England without royal licence. However, the effective defence of the forces under Charles de Blois and Du Guesclin at Auray demonstrated that close formations of well-armoured soldiers could provide a less easy target.

The use of the longbow, a popular, not aristocratic weapon, demonstrated the need for the king to draw on the support of all levels of society in his (at least theoretical) quest for the French throne. In 1363, instructions were issued requiring everyone, including the nobility, to participate in regular archery training and practice. The Reims campaign witnessed the full emergence of the mounted archer and establishment of mixed retinues (men-at-arms and archers). This in turn led to a shift in the social composition of the military community. The mounted troops gave the necessary mobility that allowed them to participate fully in *chevauchées* and for such raids to become engrained as the predominant strategy. The balanced troop composition allowed for an effective and flexible tactical response to a variety of military situations. Such forces were particularly effective when used in defensive positions, preferably prepared in advance or chosen for their advantageous terrain and natural features. The massed power of the archers could thin out the enemy at a distance and slow their advance.

The disposition of archers in general, in particular encounters, is still unresolved, at least partly due to the questionable nature of the formation described by Froissart as a *herce* in which the longbowmen operated.[51] It appears likely that troops' dispositions were not standard, but were dependent on a number of contingencies. At Crécy, the archers seem to have been used on the wings in a forward flanking position. They may have begun the battle beyond the front rank of dismounted troops to allow them to gain a little extra range. Bennett has questioned Sumption's proposition that the archers were surrounded by wagons for protection and suggests that they had a more mobile role, and that after the enemy approached, they fell back to the flanks curving slightly forward to provide crossfire. In this position, they would not have provided the vanguard with much protection. Due to the numbers involved and the lie of the land, it may be that the front was almost a mile in length. This allowed only a very light defence of the prince's division in the centre. Formations at Poitiers are less certain but, again, archers seem to have been used on the flanks (possibly at right angles). They were led by the earl of Oxford to attack the French cavalry, and were used to defend the Anglo-Gascon lines from behind earthworks.[52]

With considerations of strategy completed and the battle won, the prince invited all the captured nobles to dine with him:

> The prince himself served the king's table, and all the other tables as well with every mark of humility, and refused to sit at the king's table saying he was not yet worthy of such an honour, and that it would not be fitting for him to sit at the same table as so great a prince, and one who had shown himself so valiant that day.[53]

Geoffrey Hamelyn, the prince's attendant, was sent to London with Jean's tunic and helmet as proof of his capture. The army returned to Bordeaux and negotiations began regarding a truce and the terms of the king's ransom.

# 5 THE SIEGES OF REIMS AND PARIS (1357-61)

## TRIUMPH AND THE TREATIES OF LONDON

The constable of Bordeaux, John Streatley and William Lynne, dean of Chichester, were entrusted with the peace talks, alongside members of the prince's council and Gascon advisers including Warwick, Reginald Cobham, Nigel Loryng, Burghersh and the captal de Buch. In October 1356 they were joined by the papal legates, the cardinals of Périgord and Capocci. Early in the following year, the prince was authorised to seek a peace, and a truce was established for two years until 9 April 1359.[1]

The prince and his captive returned to England on 11 April 1357 and proceeded to London, where they were received at a glorious celebration. The next years were marked by a number of great tournaments and ongoing negotiations for Jean's release. The Black Prince also rewarded many of those who fought with in France. For the ordinary soldiers this might include pardons for various crimes, gifts of wine, timber, grazing rights and so on. Land, rents and offices were also granted and annuities were given to those of greater stature. For example, William Lenche, the prince's porter, who lost an eye in the battle, was granted the profits from Saltash ferry in Cornwall.[2] The case of James Audley shows the generosity expected of a prince and also the value of ransoms. Audley was injured in the struggle and was able to take few prisoners. As a consequence, he received the largest annuity of any of the prince's army, £400.[3] The Black Prince sold three prisoners to Edward III for £20,000.[4]

The price for the greatest prize from Poitiers, King Jean, was the subject of two treaties. Negotiations, again mediated by the papal representatives, began in June or July of 1357. The first treaty of London was signed on 8 May 1358, and involved the transfer of nearly all French lands south of the Loire and 4,000,000 gold crowns (£666,666). The French, now wracked by internal strife and dissension, were certainly unwilling and probably unable to even pay the first instalment. At this point, perhaps not even expecting a peaceful resolution, Edward III demanded an even higher price with the inclusion of Boulogne, Anjou, Maine, Touraine and Normandy, perhaps half of the kingdom of France in full sovereignty in addition to the ransom. The dauphin refused to ratify the treaty and England mobilised for war once again.[5]

# THE REIMS CAMPAIGN AND THE TREATY OF BRÉTIGNY

In 1359, Edward III's motivation was different to that which had galvanised previous campaigns. This was a direct assault, aiming for nothing less than the throne of France, and presumably influenced the change in strategy from that employed at Crécy and pursued ten years later. In all probability it was the victory at Poitiers that allowed Edward III to seriously countenance an attempt on the crown. The attempt failed. Edward hoped that he would encounter little resistance and that the gates of Reims, possibly with the aid of the archbishop Jean de Craon, would be opened to him. If this failed, he would attempt to force the dauphin into battle, employing the tactics that had been so effective in 1346 and 1356.[6] By contrast with the Crécy and Poitiers campaigns, this was not a *chevauchée* in the true sense; it was not to be an overly destructive expedition. Edward had no desire to further alienate and anger his future subjects and damage his potential tax revenue. The king did not seek to pillage and burn the land that he thought would soon be his own. The capture of Jean II and many of his nobles at Poitiers had given the English a huge advantage in the war, which they tried to convert into something tangible and territorial. The failure of the treaties of London (1358-9) resulted in a campaign to hammer home the victory of three years before and seize what was almost a vacant throne. It proved to be a campaign of long marches and lengthy sieges and, arguably, it came to nothing.

Preparatory strikes preceded the campaign of 1359-60. Lancaster arrived at Calais as an advance guard on or around 1 October and led a *chevauchée* through Artois and Picardy returning to Calais via Montreuil. Roger Mortimer followed on 22 October and raided along the coast to Étaples, which he burned before returning to Calais.[7] There was no attempt to maintain any sort of secrecy about the invasion. Edward made his intention clear, to march to Reims and there be crowned king of France. Whilst this was necessary from a political and psychological point of view, it did permit the French to strengthen the defences of the coronation city and lay in supplies of victuals and weapons.

On arrival at Calais, the army divided into two columns. The king with Edmund of Langley, Warwick, Suffolk, Oxford and Salisbury. In total, 3,000 men-at-arms and 5,000 archers commanded the main body. The Black Prince, with his brothers, Gaunt and Lionel of Antwerp, commanded the rearguard of 2,500 men-at-arms and 4,000 archers including Thomas Gray, the author of *Scalacronica*, the main source we have regarding the prince's itinerary and many of the incidents of the march.[8] The duke of Lancaster, already in the field, reinforced the newly arrived troops to form a third unit.

The advance in parallel on a broad front, perhaps on a pre-planned route, was necessitated by the need to find provisions. The prince stopped at Montreuil, Hesdin, Nesle, Ham, St Quentin and Martiers, which the French burned to obstruct his crossing, although a way was forced at Chateau-Porcien. The route roughly followed the path taken in Lancaster's preliminary raid. They were not attacked throughout the march,

> the young prince [dauphin], warned by the ill-success of his father, resolved to act only on the defensive; he accordingly prepared to elude a blow it was impossible for him to resist.[9]

*26   Seal of King Edward I (AD 1272-1307) on horseback and enthroned in Majesty. The career of Edward I laid some of the foundations for the later 'military revolution', and his ongoing struggle with the French foreshadowed the Hundred Years War. The conquest of Wales would provide Edward of Woodstock with a principality in 1343 that was the source of many of the troops for the Crécy/Calais campaigns*

On reaching Reims, the prince made camp at Villedomange. The town defences had been undergoing steady improvements for some years, a process that had been further galvanised by the battle of Poitiers. There had been no attempt to disguise the English target, unlike the 1346 operation, and accordingly the French were well prepared. Artillery had been purchased from Paris, St-Quentin and Rouen and an *artilleur* hired from Verdun. Defences were also laid in the River Vesle. The town was effectively 'enclosed' in the summer of 1358, leaving a killing ground outside the perimeter.[10] Much of the credit for the improvements to the defences in the months leading to the siege must be given to the captain of the town, Gaucher de Châtillon, seigneur of Ferté.

The eventual French victory in the war depended on successful sieges in France. Equally, it was dependent on successful fortification and defences. The ability of a town to resist siege determined who controlled the territory in its hinterland.[11] The army that came before Reims did not expect to besiege it, at least not for long. However, the walls had been strengthened following an order from the king to Jean de Craon, issued on 18 March 1356, and the defeat at Poitiers further spurred building activity. On 31 December 1358, the dauphin wrote to the captain of the town, ordering its defences strengthened and work done on the fortifications throughout 1359. Edward hoped that his close relationship with the archbishop would result in the easy capture of the city. It was a thought that had been shared by many of Reims' population. However, when Edward and his army arrived on 4 December 1359, they found strong defences and a city well stocked with soldiers and supplies.[12]

As the siege began, so did raids into the surrounding country. Eustace d'Aubrechicourt was very successful in a number of attacks along the River Aisne.[13] The prince's troops operated in concert with Gaunt's on a number of occasions. Burghersh,[14] Botetourt and many others of the prince's and the earl of Richmond's households took Cormicy and captured the lord of Clermont after a siege lasting from 20 December to 6 January. The town was burned two days later. Lancaster, Chandos and Audley, with Gaunt and Mortimer, took and burned Cernay-en-Dormois (30 December) and later, with d'Aubrechicourt, Autry and Manre. No attempt was made to assault Reims and, at best, an ineffective blockade was achieved. It adds credence to the concept that Edward simply hoped to gain the acceptance of the resident populace as their king. Efforts were continually made to convince the city of the validity of his claim and his goodwill towards the people.[15]

The siege failed due to the lack of provisions, particularly fodder for the horses and the army was forced away in search of forage. It took them to Burgundy. Near Châlons, Audley and the captal de Buch joined the prince. They reached Auxerre, staying at Égleny and suffered considerable losses at French hands:

> Several of his [the prince's] knights and esquires were killed at night in their quarters and his foraging parties taken in the fields.[16]

The king managed to secure the support of a section of the Burgundian nobility on the payment of 200,000 florins. They were further reinforced by members of the Companies, including Knolles and a number of Gascons who had 'made their way right across France by a devious route'[17] to serve under the prince. There were a number of further reverses. Flavigny was retaken from Nicholas Dagworth (son of Thomas and another of the prince's Norfolk military associates and captain of Flavigny in Burgundy) and on 24 February, Roger Mortimer, the earl of March, died during a raid at Rouvray.

A French naval attack on Winchelsea in March 1360 spurred Edward to assault Paris. The rearguard marched via Pierre-Perthuis, through the Gâtinais and east to Tournelles and Moret, suffering French guerrilla attacks *en route*. It reached the suburbs of Paris by the end of the month and set up camp in the Corbeil-Longjumeau area. Gray recounts a number of incidents that befell the prince's retinue, including the near-capture of Richard Baskerville and Brian Stapleton and other knights who met and defeated a French force near Janville.[18] However, they failed to provoke a battle, despite burning the suburbs, and the siege lasted only until 13 April, *Black Monday*, when lack of food and storm conditions took their toll and a truce was called at Brétigny.

The treaty of Brétigny[19] was a prize that Edward III would have grasped with open arms in 1340; whether it was a settlement so gratefully accepted in 1360 is another matter entirely. The Reims campaign was a failure. However it is painted, the expedition made no military gains and Edward had no opportunity to use the crown that he brought with him in his baggage train. It did acquire territory equivalent to perhaps a third of France and a very substantial ransom particularly for King Jean and also for a number of his close family and members of the high nobility. But this was not the throne, and it was not all that Edward had demanded in the treaties of London. Essentially, the question that must be asked was whether the treaty of Brétigny was enough after the crushing victory at Poitiers, the capture of King Jean and the social and political turmoil wreaked by Etienne Marcel, the *Jacquerie* and the machinations of Charles of Navarre. Perhaps it was not.

The role of the Black Prince and members of his household and retinue should not be underestimated in the negotiations leading to the treaty of Brétigny-Calais in 1360.

Stephen Cosington was involved in diplomatic activities in Normandy and elsewhere and Miles Stapleton and Nigel Loryng served as ambassadors to France between 13 August and 7 December 1360. The prince himself was sent to Calais 'pro tractatu pacis ibidem habito inter reges Francie et Anglie', for which he was paid expenses of £200 and wages of £10 a day.[20]

Anne Curry has characterised the Hundred Years War as a conflict of three treaties (Paris, 1259, Brétigny, 1360, Troyes, 1420), each of which contributed as much to the origin and continuance of the war as they did to ensuring differing periods of peace.[21] There is little doubt that the treaty of Brétigny and the failure of both sides to implement the renunciation clauses contributed a great deal as regards later motivation to fight, and it was a prime complaint of Henry V, prior to the Agincourt campaign, that the conditions of Brétigny had not been met. Nor was it only a matter of concern for those engaged in high politics. It has been suggested that the treaty and Edward III's war policy in the 1360s were the subject of allusions by Langland in *Piers Ploughman*. If correct, the treaty was not viewed favourably — the king had lessened his lordship 'for a litel siluer'. Similarly, the Prophecy of John of Bridlington, written between 1362-4 by John Erghome, urged the king not to give up his inheritance and predicted that the Black Prince would become king of France by 1405. The Anonimalle Chronicle also reported that Brétigny was 'to the great loss and harm of the king of England and his heirs for ever'. The *Scalacronica* of Thomas Gray was similarly scathing although the criticism was couched in more general terms advocating that the king should not make peace.[22]

## CHIVALRY, MILITARY SOCIETY AND A 'REVOLUTION'[23]

The treaty of Brétigny marked the conclusion of the first major phase of the Hundred Years War. It also brought to a conclusion English military success, apart from in the more distant theatres of Spain and Brittany. There are many reasons for this, the ability of the French to marshal defences being key. It was also a major period of transition in the complexion of the aristocracy and the ideology with which it associated. The Reims campaign had also marked a transition in the complement of English armies that altered the role and significance of the chivalric classes.

The decline of the feudal host, development of the contract army and changing military tactics influenced both the projected image of the aristocracy and the view that they had of themselves. The traditional role of the English aristocracy was compromised in victories founded on a tactical system that did not rely on the mounted knight. The 'Three Orders' may have been, to some extent, an artificial construct, but it had relevance in everyday life and was an accepted and ingrained philosophy. The *raison d'être* of the *bellatores* was fractured by a tactical system founded on infantry, archery and the 'common' soldier. Chivalry was founded on the battlefield but skill-at-arms was not its only criterion. The 'courtly arts' had become a standard of polite behaviour and were the foundation of a genteel education, but despite the needs for literacy and *curtesie*, the essential qualities of the *milites strenui* remained the qualities of the warrior; courage, loyalty and above all skill at arms.[24] Laudable as the prince's actions were after Poitiers,

*27  (opposite) Brass of Nicholas Dagworth, Blickling Church, Norfolk. The son of Sir Thomas and heir to various manors in Norfolk and Essex. He fought with the Black Prince in 1356-7 and by 1359 he was captain of Flavigny in Burgundy. He may have joined the prince in Aquitaine, he certainly received letters from Edward III forbidding his participation in Du Guesclin's 'crusade' to Castile. It is probable, but not certain, that he joined the prince on his own campaign in 1367. In 1373 he was granted a 100 mark annuity at the exchequer by the king and he remained closely linked to the royal household for the rest of his life. He was an envoy and diplomat to Aquitaine, Avignon, Italy, Ireland, Flanders and Scotland. He became a knight of Richard's chamber and, as such, was a focus of attack by the Appellants in 1388, alongside Elmham, Gournay and Henry Green, although they did not suffer the same fate as Simon Burley. However, despite his close royal links, the Lancastrian revolution did not damage his standing and his annuity was confirmed by Henry IV. He died on 2 January 1402*

what was truly valued was prowess, a combination of training, innate skill and boldness, such as exhibited by Sir Ralph Hastings 'who cared not two cherries for death', and Sir William Felton 'the valiant [who] very boldly and bravely charged the enemy like a man devoid of sense and discretion'.[25]

While the core of the chivalric ethic remained static, other aspects of *noblesse* were more fluid. The structure and complexion of aristocratic order was complicated as it became more socially diverse. In 1337, the Black Prince became the first English duke and other ranks would follow at both ends of the chivalric spectrum with the establishment of the esquire and gentleman as ranks and titles in their own right. With this developed a dichotomy as 'class' boundaries were blurred in some cases and reinforced in others.

The distinction between nobility, knighthood and gentility was one of degree; there was little to choose between a wealthy member of the gentry and a relatively impoverished noble, and as the opportunities for social advancement became not only dependent on military ability or a fortunate marriage. The example of the de la Pole family who rose from being East Anglian wool merchants to earls of Suffolk is a case in point. Similarly, although knighthood and chivalry were inextricably linked, they were nonetheless not synonymous. Chivalry was not a code only restricted to knights, as the emerging gentry class became both chivalrous and armigerous.

The gradations within the gentry were partially formalised in 1363, with sumptuary regulations laid down by parliament governing the dress of different social ranks, by which the lesser aristocracy were grouped according to income. Similarly, the labour legislation following the Black Death and reintroduced on a regular basis sought to restrict 'social climbing' as the game laws would do in the last decade of the century. In concert with such general attitudes, it was at this time that nobility became a question of legal definition and was divorced from its knightly and warrior overtones through its association with the parliamentary peerage. 'By the late twelfth century nobles were knights and knights were the highest social class . . .'[26] This was to change during and partly as a result of the Hundred Years War.

In addition, formerly military titles were being conferred for civilian service. This is not to say that military service had lost its importance, it could not in the context of the

28 *Tomb of William Kerdeston, Reepham church, Norfolk. A banneret who fought with the prince in 1346 and at Calais. He held lands in Norfolk, Suffolk, Lincolnshire, Cambridgeshire and Yorkshire. However, his administrative duties were predominantly confined to Norfolk — commissions of array, inquisition, oyer and terminer and, once only, of the peace. He served as MP for Norfolk between 1337 and 1360. He died on 14 August 1361*

Hundred Years War, although perhaps the triumph of the contract army changed its character. However, administrative and legal abilities were becoming highly valued. Thus, knighthood was losing its monopoly on chivalry as it passed to non-knightly ranks and as the knights themselves saw the opportunities of non-military careers. In this capacity, they could still act as the leaders of local society and the landowning elite still served the king or an overlord through an institutionalised relationship. The prince's retinue demonstrates this clearly through the changing character of the administration in which clerks gave way to soldier-administrators, men such as John Delves and John Henxteworth, before progressing to a 'professional' bureaucracy.

While they remained the recruiting captains, knights were no longer the chief defenders of the realm or the key weapons in an army. The knight now fought often dismounted, alongside lowborn soldiers, indeed often criminals, fighting for booty and a pardon. Chivalry always had financial connotations; the development of the ransom system lay at the heart of the ethic on the battlefield and in the tournament. Now however, knights fought for pay as part of a tactical system of which they were only a component. Some of the chivalric veneer was taken from them even as some of it was passed to those who fought alongside. Knighthood itself, despite a brief resurrection following early English military successes, was becoming less popular. Therefore, while this was undoubtedly a period of chivalric revival, the numbers of military active knights diminished to such a degree that action had to be taken to reverse this trend. A variety of theories have been proposed to answer the question of why the need to distrain arose: increasing costs of equipment; the spiralling expense of the dubbing ceremony; and escalating and onerous local duties have all been mooted. While plate armour and horse costs increased in the period up to the Reims campaign, the value of warhorses taken abroad by the English after the resumption of the war in 1369 was considerably reduced. This was probably due to the nature of English raiding tactics, the *chevauchée*, which necessitated the use of light, swift horses and the Crown's unwillingness to reimburse for loss of horses on campaign. The developing stratification of the lower aristocracy, the diffusion of the chivalric aura and the concurrent extension of gentility to these new ranks enabled potential knights to decline the honour and retain a comparable social position.[27]

Differing influences shaped the military aristocracy, as nobility and knighthood and chivalry, virtually synonymous for so long, became separate concepts and realities. To a degree, and only briefly, they came together in the halcyon days after Crécy and Poitiers. Edward III emphasised the military implications of chivalry, assimilating the ideals of knighthood with royal policy and dynastic ambition.[28] So it was that 'Chivalry remained a live cultural model even when, after Crécy . . . it was out of tune not only with the new military techniques but with the moral perception of the practical irrelevance and visible "frivolity" of the knight in shining armour.'[29]

The conduct of the prince's knightly retinue when on military service was governed by chivalry, particularly those aspects which found expression in the Laws of War, compounds of Christian and Classical theories bound with feudal tradition. These 'prescribed a minimum of humane and rational behaviour'[30] which fell short of the chivalric ideal but for some mitigated the worst battle conditions. They dealt with matters such as military discipline, the payment of wages, the division of spoils, military ranks and honours, duels, treaties, truces and alliances. They were chivalric rather than simply military in that pacts sworn under the law of arms were sworn on the knighthood of those concerned. In the context of a cosmopolitan knightly caste, the law of arms was international. There were, however, no international courts to implement the laws and cases were brought before the sovereign of the defendant. There were obvious difficulties in getting a fair hearing once one had overcome the immediate practical barriers of travel to the court, which was very possibly in enemy territory. The cases were heard by knights with experience of such matters who were often the official lieutenants of the lord in question, his constable or marshal. In England, cases were heard before the court of chivalry in which the Lord High Constable and the Earl Marshal presided. The constable, John Chandos, heard cases brought before the Black Prince, as prince of Aquitaine.

The effect of the crusades, romance literature and social tradition led to both an idealization of war and ambivalence towards violence allowing for an equivocal attitude to mercenaries and the *condottieri*. Although written after the conclusion of the Hundred Years War, the following passage is indicative of fourteenth century attitudes. 'War! What a joyful thing it is! One hears and sees so many fine things, and learns so much that is good.'[31] There was a direct link between chivalric idealism and the social distress and devastation caused by its implementation. Despite the courtly and literary influences and those from religious authorities, from the introduction of the Peace and Truce of God movements onwards, it is difficult to see those outside the chivalric order gaining any practical benefits from the code. For some, such as Henry of Grosmont, duke of Lancaster, chivalry prescribed a strict moral code and contemporaries saw him as an archetype of religious chivalry. He crusaded in Lithuania and elsewhere and was the author of a devotional treatise that confessed his own sins and highlighted the tension between one's duty as a Christian and a delight in the noble lifestyle. Nonetheless, on several occasions he massacred the inhabitants of a city who had resisted him, including women and children. His acts were justified by the laws of war and did not detract from his chivalric status. Geoffrey de Charny, bearer of the French royal standard who died at Poitiers, and was incidentally the first known owner of the Turin Shroud, had similar views, which he extended to the whole order of knighthood. Like Grosmont, Charny's *Livre de Chevalerie*, probably written for the Order of the Star, the French answer to the Garter, sometimes has an almost puritanical tone and contains some very similar images, particularly those concerning the denigration of the body. Charny emphasised the physical suffering endured by the knight on campaign and in battle. He viewed the life of a true knight as almost one of martyrdom. He drew parallels between the order of chivalry and a religious order but argued that no order of religion imposed greater rigours than chivalry. In much the same way as St Bernard had written of the Knights Templars so Charny wrote of the order of knighthood in general, stating that 'Through the hard martyrdom of their profession knights acted in accordance with God's will.'[32] For the majority, chivalry provided less elevated strictures although they benefited from such attitudes. The Black Prince and Bertrand Du Guesclin may be seen as leading examples of this 'secular' knighthood.[33] Away from the battlefield, the prince was seen as behaving with the courtesy and generosity expected of a knight of his station; in battle he was governed by the laws of war and the practicalities of the *chevauchée* strategy.

Before the 1346 expedition, Edward III issued strict orders to check excesses by his troops. No towns or manors were to be burnt, no churches or holy places sacked, and the old, women and children were to be spared, on pain of life or limb. This had relatively little effect, if indeed it had ever been more than propaganda. It was impossible to restrain troops whose main object was pillage.[34] As Froissart said, 'in spite of the King's orders, many atrocious murders, thefts and acts of arson were committed, for in the kind of army that King Edward led there are always villains, rogues and men of easy conscience'.[35] However, when the abbey of St Lucien near Beauvais was destroyed, the king promptly hanged 20 of the men responsible. The Black Prince's raids of 1355-6 were particularly vicious and it appears the prince was unable to prevent a great deal of devastation, such as the burning of Carcassonne after he had given explicit orders for its preservation. It was not incongruous that the leaders of the 1355 raid should spend a Sunday at a monastery whilst their men, a few miles away, were burning and looting.[36]

It has been said, 'It is impossible to be chivalrous without a horse.'[37] The knight was by definition a soldier. He had gained social and political status as a result of being a highly effective mounted warrior powerful enough, in the words of Anna Comnena, to batter down the walls of Babylon.[38] Yet, in 1346, the chivalry of France was defeated at the battle of Crécy by a combination of archers and dismounted knights and men-at-arms. It was confirmation of the end of the dominance of the mounted knight. His customary military role had altered and would further change. This shaped the ethos that sustained the knight and reinforced his social and political position. Nonetheless, knights remained an important constituent of armies although they were to adopt different tactics and modes of fighting.[39]

The increasing use and role of the longbow also compromised the influence of the knight and, it has been suggested, brought an end to chivalry on the battlefield. The devastating power commonly attributed to the longbow may have been overstated and there is much disagreement over the physical nature of the weapons concerned, let alone their deployment and effect in a battle situation. There is no doubt, however, that throughout this period the complement of armies changed and the emphasis on heavy horsed troops shifted significantly in favour of archers, both mounted and on foot. Campaigns continued to concentrate on economic warfare bent on destroying the enemy's revenue. The *chevauchée* was used to great effect by the English in the early years of the war. In addition to financial consequences, it struck a powerful psychological blow. The people suffered and the authority of the French nobility was questioned and threatened in the strongest possible manner. The battles of Crécy and Poitiers followed such *chevauchées* and it has been argued that they were deliberately provocative actions designed to bring the French to battle where the highly effective defensive tactics could be used to good effect.[40] The essential factor in the use of this new tactic was discipline. This, in itself, ran counter to the knightly quest for individual glory. It is arguable that Crécy and Poitiers were victories of professional discipline over traditional chivalric recklessness.

By the early fourteenth century, the old feudal basis of knighthood had virtually disappeared in England. The summons to the feudal levy was no more than a technical obligation, and money, not land, was exchanged for military service as the indenture system became increasingly common. As a consequence, the Hundred Years War was fought, for the most part, by paid professionals. This was true not only of the mercenary Free Companies but also the nobility who augmented their fortunes in land with the profits of a career in arms, and of the rank and file raised in England and Wales. Yet, despite the bitter practicalities of war, it was recorded and reported in very different terms. The tournament had begun as a mimic war; war was now described in terms reminiscent of a tournament. This was so because *guerre mortelle* was rare until the fifteenth century having been reserved usually for the infidel. Crécy was an exception to this.[41] Ransoms prevented wholesale aristocratic slaughter but encouraged hostilities. War was often an economic necessity for poorer knights and the rewards for service could be considerable.

*29   Coin of Edward the Black Prince 1330-1376*

The direct effect of chivalry in a military context is more difficult to pin down and may serve to show that despite the overt 'courtliness' of the Black Prince's household, his military retinue was an altogether professional military unit. In an age of discipline and defensive tactics, chivalry, and particularly mounted chivalry, was more likely to bring about defeat than victory as had happened at Crécy, Poitiers and Nájera. It was not only a French 'weakness'. During the Crécy campaign a scouting party of the first division, of which the prince was in nominal command, was detached to see if a way across the river Seine could be found for all the bridges were broken. Eventually they found a ford but it was heavily defended. The French troops on the other side taunted and bared their backsides at them. This so enraged the English that they made an ill-advised assault and were beaten back with heavy losses. Ten years later while on a scouting expedition shortly before the battle of Poitiers, the captal de Buch, Burghersh, the sire de Pommiers and Eustace d'Aubrechicourt attacked the French army. 'These Englishmen could not forebear but set upon the tail of the French host and cast many down to the earth and took diverse prisoners so that the host began to stir and tidings thereof came to the French King . . .'[42]

The members of Black Prince's retinue achieved the military success necessary for chivalric acclaim and were at the forefront of Edward III's policy. It was further supported by the atmosphere and ethos at work within the household and court of the prince. It was there in the household, in the tournament, in the *courtly* world that the prince's chivalric reputation is best exemplified, for his military success was founded on a tactical system that flew in the face of the chivalric ideal, being both dismounted and disciplined. The retinue benefited from the military success gained on the battlefield and the chivalrous and courtly milieu when not on campaign. It brought members of the retinue together through military associations of various kinds and gave them a collective identity. Many individuals who fought with the prince were marked out as worthy knights, *prudhommes* in their own right, but all benefited from the prince's reflected glory, a glory which in its way sounded the death-knell of chivalry on the battlefield.

Such a change in strategy, tactics and attitude to war begs the question of whether this constituted a 'military revolution'. Unfortunately it is difficult to ascertain the conditions under which war was fought and battles undertaken, if they were undertaken with any regularity or confidence before the period for which a number of authors have suggested that there was such a revolution. The role of the warhorse, long held to have been the mainstay and supreme weapon in the 'feudal' army, has been questioned, the importance of infantry highlighted, and the significance of the longbow interrogated. However, that infantry, well drilled, preferably experienced and occupying a defensible site, would defeat heavy cavalry in most situations does not preclude the importance of the knight and his warhorse as a savagely effective weapon both physically, and perhaps more importantly, psychologically.

Whether or not there was a military revolution in the early decades of the fourteenth century there was a change in English tactical thinking, probably spurred by a number of humiliations at the hands of the Scots. The use of dismounted knights necessitated alterations in equipment, particularly to provide increased mobility out of the saddle. Nonetheless, 'The military scene was still dominated by the heavily armed knight armed with a lance and sword even if it often happened that he fought on foot.'[43] The development of the use of infantry in co-ordination with archers was of vital importance in the English successes of 1346 and 1356. The 'revolution' was not marked by a great increase in troop numbers, especially when compared with those armies raised by Edward I. The paucity of particular records for 1346-7 does not allow for an accurate breakdown of the types of troops involved although the complement was probably in the region of 8,000 foot soldiers and over 3,000 mounted archers and hobelars. This was perhaps the largest field army raised during Edward III's reign. It was augmented for the Calais siege. The army of the Reims campaign may only have numbered 6,600 in total.

The use of dismounted troops was not an innovation, although to dismount knights, with its inherent social implications, was rare. The cavalry charge was an uncommon, if highly effective phenomenon. It could also prove very costly. The charge was not to be used as an opening gambit but as at Crécy and at Poitiers, troops were remounted towards the end of the battle after the archers and dismounted troops and infantry had done their work. The manoeuvre of the captal de Buch at Poitiers in which he led a cavalry force to attack the rear of the French army was decisive, as was Calveley's similar action at Auray, and it was also undertaken at Nájera. This pattern was rare; after Bannockburn there was scarcely a battle in which the English chivalrous class fought on horseback.[44]

The early victories and those at La Roche-Derrien, 1347, Taillebourg, 1351, Ardres, 1351, Mauron, 1352, and Poitiers in 1356 have not all been attributed to an Anglo-Gascon tactical approach. Jim Bradbury maintained that the French failures were the result of not developing a type of infantry to match the pikemen and infantrymen of other nations. Perroy attributed the English victory of 1346 to numerical inferiority that forced Edward 'to resort to improvised ruses, of which, in his heart of hearts, he was somewhat ashamed'.[45] Rogers states that the early victories that were so influential only occurred because of peculiarities of terrain and the mistakes of enemies.[46] The theory of an English battle-seeking strategy is open to question but it would seem likely that, particularly at Poitiers, the prince could have avoided battle if he so wished. Philip VI's tactics in the 1330s and early 1340s proved highly effective. The rashness of Audrehem at Poitiers and the failure of Enrique to listen to French advice not to give battle before Nájera brought about defeat.

The characteristics of the wider strategy and more narrowly focused tactics were, by the beginning of the prince's military career, based around an experienced and professional body of men, both in the wider military community and within his own retinue and household. The basic characteristics of the English battle formation remained constant from Dupplin Moor to Agincourt. The disposition of troops was crucial to the English and Anglo-Gascon victories, and the arrangement of troops at Crécy followed the pattern instigated by Northampton at Morlaix. The most significant element of the strategy and the close-quarter tactics that supported it was the necessity to entice the enemy to attack; these tactics were essentially defensive. For this reason, men-at-arms were dismounted and, when possible, the battlefield was prepared with defensive contrivances to protect the foot soldiers from enemy cavalry with trenches, stakes and other items.

The role of archers in English victories has also been questioned in recent years and some have suggested that rather than causing the disruption and destruction traditionally associated with the English and Welsh bowmen, that archery was a less potent weapon. The disposition of these archers is a particularly vexed question, hinging on Froissart's use of the word *herce* to describe their formation. All that can be said with certainty is that the archers flanked the dismounted troops and took a strong defensive position.[47] This was the case at Crécy and Poitiers followed this same pattern, hardly surprising given that the prince and his commanders had seen the effectiveness of such a formation ten years previously.

The English successes in France can be attributed to the psychological and economic effect of the *chevauchée*. The war was fought in the heart of France and '[b]y 1355 it is clear that the English were using destruction of territory as a deliberate weapon, designed to reduce the resources available to the Valois monarchy and discredit it in the eyes of its subjects'.[48] Raiding tactics also meant that the English and their allies could choose the theatre of operations and, in the case of Crécy and other clashes, the battlefield itself. These factors coupled with the professional nature of recruitment to establish a highly effective fighting force and military tradition that bred success of itself.[49] These battlefield tactics, although not the overall raiding strategy, were again to be useful and effective in Spain.

Perhaps in English terms, revolution has been too closely associated with military success and that success based primarily on two battles. The Black Prince's retinue at Crécy and Poitiers was central to English victory, forming the core of the vanguard and the heart of the army in each case. As the chief figures in the retinue fought together, the expeditionary forces developed an organised command structure and high level of discipline. It was these factors which, when used in concert with other developments in equipment and tactics, were the main elements in the early English triumphs in the Hundred Years War. As a military leader the Black Prince was both following and setting an example of 'good practice'. It was a model primarily based on what he and members of his retinue observed in 1346. The campaigns of 1355-6 displayed courage, even foolhardiness, but the strategy may have been out of his hands in the absence of support from Lancaster. Poitiers itself was a tactical triumph and even if he was following a

*30 Richard II the contemporary portrait in Westminster Abbey*

successful pattern, the prince must be given great credit for its success. The military aspects of the Nájera operation were more mixed. The campaign strategy was poor and it was only Enrique's willingness to fight, and fight in a manner at odds with the advice of Du Guesclin and Audrehem, which gave victory to Pedro and Edward.

The retinue of the Black Prince proved to be a highly effective military unit when used in offensive situations, although it fought its pitched battles using defensive tactics. Recruitment was rarely difficult but there were ongoing problems with regard to paying and supplying the troops, most evidently in the sieges of 1359-60 and after Nájera in 1367. Cornwall provided much of the foodstuffs, Cheshire many of the soldiers, although the recruiting captains were drawn from much further afield, and Wales a large proportion of the money. The individual success of the prince's retinue was underpinned by a national war effort, which in Edward of Woodstock became something of a national icon. The health of the Black Prince mirrored the English military condition. The early successes were attributable to a relatively small number of commanders, many of whom found inclusion in the Order of the Garter. Many of the prince's retinue were founder members of that august association and many others would later be granted a stall in St George's

31 *Sir Miles and Lady Stapleton. Miles was a founder knight of the Order of the Garter. With Richard Stafford and Nigel Loryng he investigated violations of the Treaty of Brétigny*

chapel. Even when the principality of Aquitaine had been broken and the prince had died the reputation of the retinue and of its members remained. The prince himself was used, time and again, as a model by which his son should be judged and those who had fought with him, many of whom were very fine soldiers in their own right, retained something of his aura and the acclaim from Poitiers. Some of these men were soldiers through and through, but others had wider responsibilities, in local society and in parliament. Many more were members of the prince's household and officials in the administration of his estates. That administration provided the retinue with rewards and underpinned the financial costs of the military campaigns. These two elements were inextricably interwoven. However prosaic and distant it may have seemed on the plains outside Poitiers or on the banks of the Najerilla, the victories that would follow, the opportunities to implement the tactics which would lead to the capture of King Jean and Du Guesclin, came about, in part, through such concerns as demesne farming in Wales, tin mining in Devon and Cornwall, and the wine trade in Aquitaine.

# 6 THE PRINCIPALITY OF AQUITAINE (1362-67)

The Black Prince married Joan of Kent on 6 October 1361 at Lambeth in a ceremony conducted by the archbishop of Canterbury, Simon Islip. The pair had required a papal dispensation before the wedding could take place because they were related within the third and therefore prohibited degree.[1] It was not the match his father had wanted, nor can it have been enjoyed greatly by a knight of the prince's household, Bernard Brocas, a 'tres bon chevalier qui moult grandement avoit servi le prince et pour lui tant en ses guerres que autrement avoit moult travaillié'.[2] Bernard had been made an esquire at the landing at La Hogue in 1346 and fought with the prince at Crécy, Poitiers (although not in the 1355 expedition) and would do so again at Nájera. He had seen service in Normandy in 1359 and 1361, in which year he asked the prince to act on his behalf in asking for the hand of the recently widowed Joan Holland. The prince approached the countess of Kent but almost immediately married her himself.[3]

Joan remains as 'shadowy' a figure as her husband, and like him she was not referred to by her famous soubriquet in any contemporary literature. The Fair Maid's father was Edmund, earl of Kent, the sixth son of Edward I, and she was raised at court after his execution. It seems likely that Edward and Joan knew each other from an early age since Queen Philippa was closely involved with her upbringing. She is most renowned for her marital entanglements; after contracting a marriage to Thomas Holland, he was called abroad on military service and during this time she was convinced or forcefully persuaded by her family or the crown that she should marry William Montague. On Holland's return, he found his wife married to the earl of Salisbury. His military rewards and booty enabled him to press a case before the pope that eventually resulted in the annulment of Joan's marriage to Montague and her reunion with Holland. In 1352, the death of Joan's elder brother led to her acquisition of the title countess of Kent, and Lady Wake of Liddel and Holland received the title of earl of Kent soon before his death in 1360.[4]

## GOVERNMENT, COURT AND CHARACTER

The Principality of Aquitaine was created on 19 July 1362 and formed the basis for some of the most contentious events of Edward's career, and is the area that has received some of the least historical attention.[5] This is predominantly due to the scarcity of available sources. The failure of the prince's administration to enrol accounts at Westminster as its predecessors had done and successors would do, in addition to the loss of the Gascon register, leaves one reliant on other, more oblique documentation.

Much of the interest in the prince's rule stems from its consequences. The reopening of the war in 1369 has often been attributed to the poor relations established by the prince with the indigenous nobility and to the general attitude and arrogance displayed by the English administration. Sir John Chandos, who as the king's lieutenant paved the way for the arrival of the prince and accepted the territories resulting from Brétigny on behalf of the monarch, initially established that administration. It was not a simple task, the Rouergue in particular was most reluctant to become 'English' as were many towns, but with no outside support they were forced to submit. Belleville was a difficult area and the French argued that it had not formed part of the treaty and Ponthieu and the viscounty of Montreuil also proved troublesome. It is often stated or implied that, had Chandos remained in office, the collapse of the principality might not have been so precipitous or complete, indeed that it might not have happened at all.[6] The evidence for this is slim and does not take account of the very different political conditions at work in the early years of the 1360s compared to the first decade of the reign of Charles V.

The intrinsic importance of the local nobility in the governance of any late medieval kingdom is as evident as the consequence of a failure to maintain good relations with those nobles. As Edward II, Isabella and Richard II discovered this was not always easy. How much more difficult might it have been if they had been at war with such disaffected elements for over 20 years prior to gaining power, and if the lands and reputations of those elements had been the target of one of the most thorough examples of the *chevauchée* and the devastation that accompanied it, which had been seen in the war up to that point? From the outset there was vigorous opposition to the Brétigny settlement; Pierre Bernard, count of Périgord, Jean d'Armagnac, Pierre Raymond de Comminges and Armand d'Eauze, vicomte de Castelbon, denied the right of the king of France to give them over to a new sovereign. Similarly, Gaston Fébus, always looking to play off the Plantagenets and Valois against one another, refused to do homage for Béarn, which he considered a sovereign allod and tried to assert his claim to Bigorre.[7]

The principality of Aquitaine is often glibly referred to as making up about a third of all France without much consideration for what the governance of such an area would involve. It was perhaps five times as large as the duchy Edward III had inherited in 1327, consisting of 24 bishoprics, two archbishoprics (Auch and Bordeaux), and 13 *senechausées*. The geopolitical structure of this entity had little in common with the Gascony that preceded it and on which structures and modes of government the administration of the new territories depended.[8] The principality was also, very much, a frontier region, not only against the uncertainties of Navarre and Charles the Bad but also the very particular boundaries of the Atlantic and the Pyrenees. Furthermore, the hugely expanded inland borders proved only too vulnerable to assault (in those areas where allegiance was not freely returned to the French) after the collapse of the treaty in 1368/9. The traditional 'English' duchy of Gascony had formed a linguistic and ethnic unit while the principality was a wholly artificial political construction. Analogies might be drawn and vestigial associations made with the Angevin Empire, but although English royal memory may have been long, there was little sympathy among the inhabitants of the surrendered territories. By contrast, the Gascons, although fiercely independent, looked to England and the population did not consider itself to be occupied by a foreign power. For France, the frontier of Gascony was a march comparable to those in Scotland and Wales, with which the prince and his officials were well acquainted. Similarly, the area was also highly fortified not as a result of conquest but political fragmentation. Those castles under Anglo-Gascon control formed what has been described as the 'nervous system of the administration'[9] giving command of communications and supply routes by both road and water. Unfortunately, from the point of view of central government, sites within the old duchy and certainly beyond its borders were held by independent members of the nobility who bitterly resented any attempt to curtail their local authority either by representatives of the king of England or their neighbours.

The principality was a complex, internally dissonant body, founded on little less than military conquest and with common traditions only so far as they might be described as 'Angevin'. 'L'Aquitaine repose sur un equilibre complexe où intervient tout une suite des forces différentes. Elles depend essentiellment d'une mentalité anglo-gasconne.'[10]

The transition of territory and authority began in October 1360 and the first major town to be handed over was La Rochelle. There were two main tasks, 'reorganisation administrative d'une part, d'autre part effort considérable pour assurer l'application de la paix'.[11] On 1 July 1361, John Chandos was charged with annexing the new territories, and Richard Stafford and William Farley were chosen to take responsibility of the administration. Neither of these were long-term appointments; Stafford, the seneschal, had left office by 12 January 1362, and may have been replaced by Chandos in the greater office of constable of Aquitaine; Farley died on 11 September 1362 although his final accounts were not handed in until 1365.[12] Several other members of the prince's retinue were important in overseeing the transfer of territories while others were concerned with making preparations for his arrival. These included Nigel Loryng, William Felton (an old military companion of the prince's, later to be seneschal of Poitou, and the Limousin), Adam Hoghton (bishop of St Daid's and chancellor of England, 1377-8) who was responsible for annexing Bigorre, Thomas Driffeld and Stephen Cosington.[13]

The three great offices of state were the constable, seneschal and chancellor. The first to hold these offices in the principality were Thomas Felton (William's kinsman but not his brother), John Chandos and John Harewell, the constable and chancellor of Bordeaux (1362-4).[14] The seneschal was the head of government with a variety of changing duties. He presided over the council and the judicial business of the court of Gascony. The constable of Bordeaux was the next most important official accountable for financial matters. He paid the salaries of most officials, received their accounts and was guardian of the seal.[15] The constables of Bordeaux came from a variety of backgrounds with previous experience in the duchy or having served the Black Prince before his arrival in Aquitaine. Bordeaux, with its population of 20,000-30,000, was the administrative capital of the principality and the constable was the chief financial minister. He was based at the castle of the Ombrière where he received revenue and made payments for which he had to account at the exchequer. He reviewed the accounts of lesser officials and had a variety of other duties, which required an extensive staff. These duties included the management of supplies and victuals, the supervision of coinage and the upkeep of castles and fortresses.

*32   Coin of Richard II 1377–1399*

Authority in Bordeaux was concentrated in a very few individuals. If they failed to be effective, it damaged the whole administration. John Streatley (in office 28 April 1348 – 12 September 1350 and 18 January 1354 – 1 July 1361) assisted Chandos with the transfer of lands and was a frequent member of the prince's council and had also served him as an envoy. He was chancellor of Guienne from 1362 to 1364. Chivereston and Streatley stayed for a time at the head of the Aquitaine administration. William Farley had been keeper of the wardrobe of the duke of Gascony and succeeded Streatley as constable (20 September 1361) at the time of the handover of territories with William Loryng as his lieutenant. He travelled to Gascony around the same time as Stafford and Nigel Loryng (*c.*July 1361). Farley received the first accounts but died of plague soon after.[16] It was after this that the administration began to develop. Bernard Brocas was controller and receiver of the money due to the king at this time. He was the most experienced Englishman in south-western French financial affairs having served as controller to Nicolo Uso di Mare, John Streatley and Farley and in 1357 he had also been keeper of the seal. He succeeded Farley on 9 December 1362 with responsibility to collect all revenues due to the king until 19 July 1362 when he had created the principality. If his activities and practice were followed by the prince's officials then accounts were very closely scrutinised. John Ludham graduated from being the prince's clerk to become constable. The next most important fiscal officer was the controller who was also based in the Ombrière and kept a counter-roll of the constable's records and whose salary was half that of his superior. There was also a *memorandus* to guard the castle archives. Other officers included the judge of Aquitaine, the provosts with authority over towns, the bailiffs and reeves with responsibility for districts.[17]

The centre of authority was the court and it was shaped with the character and in the image of the prince himself; 'L'atmosphere de la cour, au milieu de laquelle il évoluait, était brillante, et il avait probablement l'habitude de s'imposer à sa place, parmi beaucoup d'hommes de naissance et de talent. Dans ce milieu, l'exercice d'armes était une activité essentielle, et chacun s'y trouvait rompu.'[18] The prince's household and administration in England and Wales had been geared towards warfare and it continued to be so in Aquitaine.

> Every day there were more than eighty knights at his table and four times as many squires. They jousted and held revels at Angoulême and Bordeaux; all the nobles were there, joyful and happy, generous and honourable; and all his subjects loved him well because he did so much good for them.[19]

The prince was accompanied to Bordeaux by a retinue of 250 men-at-arms, including three bannerets, 60 knights and 320 archers, and feed was requisitioned for 1,000 horses.[20] A large number of ships were needed to transport such a retinue as well as those who had been involved in overseeing the transfer of lands after Brétigny.[21] The prince was delayed until April 1363 because of the lack of available ships.[22] A strong military presence was vital; frontiers had to be defended against the Free Companies and in wariness against French incursions. The military character of the court was certainly not all for show, prior to the Spanish expedition of 1367 a number of the court were involved in the battles of Cocherel and particularly in the victory for the Montfort claim to Brittany at Auray.[23] Thus, while there was a formal peace between England and France (or perhaps a cold war), both countries continued to support opposing sides in extraneous conflicts.

The scarcity of administrative and other 'formal' sources means that we must rely more heavily on the evidence of Froissart and other chroniclers. Their reliability is, of course, in doubt and their manipulation of detail and character may leave one with a somewhat skewed impression. The following statement shows the opportunities for distortion and is also indicative of a broadly held opinion of the prince. 'Under his [Froissart's] improving touch, Edward the Black Prince, no longer appears the vicious tyrannical despot he actually was, instead he emerges the chivalrous knight . . .'[24] Edward's character *is* open to question. It has been shrouded in chivalric propaganda and was subject to only the mildest criticism in his lifetime. However, he must be judged by the standards of his own age in which it was entirely possible to be a 'vicious, tyrannical despot' and a chivalrous knight at one and the same time. In much the same way, the leaders of the mercenary Free Companies, men such as Robert Knolles and Gregory Sais, who often found themselves in the prince's service, were considered praiseworthy by Froissart and Cuvelier despite their lowly birth, questionable tactics and loyalty which was strong for as long as they were paid.[25]

Despite the years of the war, French and English knights considered themselves as part of the same international brotherhood. Beyond a shared adherence to a code of conduct and culture, knightly solidarity could also be expressed in a more binding way. Brotherhood-in-arms had developed from Germanic roots into a legal association with many connotations; it certainly provided the legal basis for a profitable commercial relationship. Hugh Calveley and Bertrand Du Guesclin formed such an alliance. They fought together and on opposing sides during the Castilian civil war, which brought the Iberian peninsula fully into the arena of the Hundred Years War. Calveley served with Du Guesclin to depose Pedro the Cruel in favour of his half-brother, Enrique of Trastamara.

Calveley was recalled to the English side in 1367 when the Black Prince became involved. At the battle of Nájera, Du Guesclin was captured but in accordance with their agreement Calveley paid part of his ransom.[26]

Despite such links, the chivalric ethos which the prince brought to Aquitaine was not necessarily the same as that which already existed there. In England and Northern France, the ideal of knighthood tended to merge with one of loyalty and duty to one's lord. This may not have applied in Occitania.[27] Southern French literature laid stress on *largesse* (ostentatious generosity), friendship and voluntary aid while the weakness of 'feudal' bonds is indicated by the advocation of a sense of loyalty between companions or equals rather than between lord and vassal. There was also an emphasis on individual rights to inherit and on fighting to uphold one's rights and those of one's allies. This is not to say that concepts of loyalty and duty did not exist but that they were not fixed or clearly delineated responsibilities. Thus, the knightly ethic of the south was a very pragmatic one: there was no sense of disdaining conflict with one's inferiors or showing mercy. In this sense, there is little evidence of a chivalric ideology or attempt to cultivate a particularly 'knightly' way of life although there was a strong courtly culture. This had been disseminated and encouraged by the troubadours for whom the ideal court had a harmonious social atmosphere, characterised by music and female company, in which gifts were freely dispensed. Princes should not be aloof but discriminating, tactful and willing to take advice. The cardinal sin was avarice, the opposite of *largesse*, and this was often indicated by the lack of feasts hosted by a prince. This was not a charge of which Edward could have been accused. According to Froissart, the early years of the principality seem to have been taken up almost entirely with feasting. From the arrival at La Rochelle where the prince and Joan were met by Chandos with a 'belle compagnie de chevaliers' there was feasting and festivities and the giving of gifts and beautiful jewels. After the prince had received the oaths of homage from his great vassals during his tour of the principality Froissart tells us that he could not record all the feasts, the honours done to the prince nor all those that came to see him.[28]

The troubadours also levelled criticism at princes and courts in which the sway of flatterers, administrators and bureaucrats was seen as too extensive. If such beliefs were representative of wider opinion then attitudes and behaviour evident in the Black Prince's court could be seen as both delighting the indigenous nobility and yet also contributing to the eventual collapse of the principality. Blame for the souring relationship of the prince and his greater vassals and their eventual rebellion has been attributed to the prince's haughtiness and his unwillingness to allow the Gascons any part in government. The prince was said to force his greatest vassals to wait days to see him and then leaving them on their knees for a quarter of an hour.[29]

With regard to other courtly pursuits, it is usual to see the Black Prince as a man with little or no interest in the literary or academic. However, there was a literary circle around him, book owners and authors in their own right, men such as Simon Burley, Richard Stury, Philip de la Vache, Lewis Clifford and John Clanvowe.[30] In Languedoc there was a long-standing literary tradition and among the prince's neighbours was Charles of Navarre who became the patron of Guillaume de Machaut some time after John of Bohemia had died at Crécy, according to some at the hand of the Black Prince. It may have been from John that the prince acquired the device of the three ostrich feathers, one of the earliest stable non-ordinal badges. It first appeared on a seal shortly after his appointment as prince of Aquitaine.[31]

As elsewhere, there was a long tradition and powerful culture of hunting in southern France. In Gaston Fébus, the prince had a neighbour who was an acknowledged master of the art as is shown in his *Livre de Chasse*.[32] In organising a meeting in which the prince hoped to secure Gaston's homage for Béarn, the count of Foix asked that Chandos' hounds be brought so that he might see them. The sport was considered an essential part of chivalric and military education. Hawking was also extremely popular and the great ceremony that accompanied such events is evident in *Sir Gawain and the Green Knight* that may have been written for an English audience abroad. The prince had, prior to 1362, maintained a considerable number of hounds and falcons for hunting. It does not appear that these or at least all of them were brought to Aquitaine, as there are references in the *Register* regarding falcons being transferred to the prince's manor of Wallingford for the season after he was resident in Gascony.[33]

The prince spent lavishly on clothes and jewels and moved more quickly to ensure the presence in Bordeaux of his goldsmith and two embroiderers than he did to ensure his administrators had enough money for their own expenses.[34] There was a great deal of concern with garments as many chronicles and the sumptuary laws demonstrate. Richard II was subjected to heavy criticism for his expenditure on clothing; it may have been a trait he inherited from his father and mother. Records exist of the payment of £715 to an embroiderer for work for the prince, Joan and her daughter, while in 1362, £200 was paid for jewelled buttons for Joan, the equivalent of the wages of a Master-Craftsman for ten years. The princess seems to have become a sartorial icon and many followed her style of dressing in tight-fitting garments of silk and ermine with low-cut necklines and wearing pearls and precious stones in her hair.[35]

The importance of music in the prince's household, throughout his life, is evident in records of the purchase of instruments and payments to minstrels.[36] In 1352, the prince was sent four silver-gilt and enamelled pipes along with a bagpipe, cornemuse and drum by the count of Eu, who had been captured at Crécy.[37] In 1355, these instruments were given to Ralph of Exeter and John Martyn, minstrels in the prince's employ.[38] For the journey to Gascony in 1363, the prince was accompanied from England by six minstrels dressed in ray, a broadly striped cloth. The rates of pay were probably similar to those of the king's minstrels, 20s. a year in peace, $7\frac{1}{2}$d. or a shilling a day on campaign and this military facet of the minstrels' life should not be overlooked. In addition to standard wages, minstrels probably also received generous tips.[39] Music played an important part in both court ceremonial and general entertainment. Before the battle of Winchelsea, Edward III enjoyed hearing his minstrels play a German dance that Chandos had learned.[40] Southern France was an excellent area for musicians to find employment and also to gain inspiration and exposure to one of the most important composers of the age. Both Charles of Navarre and Gaston Fébus were patrons of musicians, the most significant of whom was Guillaume de Machaut, the most important figure of the French *Ars Nova*, and the most distinguished composer of the Middle Ages, particularly renowned for his four-voice *Messe de Notre Dame*.

Chivalry throughout Western Europe was undergoing change in accordance with varying military tactics and a number of socio-political developments. In the principality, such changes were reinforced by differing traditions and England and Aquitaine were sometimes at odds with one another. This is not to say that chivalry was dead. On the contrary, in the prince's court, chivalric traditions were reinforced by the influence of secular orders of chivalry, such as the Garter, of which the Black Prince and members of his retinue were important members. Chivalry also remained intrinsically linked to the crusade. The crusading movement had lost impetus after the fall of Acre in 1292 and the destruction of the Order of the Temple in 1314. However, one of the great courtly occasions in Aquitaine was the visit of Peter of Lusignan, king of Cyprus, in 1364. Peter had toured Europe passing through Avignon, London and Paris in search of support for a crusade. He was met at Angoulême where there was held 'une très grosse et noble feste'. He encouraged many to join his crusade including Chandos, Thomas Felton, Nigel Loryng, Richard Punchardoun, Simon Burley and Baldwin Frevill, although the earl of Warwick was the only one to take up the offer. Peter's visit lasted for a month. The festivities that accompanied the visit were combined in some accounts with the birth of a son to the prince and Joan, in early March 1365 at Angoulême.[41] On 27 April, a splendid tournament was held to celebrate the birth of Edward of Angoulême and the 'churching' of his mother. Accounts of the event vary; Froissart for once appears to be quite restrained, merely stating that 40 knights and 40 esquires comprised the princess's entourage. The Chronicle of the Grey Friars of Lynn states that Joan's retinue consisted of 24 knights and 24 lords and noted the presence of 154 further lords and 706 knights at the festivities. The prince stabled 18,000 horses at his own expense and the celebrations lasted for ten days. The cost of the candles alone was said to be over £400.[42]

There were certainly political benefits in maintaining a lavish court beyond the munificence usually expected of a sovereign. The Languedocian culture that delighted in conspicuous consumption demanded a magnificent court. It helped to placate the nobility and gain their support, at least for a time. Accusations that luxurious living led to the prince's downfall have been made, and the expenses of the court and household were very large but were almost insignificant beside the military expenditure occasioned by the Nájera campaign and the administrative costs of running a hugely enlarged and financially disparate state with machinery and organisations designed for a much smaller province.[43]

## 1367: Nájera, The Beginning of the End

Endemic, if not constant hostilities changed the complexion of England, France and those other states that were dragged within the orbit of the Hundred Years War, and the demands of that conflict and the pressures which it engendered did not end during the all too brief periods of truce. The development of the contract army created a surplus of military manpower in peacetime that banded together in the form of the mercenary Free Companies, ensuring that in France (official) peace with England did not mean an end to military activity. Rather 'war became a full-time occupation, one in which mercenaries served as the undisciplined instruments of royal policy'.[44] The practical problems of bands of unemployed mercenaries roaming the French countryside were real enough and further enhanced by contemporary attitudes to combat, conflict and the bearing of arms. War had acquired a social mystique providing a means for the ennoblement of the common man. In Froissart's habitual phrase, any man could 'better himself in the profession of arms'. The mercenary forces seized upon such attitudes, and the religious and idealistic justification of chivalry made it difficult to recognize the actions of soldiers for what they were. In this context, chivalry did not limit war but quite the reverse. Chivalry also underpinned the potential financial benefits that could be accrued in war and it was in the interests of the military classes to maintain that state of affairs. Froissart was not unaware of the brutalities of war or that strategic considerations could overcome the code of chivalry and that ransom money was the prize for which men fought. Nonetheless, he seems to have been completely taken in by the spectacle of battle. He made little distinction between mercenaries serving the highest bidder and knights serving their king or prince as indentured retainers. The distinction was, in any case, becoming very uncertain. Professional captains such as Calveley, Knolles, Nicholas Dagworth and Walter Hewitt (who was very active in the Breton civil war) thrived in the Hundred Years War. They proved to be a very considerable military force at Auray (1364) and in 1362 when the Great Company defeated French royal forces under Jean II's chamberlain, the count of Tancarville, at the battle of Brignais on 6 April 1362. The mercenary forces were led by Seguin de Badefol and the defeat has been compared to both Crécy and Poitiers. There were some tactical similarities between the encounters and it is possible that de Badefol and a number of the routier commanders fought on the plain of Maupertuis in 1356.[45]

The defeat at Brignais may have contributed to a change of attitude in France, compounded by the accession of Charles V. If the Free Companies were not to be defeated then perhaps they could be encouraged to go elsewhere and if in so doing they might further French interests then so much the better. The destination chosen was Moorish Spain; the purported intention, a crusade to drive the enemies of Christ from the Iberian peninsula; the real purpose, to expel the Companies from France and to replace the English allied King Pedro 'the Cruel' of Castile with his half-brother, Enrique 'the Bastard' of Trastamara.

The prince was not unaware that steps were being taken for military action and in November 1365 he sent a number of his household officials to Avignon to observe the crusaders receive a papal blessing and funding for the crusade. He may well have been taken in by the ruse and seems to have given his blessing for many of his associates to participate in the crusade. It was when his father took belated steps to prevent English involvement in the campaign and indeed ordered that Du Guesclin should not be allowed passage over the Pyrennees that preparations in Aquitaine began to take shape.

The Black Prince had the most to lose from a French allegiance with Castile, so close to the borders of Aquitaine. The means by which he undertook the Nájera campaign highlights the apparent inconsistencies of the chivalric ethic and of military service, which were nonetheless permitted and indeed lauded in the chronicles of Froissart and others. Many of those members of the Companies that Bertrand Du Guesclin led to Castile and who were actively involved in the deposition of Pedro were English and Gascon and were recalled by the prince to serve in his own expedition, designed to reverse the political situation for which they were responsible.

The motivation for, and conditions that surrounded, the Spanish campaign of 1367 were very different and less certain than those of the prince's previous military operations. The expedition has been described as 'something of a crusade for an abstract principle'.[46] The enemy as well as theatre of operations was changed, although Enrique had French support. Perhaps, like the expeditions of 1346, 1355-6 and certainly 1359, it was a campaign for a throne, although not the throne of France, and in strategic terms, while the army tried to live off the land, it was not a *chevauchée* after the model of 1355.

The prince's advisors questioned the wisdom of committing troops to Pedro's cause. He was counselled that;

> . . . it is reasonable that you should be content with what you have, and not seek to make enemies. It is well known that Don Pedro of Castile . . . is now and has always been, a man of great pride, cruelty and wickedness. Through him the kingdom of Castile has suffered many wrongs and many valiant men have been beheaded and murdered without any just cause . . . He is also an enemy of the Church, and has been excommunicated by the Holy Father. He has had the reputation . . . of being a tyrant, and has always, without any justification, made war on his neighbours, the Kings of Aragon and Navarre whom he has tried to dethrone by force. It is also generally rumoured and believed that he murdered his young wife, your cousin, the Duke of Bourbon's daughter . . . For everything that he has suffered since is merely God's punishment.[47]

A Trastamaran propagandist might as well have written this speech, attributed by Froissart to one of the prince's council. Rebellion against Pedro was justified since he was a tyrant and enemy of Christ, although Knighton blamed the pope for the usurpation of Pedro's throne. These same arguments were presented to the prince before the battle of Nájera.[48] The proximity of Aquitaine had considerable implications with regard to the participation of any of the Iberian kingdoms in the Anglo-French war, as did the Castilian fleets in the maritime struggle. In addition to this, the prince's own desire to be again involved in a military campaign cannot be ignored. Support for Pedro in a successful coup would replace the Francophile Enrique providing military and, more particularly, naval assistance, with a galley fleet capable of summer operations in northern waters. Enrique had, by 1365, been offered financial assistance from Aragon, France and the papacy. By deposing him, the prince would have an ally on his border. Furthermore, England, although not the prince personally, was obliged to lend Pedro assistance in accordance with the Anglo-Castilian treaty of 1362.[49] Consequently, Martín López de Cordoba was sent to remind Edward III of this and urge his support. On 6 December 1365, the king issued an order, forwarded to the prince at Bordeaux, forbidding Englishmen to fight his Castilian allies. López also probably managed to dispel the worst prejudices about Pedro and 'transmit a sense of Enrique's pro-French villainies'.[50] He may well have stopped in Aquitaine on his way home to deliver the same message.

The role and importance of the Castilian galley fleet in the war may have spurred the prince to involvement in the civil war in 1366-7. From the end of the thirteenth century, the French and English had made diplomatic efforts to secure the support of Castilian naval power. It became of marked importance after the treaty of Toledo in 1368, which provided Charles V with the support that brought him victory at La Rochelle in 1372. Throughout the decade, the Castilians raided along the English southern coast. In 1374, the Isle of Wight was attacked. In 1375, 30 English ships were burned in the Bay of Bourgneuf. In 1377, French ships collaborated with the Castilians harrying the south coast of England. Rye was captured, Lewes was burned, the Isle of Wight overrun, Plymouth and Hastings were burned and Portsmouth and Dartmouth attacked. Winchelsea and Gravesend were assaulted in 1380.[51] The failure of the English to ensure there was a sympathetic ruler in Castile proved to be costly.

The importance of an Anglo-Castilian alliance is, in this context, clear and may lie at the root of the prince's willingness to be involved in the 1367 expedition. This is not, however, apparent in contemporary sources. Chandos Herald provides no clue as to the prince's motivation except that he considered it the honourable course of action. It has been seen as an essentially personal campaign in that 'the Black Prince was supremely confident in English military superiority and caught up in his own legend';[52] it was a long time since the last campaign, and even longer since the glory of Poitiers. According to Froissart, the prince ignored the advice of Chandos and others on the grounds that 'c'est contre droit et raison d'un bastart couronner et tenir à terre et royaumme'.[53] If this was an attempt by the prince to maintain the true order of succession, it is tempting to speculate about anxiety concerning his own family. His own legitimacy was not in doubt but his marriage to Joan was controversial. The marital entanglements of the Fair Maid of Kent may well have been instigated by her family and by the Crown, yet she was still viewed as something of a 'fallen woman'. The prince had been counselled against the marriage by the archbishop of Canterbury for the very reason that the legitimacy of any offspring could be challenged. It turned out to be prophetic, as Bolingbroke was to question Richard's birth. Joan's pregnancy may have brought such thoughts to the fore. Edward of Angoulême, although still alive, was a sickly child unlikely to survive to inherit the title of king of Galicia offered by Pedro. The Nájera campaign may have been a statement associating the prince with the cause of legitimacy and particularly with the legitimacy of his newly born son, the future Richard II.

That the English would attempt to support Pedro was probable from the moment Enrique received French assistance. The initial motivation may have come in fact from England. On 8 May 1366, Thomas Holland, the prince's stepson and Nigel Loryng were ordered to Gascony and further reinforcements followed behind. Negotiations were opened with Charles of Navarre, necessary because of Enrique's alliance with Aragon as he controlled the remaining passes through the Pyrenees.[54] The prince's own preparations were further galvanised by the collapse of Pedro's position in Castile. The prince met Pedro at Capbreton in August and the negotiations culminated in the treaty of Libourne on 23 September.

The prince undertook to advance 56,000 florins to Charles of Navarre on behalf of Pedro. The expenses of the prince's retinue and those of the Gascon lords were assessed

*33, 34, 35 (above, below and opposite)*
   *Thornham Parva retable. Created c.1340 for the Dominican priory at Thetford. The prince and his retinue were regular patrons of the mendicant orders. The polytich wa broken in the Dissolution of the Monasteries and its partner is in the Musée de Cluny, Paris*

at 550,000 florins, based on the supposition that the campaign would last no more than six months. By the time the army left Gascony this figure had risen to 1,659,000 florins (£276,500).[55] The treaty proved to be a disaster and it can only be assumed that the prince knew full well that Pedro would be unable to fulfil his side of the bargain and hoped to exploit the situation once his ally was reinstated in Castile. Certainly 'it is clear . . . that neither the prince nor Charles put much trust in Pedro'.[56]

These discussions were common knowledge and the response, at the instigation of Pere of Aragon, in January 1367, was discussions between Enrique and Charles of Navarre. Charles agreed to break his agreement with the prince and Pedro and oppose their advance into Castile. It was rescued initially only by the action of Hugh Calveley whose raids on Miranda and Puenta-le-Reina forced Charles of Navarre to return to the allied fold after having given his support to Trastamara.[57]

The prince was also responsible for the defence of the principality of Aquitaine during his absence. Measures were put in place to guard against the ravages of those members of the Free Companies not involved in Spain. Much more significant was the alliance made by Louis of Anjou, Pere of Aragon and Enrique, made with the assent of Charles V, aiming to attack both Navarre and Aquitaine. James Audley remained behind and was entrusted with the defence of Aquitaine. In addition, during the peace following Brétigny, measures were put in place for the defence of the realm and particularly Wales. It may have been that there was a fear of a retaliatory Castilian naval raid when the Nájera campaign was underway.[58]

The prince mustered his army, which numbered between 6,000 and 8,500 troops (between a third and a half recruited from the Great Company) at Dax and crossed the Pyrenees in three main groups. The lack of wardrobe accounts, the dearth of information from Aquitaine and the few remaining indentures mean that there is limited evidence for the Nájera campaign. The main source for the operation is the account by Chandos

Herald, which is so complimentary of the role of John of Gaunt that it has been suggested that it was a propaganda piece to further his Castilian ambitions, although Richard II may be a more likely patron.[59] He received a letter from Enrique on 28 February that, rather than asking the prince where he wished to meet for battle as suggested by Chandos Herald, was both an attempt to placate the invaders and show Enrique's determination to defend his kingdom.[60] Previously, he had requested the return of Du Guesclin, then passing through Aragon on his way back to France. Thomas Felton led a reconnaissance mission to spy out the enemy army, based at Santo Domingo, to prevent Pedro reaching Burgos. This party included several notable members of the prince's retinue including William Felton, two scions of comital families in Thomas Ufford (knight of the Garter) and Hugh Stafford (son of Earl Ralph, who served the prince consistently from 1359), Knolles and Simon Burley. There is some confusion about which Felton led the operation; Russell states it was William, kinsman of the seneschal of Aquitaine, Chandos Herald and Froissart indicate that it was the seneschal himself, and Barber maintains that both were involved and the force was led by Thomas. As William was seneschal of Poitou and Thomas, seneschal of the principality, it would seem likely to have been the latter that led the expedition. The contingent, made up of 200 men-at-arms and archers, was guided quickly across Navarre.[61] They crossed the river at Logroño and camped at Naveretta. After trying to establish what force Enrique had established at Santo Domingo, a raid was made on the watch in which Simon Burley captured the knight in command and other prisoners were also taken. From these, the reconnaissance party established the strength of Enrique's army and sent messengers to inform the prince. The result of these reports was what Russell describes as 'a first-class strategic error', but Fowler has explained in the context of the movement of Enrique's troops and mistrust of Charles of Navarre.[62] Rather than taking the safe crossing of the river at Logroño and the relatively easy route thereafter to Burgos, the prince determined to follow the road from Pamplona into Álava and then travelled south-west to cross the Ebro at Miranda. The uncertainty of the position of Charles of Navarre may have prompted Edward to open another line of communication with Gascony. After a difficult journey the army arrived, short of provisions, in Salvatierra, which surrendered to Pedro. Enrique, at this point, did have an opportunity to effectively end Pedro's aspirations of regaining control. Had he followed the advice of Charles V and both Du Guesclin and Audrehem, the English army would have been bottled up in Álava until lack of supplies forced a retreat.

> . . . the King of France sent letters to King Enrique urging him to avoid fighting a pitched battle but to carry on the war in other ways, since he could be certain that the Prince came accompanied by the flower of the world's chivalry, but they were not the sort of men to stay for long in the kingdom of Castile and would soon go away again . . .[63]

However, to do this, Enrique had to admit military inferiority. Politically it was necessary to show a position of strength and confidence to the Castilian nobility; militarily it was disastrous. The decision mirrors that taken by Philip VI in 1346. Felton informed the prince of Enrique's advance to Vitoria. The reconnaissance party kept ahead of the

Castilians and eventually halted at Ariñez. The prince led his army to Vittoria but was not met by the Castilians. Indeed, 'The Bastard was not yet in sight, but was on the plain on the other side of the mountain.'[64] In fact the Trastamarans had based themselves at the castle of Zaldiarán from where they sent out the *jinetes* to harass the Anglo-Gascon foraging parties and a major attack was made on Felton's outlying force led by Don Tello, the Bastard's brother. He may first have defeated a small unit under the command of Hugh Calveley. It was perhaps a feint that took place while the main assault was made on Felton. Alternatively the vanguard may have been attacked after the defeat of the English at Ariñez, the chronology is somewhat confused. William Felton was killed and many prisoners were taken including Richard Taunton, Gregory Sais (a Flintshire knight and captain of Beaumont-le-Victomte), Ralph Hastings, Mitton and Gaillard Beguer. The defence of Ariñez allowed the prince time to organise his defences although it seems that the measures taken to secure the army were not of the highest order since the perfidious king of Navarre successfully arranged for himself to be 'captured' by Oliver de Mauny, while out hunting on 11 March. This event, in combination with dwindling supplies, forced the prince to abandon his position in Vittoria. Another arduous journey brought the army south-east to Los Arcos and then south west to Navarette, crossing the Ebro at Logroño. In the meantime, Enrique had taken up a defensive position at Nájera, where he had been defeated in 1360, which had the only bridge crossing the Najerilla. On 1 April, the prince replied to Trastamara's letter of 28 February and then deployed his forces to settle the matter. This was made much easier since Enrique, in a manoeuvre reminiscent of the battle of Maldon, abandoned his highly defensive position and crossed the river to fight in a site that 'offered no tactical advantages whatever'.[65]

The prince's troops remained deployed as they had during the crossing of the Pyrenees. The vanguard was led by Chandos and Lancaster, with the two marshals Stephen Cosington and Guichard d'Angle, John Lord Devereux with his sons and the lord of Rays commanding the English contingent of about 3,000 archers and men-at-arms; with them were Calveley, Knolles and Olivier de Clisson. The main body, commanded by the prince, contained his personal retinue, most of the troops of the Great Company, Pedro's Castilian forces and deserters from Enrique as well as the Navarrese forces now commanded by Martin de la Carra and the Mallorcans. It may have numbered some 4,000 soldiers. Armagnac and Albret held the right wing whilst on the left was the captal de Buch with men from the Free Companies and Foix. Both wings contained about 2,000 men.

Enrique's force was perhaps half the size of his opponents' although it was fresh and well supplied. The English forces were better equipped and had a more organised command structure. Furthermore, they had been under arms together on campaign since February and many were old comrades in arms. Of greater importance were the disadvantages of the Trastamaran army. A divided chain of command underpinned a wide divergence in skill, tactics and equipment. They had, in Du Guesclin and Audrehem, an opportunity to use the experience and knowledge of two of France's finest soldiers who were used to English tactics and military methods. They were ignored. Du Guesclin did manage to have the *jinetes* more heavily armoured to protect them from the English archers but he could not convince the Castilian and Aragonese knights to fight on foot.[66] Russell makes much of the national differences among Enrique's army and while this may have undermined the structural unity of the army, it is unlikely that the Anglo-Gascon army was an example of solidarity and fellowship. The differences between the prince and his Gascon lords were already evident and the action of the prince in reducing the number of soldiers Albret had to bring on campaign was seen as insulting, as was his response to the prince. The ransom that Albret owed Gaston Fébus of Foix had left him in financial difficulties. The more soldiers he brought on campaign the more money he could 'cream off' the wages paid by the prince.

The crucial area of battle was the right flank that attacked the Trastamaran wing under Don Tello who fled. This allowed the captal de Buch to deal with the footmen, which in turn permitted Percy, Walter Hewitt and others on the left flank to support Gaunt in the vanguard. Du Guesclin was thus enclosed on three sides by the English flanks and vanguard. The main body of the army was then brought up. Enrique had been unable to support Du Guesclin and now attempted to make an attack on the prince but again the archers kept him at bay. Although Enrique rallied his troops three times, eventually they and he fled the field. The routed army was pursued to its banks by Jaume of Mallorca and the reserve cavalry, where many were killed and drowned.

The failure of the Castilians at Nájera was partly due to morale, numerical inferiority and surprise at the route taken by the prince from Navarette but, more importantly, it was a battle Enrique never had to fight. The invaders could have been bottled up in Álava long before they reached Nájera. Even when they arrived there it would have been entirely possible to hold the bridge over the Najerilla until the invaders' supplies gave out. Even so, once the decision to fight was made, the conservative Castilian nobility did not make use of the knowledge their French allies had gleaned from earlier encounters with the English. Apart from the Order of the Band, the Castilian knights remained mounted, the troops and horses were lightly armoured and suffered greatly under the attacks of the English archers. The Anglo-Gascon campaign as a whole was poorly organised and certainly entered into with little thought of the consequences and cost. The manoeuvres that brought the prince's army to Nájera exhausted his army unnecessarily and could have ended the campaign without any sort of major engagement. Nonetheless, the movement of 10,000 soldiers with their horses and baggage through the pass of Roncevalles, some 3,500 feet above sea level, in the cold of February, was a logistical triumph.

Nájera was only the second major encounter of which the prince took command. As at Crécy and Poitiers, the terrain, the disorganisation and recklessness of the enemy were vital elements in his success. At Nájera the prince was able to advance, masked by the hill of Cuentos, appearing on the Castilians left flank at daybreak, leaving a gentle downward slope between himself and the enemy.[67] The knights dismounted and the vanguard advanced under the cover of archer fire. Chandos Herald describes the knights as armed with lances, which were presumably cut-down. It may be that they advanced further than intended and came into conflict with the Trastamaran vanguard led by Du Guesclin, which had swung around to face them and 'caused them much mischief'. It was during this exchange that Chandos was knocked to the ground and wounded through the visor by 'a Castilian, great in stature — by name Martin Fernandez'[68] whom he managed to kill. It may have been this wound which left him blind in one eye and was partly responsible for his death at Lussac.

The surprise gained by the hidden movement behind Cuentos gave the English a great advantage. This certainly can be attributed to the prince and/or his advisers. It is difficult to say if the tactics used at Nájera were the prince's own or whether he simply put into practice those that had been developed by the English over a number of years. It is certain that the total lack of a command structure in the Trastamaran army allowed the English to attack them as separate units rather than a single fighting force. The vanguard, under the command of Du Guesclin, was effective but enclosed by superior numbers and not allowed to manoeuvre. Victory was secured with a very small number of Anglo-Gascon casualties. According to the letter sent by the prince to his wife that was later circulated in England, only Sir John Ferrers, among the English nobles, was killed. He was referring only to the battle itself, as it is clear that William Felton died in the earlier engagement at Ariñez.[69] This letter provided the basis for the account of the battle in the Anonimalle and Canterbury chronicles and that of John of Reading. If the tactics used at Nájera were a culmination of those developed throughout the Edwardian 'military revolution' then it does not lessen the prince's reputation. He was using a successful system known to many of his soldiers and using it to very good effect.

That the Black Prince had some skill as a general is not in doubt, although the example of the Spanish campaign shows a limited regard either for political realities or some aspects of the subtleties of wider military strategy. As a leader of men however, he had great personal qualities. Furthermore, he inherited a military structure that was highly effective and efficient both in the preparation for war and on the battlefield itself. English military successes, including those of the Black Prince, were due to effective recruitment, reinforcement and financing, the provision of the necessary supplies of arms and victuals, and the support of the country at large for the king's objectives in France. On the battlefield, the prince adopted the tactics that had developed throughout the fourteenth century and, apart from in 1367, his expeditions and campaigns were part of a wider strategic plan. The prince's retinue was extremely effective in implementing these methods. The strategy and tactics used by the prince and put into action by his retinue were to be highly influential although they were not, in themselves, innovative.[70]

The consequences of the battle were momentous. It became apparent that the alliance would not last for long. Fractures began to appear over the question of prisoners, many of whom Pedro, being a political pragmatist, wished to execute and whom the Black Prince, in all but one case, being an impecunious knight, wished to ransom. The marshal Audrehem had been taken prisoner by the Black Prince at the battle of Poitiers, a ransom was fixed and he swore to be a loyal prisoner and not to take up arms against the prince or his father until the ransom was paid unless it was in the company of the king of France or one of the princes of the *fleur de lys*. The ransom was not fully paid when in 1367 he fought in the company of Du Guesclin and Trastamara and was again captured and charged with treason. Since the prince was personally involved he convened a court of 12 knights to hear the case. The laws of knighthood before this court bound equally the prince and Audrehem, but the judges had been chosen by the prince not to hear a case of arbitration but a criminal trial. Audrehem's defence was that he had not armed himself against the prince but Pedro and on the basis of this argument he was acquitted. Matters such as this provided legal precedence and this case was used as evidence in the Parlement of Paris 23 years later.[71]

*36   Seal of Edward III (AD 1340-1372)*

Around this time, the prince began to succumb to the illness, variously although uncertainly diagnosed as dropsy and amoebic dysentery, that would lay him low and eventually claim his life. His army was also suffering with dysentery and probably malaria and had limited supplies. As wage bills rose, attempts were made to ensure that Pedro kept his part of the bargain but he could do little until he established his regime. Relations worsened as Pedro attempted to renegotiate the stipulations of Libourne and refused to make the required territorial concessions. Eventually, the sums were reassessed and agreed at a ceremony in Burgos cathedral on 2 May and Pedro's daughters remained as hostages in Gascony. Efforts were made to raise funds through loans and taxation as Pedro certainly wanted to be rid of the prince and the Companies who, in particular, were becoming restive and as time passed and supplies lessened, some even considered the chance of continuing employment in Castile, communicating with Enrique with advice that he not begin another campaign while the prince was still in the country. Negotiations were opened with Pere of Aragon with a view to seizing Castile, the ambassadors being William Elmham and Hugh Calveley, now something of an expert in Iberian affairs. Events prevented such an attempt; Pedro advised the prince that it was impossible for him to raise the necessary money while the prince and his army were still present, and more significantly Edward learned of the likelihood of Enrique attacking Aquitaine. In the middle of August, the army began to withdraw and returned to Aquitaine, soon to fracture.[72]

The prince's interests in Castile did not end when he re-crossed the Pyrenees.

> . . . until his eventual return to England, the prince . . . was continuously engaged in intense diplomatic negotiations with various Iberian rulers, the aim of which was to mount another military invasion of Castile, in alliance with them. One of its chief purposes was to secure the Castilian crown for himself.[73]

# 7 THE RECONQUEST OF AQUITAINE (1368-71)

In 1368, the prince's reputation was at its height, confirmed militarily by Nájera and founded on a glorious principality in Gascony and his English demesne. It was also founded on the close circles of the military retinue, the knights of the prince's household and the administrators that governed his estates.[1] The Black Prince's retinue grew with his appointment as earl of Chester, duke of Cornwall and prince of Wales. It was tempered in the Crécy campaign and came into its own ten years later at the battle of Poitiers. It was, without doubt, one of the most significant groups in late medieval England and included some of the most fêted individuals from the years that marked the high point of England's European reputation.

Men were drawn to the prince's service because of the potential financial rewards and his military reputation. Furthermore, he was the heir apparent and, as such, his influence at court was considerable and could be used to bring his servants and retainers to the attention of that greatest of patrons, the king, an office and dignity which would, in time, be held by Edward of Woodstock. This not only made the Black Prince an attractive employer but it dictated the make-up of his retinue and was evident in the manner by which he recruited and rewarded its members.

The nature of the prince's demesne also influenced the complement of his retinue. Wales, Cheshire and Cornwall were not areas rich in highly influential members of the aristocracy who could bring their own followings within a greater affinity. Therefore, although the prince did recruit heavily within his own demesne, the retinue was by no means exclusively made up of those from the west. Rather men were drawn to his service from throughout the country, and perhaps surprisingly, a significant number of prominent individuals came from or had close connections in East Anglia, particularly Norfolk. The prince's only tenurial interests in the county were at Castle Rising and he also had rights to the tollbooth at Lynn. The region certainly did not have the martial, indeed the aggressive, reputation of Cheshire or Wales but it was there that the Black Prince found some of his most loyal and militarily active servants.[2]

The war was the primary purpose of the retinue and the strategic and tactical manner in which it operated in the field was critical to the prince's military success. The prince benefited from the inclusion in his retinue of a number of skilled and experienced soldiers as well as others who were involved in his expeditions or assigned to him by the king. The 1355-6 campaigns provide the best example of the operation of the command ranks in the field. James Audley, Chandos, Baldwin Botetourt and, occasionally, Bartholomew Burghersh 'were the prince's handy men for field work, Richard Stafford was assigned to special tasks . . . Wingfield . . . [was] . . . "head of the office" and that these men who [knew] one another [well], formed a group bound by friendly relations to one another and by common loyalty to their chief; they were part of the "permanent staff".'[3]

Such men as these were at the heart of the prince's armies and the divisions he led in the royal campaigns of 1346 and 1359-60. Their role in a number of particular instances highlights their importance and particular aspects of their military service. This is again particularly evident in the *chevauchées* of 1355-6 and at Poitiers where the earl of Warwick and Reginald Cobham led the vanguard with John Beauchamp, Roger Clifford and Thomas Hampton, the standard-bearer. The main body was under the command of the prince with Oxford, Burghersh, Willoughby d'Eresby, Roger de la Warre, Maurice Berkeley, John Bourchier, the captal de Buch, the sire de Caumont, Montferrand and Thomas Roos, mayor of Bordeaux. The rearguard was commanded by Suffolk and Salisbury with Guillaume de Pommiers.[4] When Armagnac's army came within nine miles of the English rearguard near Carbonne the prince wrote

> At this we marched towards them, sending on Bartholomew Burghersh, John Chandos, James Audley, Baldwin Botetourt and Thomas Felton and others . . . to get definite information about the enemy. They rode on towards the enemy until they came to a town where they found two hundred of the latter's men at arms, with whom they fought and captured thirty-five of them. This made the enemy retreat in great fear.[5]

All apart from Audley held posts in the household or administration in addition to their military offices and he later held office in Aquitaine. The retinue was thus composed of individuals with vested interests in the prince's success in a number of areas, and were similarly driven by the need to finance the campaigns. What has been said of the victory at Poitiers can be said of the prince's military career in its entirety and the reverse may be said of certain aspects of his political and diplomatic style: '[a]t the core of the English success was the good working relationship between the prince, his chief officers and their men, a relationship which . . . evolved during the . . . weeks of campaigning, but which hinged on the presence around the prince of a group of tried and trusted knights. To them, as a group, belongs credit for the victory; to the prince belongs credit as primus inter pares.'[6]

The purpose of the prince's retinue was primarily military. It goes without saying that an army was expensive, that it needed supplies, food, horses, arms, armour, and during this period of increasing professionalism, it needed to be paid. The prince was supported in all his campaigns except the Spanish expedition by the royal exchequer, but a very considerable bill still had to be met from his own resources. Thus his estates, rights and other sources of income needed to be exploited, collected and maximized. Such duties were also the tasks of the retinue. Household and administrative offices throughout the prince's extensive demesnes provided additional employment for many members of the prince's retinue. In some cases, such as John Chandos' appointment as master-forester of Cheshire, the posts were simply sinecures to reward past and future military service, but others undertook important duties, which directly or indirectly sustained military operations and the grandeur of the prince's household. Their efforts were not always adequate and this became particularly apparent in 1359 when, despite the ransoms and booty taken at Poitiers, in preparation for the Reims campaign, Edward had to take out loans of at least £21,350. His creditors included Richard FitzAlan, earl of Arundel,[7] the Malabayala family,[8] assorted members of the lay and episcopal aristocracy[9] and members of the London merchant community.[10] Of this sum, Sir John Wingfield, governor of the prince's business, negotiated a loan of 20,000 marks.[11] Therefore violence or the capacity for violence, perhaps more correctly the prowess of the knight, the skill at arms of the infantryman or archer was not the only criterion by which the prince recruited. Wingfield was a knight who fought with the prince in 1355 and at Poitiers, but his value was far greater as an administrator and financier than in the front line.

Certain members of the retinue also played a role on the domestic political stage. A survey of parliamentary members in the retinue throughout the prince's adult life reveals 36 or 37 individuals who sat in the Commons of which three represented two different constituencies. This is a very considerable number but does not necessarily indicate that there was a deliberate 'Westminster' policy.[12] The presence of individuals in the Commons may not have been the consequence of a calculated strategy. The prince recruited widely and among men of high calibre, it is no surprise that a number of these sat in parliament. In accordance with the extended geographical character of the retinue, the prince retained or had links to men who sat in constituencies throughout the country. He does not appear to have 'swamped' any particular regions with his familiars, although Norfolk, Herefordshire and Cornwall tended to return members who can be associated with the prince on a fairly regular basis. The majority, although by no means all the appointments were dated to the last decade of the prince's life. This may indicate an increasing interest in domestic politics but there is little evidence to corroborate this. More probably, these years marked a period in which the members in question were older, more respected in county society, less militarily active and thus more likely to take up seats in the Commons.

The means of recruitment to the prince's retinue are something of a 'grey area'. It is uncertain how or if individuals were approached or if they directly sought the prince's patronage. It can be supposed that 'word of mouth', local influence, family ties, nepotism and military and administrative experience all had a part to play. The prince's retinue formed something of a core and model among the great bastard feudal associations of the day and the opportunities for overlapping military and administrative service among the great affinities and retinues of the day were very great. The inter-relation of the royal households of Edward III and Richard II, the Lancastrian affinity of both Grosmont and Gaunt, and the Black Prince's retinue shows the fluidity of service between these institutions. This is in no way surprising, especially if the prince is viewed as the future Edward IV and his retinue as the king's household in waiting. It must be remembered that the knightly community was small and closely connected on a number of levels and through a variety of vertical and horizontal associations.

As there were only four major campaigns to speak of in 21 years, the role of the retinue was governed by extended periods of peace and truce even as it was shaped by the hostilities. In the 'close season', some of the retinue fought elsewhere, with Chandos and the captal de Buch in Brittany, some with Du Guesclin in Spain. Others sat on commissions of array, of oyer and terminer, as members of Parliament, and as such, they cared for their master's interests and those of fellow members of his retinue. Others saw diplomatic service further abroad. Political, household, diplomatic and military service in the retinue of Edward the Black Prince were within the broad range of national policy and also reflected trends and practices evident among other contemporary 'bastard feudal' associations. However, the retinue itself was different, being in some aspects anachronistic, particularly in its structure and yet in other way, highly innovative. It combined facets of innovative bastard feudal practices by its 'artificiality', its distance from its tenurial roots, with the practices and traditions of earlier times.[13]

While the 'synthetic' nature of the retinue contributed to its success, the same could not be said of the principality of Aquitaine — an almost fictional political entity. A typical account of the failure of the principality attributes it to the poor relations between the prince and his nobles, the financial exactions demanded of them and their vassals and the arrogance displayed by the *English* officials who governed as if they were in occupied territory. But of course they were and for the most part this was not a Gascon revolt but an Aquitainian one.

The economic foundations of the principality of Aquitaine had always been, at best, shaky. The years in which Gascon revenues were accounted as being as valuable if not more so than all English Crown lands were long gone. The principal wealth of the duchy was based on viticulture and by the 1360s wine exports were at less than half pre-war levels. Furthermore, and somewhat ironically, peace may not have been a beneficial economic state. The 'war dividend' had taken a number of forms. First, the spoils of war had been considerable, certainly for a number of Gascon captains who in their turn contributed a considerable, if unquantifiable, amount to the local Gascon economy. Secondly, the duchy had been and remained the focus of the quarrel that lead to the outbreak of the Hundred Years War, and the consequent military activity had encouraged a variety of 'secondary industries' to develop in support of the war effort. These included the Bordeaux armourers, the iron-founders of Bayonne and the financiers that dealt in loot and ransoms. For those involved in such activities, the end of hostilities brought limited benefits.

Alongside the economic decline of the duchy, the new principality could not depend on support from the Crown. After a large subsidy prior to Edward's departure for the principality, there were no payments to the Gascon exchequer until the reopening of hostilities. The principality was to be self-sufficient but the effects of war, plague and administrative confusion during the period of the handover meant that the estimated value, if it could be determined, could never be realised. The Grand Custom (*grande coutume*) on wine, traditionally the major source of revenue, was at a low point and the opportunities of war, in terms of confiscations of land and property from 'traitors' and the defeated, that had previously covered the gap were no longer available. In addition, expenditure, with the arrival of the prince, ballooned.

Sumption estimates that the prince's household expenditure averaged about £10,000 per annum.[14] It is difficult to be certain about this due to the nature of the composite account enrolled by Richard Fillongley in 1370-1, the only evidence for principality finances. Fillongley's account notes the prince's household expenses during the time of

37  *Shield with the Royal Arms, from the tomb of Edward, the Black Prince in Canterbury Cathedral Church, 1376*

office of Hugh Berton and Alan Stokes (treasurers of the wardrobe) as being 211,773 *l.g.* (approx. £41,800) which was nearly half the income of the principality (445,849 *l.g.*, approx. £88,070). On this basis the prince's household expenses were generally in line with those expected of a great magnate, about half his annual income. However, the figures recorded in Fillongley's account only deal with the period of Berton's and Stokes' treasurerships (at most from *c.*1359–*c.*1365). If the account deals with a period of approximately five years, then average annual household expenditure in Bordeaux was nearly £8,400 but judging by the tenure of the treasurers, it seems that the prince was only resident in Aquitaine for two of them. Details are not included of the treasurership of John Carleton, from *c.*1365. Fillongley's figures only allow him about £8,000 before going into 'the red', less than one year's expenditure at average levels over the last five years. There can be little doubt that this average was much lower than the true amount the prince spent and that Carleton had to fund annual expenditure on the court at a much higher level. It is possible, although unlikely that the account only covers the period from *c.*1363–6 and consequently annual household expenditure could have been somewhere in the region of £20,000.[15]

The reason (or excuse) for the rebellion that was to lead to the resumption of the war and the collapse of the principality was taxation, specifically the *fouage* levied in 1368. Taxation had always been a thorny problem in Gascony; even in the 1340s, the English had never been able to institute a regular system. However, the hearth tax was by no means a new imposition in Languedoc and had been exacted by Armagnac as lieutenant of Guienne on a number of occasions and often at a higher rate. Additional taxes were also demanded for the ransom of King Jean after Poitiers as well as the *gabelle*, the salt tax.[16] Under the prince's regime direct taxation accounted for 36% of income and, until 1368, it generated comparatively little opposition. In June 1364, the prince had levied a *fouage*, with the approval of the Estates of Aquitaine as a rate of 3s. 4d. In September of the following year it was again imposed at half that rate (1s 10d). Following the (financial) debacle of the Nájera campaign, the Estates voted for an annual tax of 2s. for an indeterminate period in return for certain concessions.[17] The nominal yield on a 2s. tax was £5,400. Pedro's recalculated debt to the prince was about £385,000 (2,720,000 florins) which would require this level of imposition to continue for something over 71 years if that was the only outlet for the taxation. Froissart attributed the plan to John Harewell, chancellor of Guienne.[18]

It is, of course, arguable that Gascony itself, not the greater Aquitaine, could not be governed by a resident English lord; examples abound of the failure of such schemes but the situation in the principality in the 1360s went beyond previous experience and was exacerbated by social, cultural and political traditions. For example, the traditional seigneurial right to make private war was tenaciously upheld throughout Languedoc and the Valois kings had had little success in curbing such instincts. The main example of such strife was the Foix-Armagnac feud. The authority and territorial holdings of these protagonists were such that a network of alliances had developed, subsuming many other issues within that struggle. In 1362, at the battle of Launac, Gaston Fébus, count of Foix, defeated the Armagnac faction, which included the Albret family. The enormous ransoms that were demanded may well have encouraged the appeal to Charles V due to the financial benefits which Valois loyalty would bring.[19] Armagnac's ransom after Launac was about £42,500. Seeking allies and stability and showing some diplomatic instincts, the prince had assisted with payments, and prior to the Spanish campaign, Armagnac owed Edward £8,300. However, Pedro's failure to fund that expedition left the prince indebted to the count for war wages amounting to about £28,300. With the loan repaid several times over, Armagnac had freed himself from his difficult obligation and could return to his natural allegiance. The subsequent appeal to Paris included Albret who had also suffered financially in the expedition across the Pyrenees and like Armagnac was suitably remunerated for his change of heart. He was granted a pension of 10,000 *l.* by Charles V and marriage to the king's sister.[20]

The 'Gascon' revolt has also been attributed to the nature of the prince's administration and his personal relations and those of his chief officials with the Aquitainian nobility. Certainly, this reason has often been highlighted as among the main causes of the collapse of the Brétigny agreement. It should be noted however, that such attitudes had probably been fomented in secret by Charles V and Louis of Anjou. In this regard the issue of the prince's personal style of rule is crucial.

Chapter 17 of Machiavelli's *Prince* asks if 'it is better for a prince to be loved or feared'. The resolution of the argument is that since love is out of a prince's control, and fear is something he can instil, the latter is the preferable option for governing effectively. The story in the *Anonimalle Chronicle* of the prince forcing some of his nobles to wait on their knees for 15 minutes before addressing him also puts one in mind of a later incident. Queen Elizabeth I was arguing with Lord Burghley. Burghley by this time was an old man; he was also a subject and thus required to remain on his knees when addressing the queen. Commentators at the time were startled by the queen's kindness when she called, not for Burghley to rise, but for a cushion for his knees. The comparison has often also been drawn with Richard's court which will be discussed further below. Clearly the situations are not directly comparable and concepts of kingship (and queenship) had developed and nor, clearly, was the Black Prince a king, but nor was it necessarily something very far out of the ordinary; what was different were the cultural and political forces at work in Aquitaine.[21]

It has been strongly argued that the 'anglicising' of the Gascon/Aquitainian administration was another key element that caused the discontent that erupted in 1368. The choice of officials was often governed by political motivations and most of the new seneschals were English and predominantly military men such as William Felton, seneschal of Poitou, and Richard Totesham, seneschal of Angoumois and governor of La Rochelle.[22] Nonetheless, some effort was made to offset such appointments and there may have been a programme of establishing concentrations of politically supportive families in various towns and cities.[23] In an attempt to win over the port of La Rochelle, Edward III chose several of the chief officials of Saintonge from among the municipal elite. William Seris was appointed president of the sovereign court, to hear appeals from Saintonge.[24] He also became governor of Benon. However, he returned to the French fold in 1369 and Charles V rewarded him with the office of president of the Parlement of Paris.[25] By contrast, the Poitevin, Guichard d'Angle, King Jean's seneschal of Saintonge, was retained in office and gave his full allegiance to England. He became the master of Richard II's household and was rewarded with the earldom of Huntingdon.

A comparison with that area where the prince also experienced difficulties in dealing with his nobles, the March of Wales, may be useful. There it was believed most constructive to affect 'a surrender of power into the hands of those who were already the economic and social leaders of the community'. The English did not have any form of traditional power base in much of the new principality and despite their efforts they failed to create one. Similarly in Wales, while the Black Prince employed Welsh officials particularly for raising revenue, the key posts went to Englishmen with the result that 'The feeling that they were "outsiders" in the governance of their own country was not an insignificant cause of disaffection on the part of Welshmen . . . it almost certainly played a prominent role in the build-up to the Glyn Dwr revolt.'[26] This should not only been viewed in ethnic and racial terms however, as exploitation of the Welsh by Welshmen was certainly not unknown. For example, Rhys ap Roppert, who was descended from Ednyfed Fychan, the great minister of Llewellyn ap Iorweth, prince of Gwynedd, served as escheator of Caernarvon and Merioneth from 12 December 1347 and leased the offices of sheriff and *raglot* of Flint for two years from 3 December 1353. He was an extremely repressive official and exploited his position for his own benefit; it is unlikely that he brought much profit to the Black Prince. His sons, Ieuan and Magod, fought with the Welsh *condotierre*, Owain Lawgoch, on the side of the French and Rhys was accused of sending money to them.[27] However, despite the similarities between Wales and Aquitaine, the governmental procedures enforced by the new regime in the greater Gascony compared closely to those that had been employed by Jean II. French administrative practices (if not personnel) were maintained in the newly acquired *seneschausées* although most of the new seneschals were English.

The period of the principality was a time of constant political reassessment, a process that continued in the 1370s. Loyalties were elastic and transitory, a state conditioned by both culture and politics. It is brought sharply into focus in the role of the Great Companies and individuals therein. For example, it is particularly interesting that in the interval between the battle of Launac and the peace settlement, that the Armagnac faction recruited members of the Companies led by John Amory and John Creswell, both close associates of the Black Prince. Amory, in the way of such things, had fought with Gaston Fébus against Jean d'Armagnac at Launac. Elsewhere there were links to Navarre that give the lie to the suggestion that this was a period of peace. The captal de Buch and Chandos, as constable of Aquitaine and more particularly as lord of Saint-Sauveur, were to lead twin forces against King Jean although in the event, matters changed and the Navarrese were defeated at Cocherel. The clearest example of such flexibility with regard to service was in the Spanish campaigns: Du Guesclin's so-called crusade which toppled Pedro the Cruel from the throne of Castile and the Nájera expedition led by the Black Prince that replaced him albeit briefly. Among Du Guesclin's commanders were Hugh Calveley, Mathew Gournay, Walter Hewitt, John Devereux and Stephen Cosington, all of whom then fought with the prince to reinstate the monarch they had so recently deposed. With regard to the Companies and the prince's regime, it should be remembered that during the bulk of the lifetime of the principality, Aquitaine enjoyed a far more peaceful time than the rest of France. It did not suffer the depredations of the *condottieri* until very late in the day. Indeed, it might be argued that the tide turned against the Black Prince and the English, when they could no longer depend on the support of the Great Companies.[28]

*38 Brasses to Sir John d'Abernon (c.1330) and his son, Sir John d'Abernon (c.1345), in Stoke D'Abernon church, Surrey. Note the differences in arms and armour with the later brasses. There were family links between the Surrey d'Abernons and the keeper of the prince's fees in Cornwall, also called John Dabernon*

If the prince was more or less responsible for the conditions that led to the loss of the principality, he was entirely responsible for the chief instrument that confirmed (if not precipitated) that loss. The ransoming of Bertrand Du Guesclin after his capture at Nájera was certainly 'crass stupidity'.[29] After once again securing the Castilian throne for Enrique, he returned to France, was appointed Constable, and fought against his former captor in Aquitaine from July 1370. He took advantage of, and brought about, military advances in tactics and recruitment which resulted in a great upturn in French fortunes.

The rebellion that allowed the participation of Du Guesclin was not spontaneous, not in the cases of Armagnac and Albret, and certainly not for those that followed in returning to French royal allegiance. The count of Périgord waited some time to see 'how the wind was blowing' despite being offered 40,000 francs by Charles V. However, once momentum was gathered fresh appellants appeared in the hundreds, mainly from the regions in Aquitaine of the 'Languedoc' bordering 'France'. Motivation varied, patriotic sentiment certainly played a part, various long-standing disputes with the prince or his officials including questions of failed litigation over land following the transfer of territory after 1360 were also a cause for rebellion. Bribes were offered to others such as the viscount of Castelbon. In most cases the *fouage* was only an excuse although it may have been symbolic of other grievances.[30]

The prince may well have been aware of the worsening political climate and took suitable precautions; there were considerable movements of troops from England to Gascony in the later months of 1367. Such stalwarts as Duncan Felton, John Thurston (Chandos' yeoman), James Audley (possibly not Chandos' companion-in-arms since he was described at this time as the prince's esquire), Robert Morley, John Harpeley, John del Hay, and Aubrey Vere (the future earl of Oxford), together with reinforcements set sail for the principality or received letters of protection and other documentation regarding their service there. Measures were also taken in England and Wales for the defence of the realm.[31]

On 22 December 1368, the duke of Anjou wrote to the nobility of Aquitaine regarding the incipient return of hostilities and commenting on the prince's rule. He spoke of the 'ordonnaces, indictions et exactions de fouages et autres griefs et nouveletés à eux faites par nostre cousin le prince de Galles, duc de Guyienne et autres seneschaux et officiers de dits pais pour luy'. Phrases such as 'droit, raison [et] justice' were interspersed with economic arguments and emotional and nationalistic appeals regarding 'grant amour et loyauté envers eux aux preddecesseurs de mondit seigneur, roys de France'.[32] It appears to have been very effective. In January 1369, the prince was summoned to Paris to answer the appeals. He refused, although Froissart and Chandos Herald claimed he did offer to visit the capital in the company of an army. Further reinforcements were dispatched from England adding to those the prince had been raising since his return from Spain.[33] They mustered at Northampton in the winter of 1368/9. John Montviron, the prince's marshal of the household, oversaw the arrays in north Wales, which were co-ordinated by the justice and chamberlain.[34] Others were recruited from Cheshire, the array probably being organised with the assistance of Thomas Wetenhale, seneschal of the Rouergue. The Northampton muster gathered in September 1368 and included 369 men-at-arms and 428 archers; it did not arrive in Aquitaine until April of the following year. Many of them

*39  Coin of Edward the Black Prince*

served with Audley and Chandos in Poitou and Saintonge.[35] Further reinforcements were sent in 1369, including retinues under the command of Gaunt and Walter Hewitt.[36]

The erosion of the principality began in the Rouergue. Najac was the first town to abandon fealty to the prince on the appearance of forces commanded by Louis of Anjou.[37] This may have taken place even before the proclamation of the count of Armagnac, issued at Rodez on 22 February 1369. Intermittent fighting began in the district (a major area of support of the count of Armagnac) in the spring. On about 9 January, the count's son (also Jean) took the castle of La Roque-Valsergue and used it for a base for further incursions into the Rouergue. The defence of the province, organised by Thomas Wettenhale (seneschal), David Cradock (his deputy) and James Mascy (castellan of Millau), was hampered by a lack of troops and these three retreated to fortresses at Villefranche, Castelmary and Millau respectively. The revolt quickly spread; by 18 March over 900 castles and towns in Armagnac, Rodez (the town had opened its gates to the invaders on about 19 February), Limoges, Quercy and the Agenais had deserted the prince. Further noble support had also been lost, including the vicomte de Rochechouart and the lords of Chauvigny and Pons although loyalty to the English proved to be stronger in the north.[38]

This was not purely a rebellion, Valois support was conspicuous; the French force was estimated to be around 4,000 strong and commanded by Raymond de Rabastens, seneschal of Toulouse, acting in the name of King Charles V, whose claim to the lands of the principality he vigorously and vociferously upheld. He was supported by Jean d'Armagnac.[39] Such action demanded that all available strength be diverted to the principality. Possibly as a result of the prince's failing health, Chandos was recalled from retirement at Saint-Sauveur in Normandy, Knolles was brought in from Brittany and Calveley from Spain. Armagnac's lands became a base for launching attacks and were also the focus of English retaliation. Chandos tried to draw the French away to Toulouse and Albi and then north to Quercy. Further English reinforcements arrived throughout 1369, most notably the forces led by the earls of Cambridge and Pembroke. They linked with Chandos after failing to hold Périgord and captured La Roche-sur-Yon. James Audley, one of the mainstays of the English resistance, died during the siege. On 30 November 1369, Charles formally announced what he was actively acquiring the confiscation of Guienne and it was once again a time of war.[40]

By the end of 1369, Rouergue, Quercy and the Agenais had been lost and Bigorre and Comminges were unlikely to remain loyal for long. Partly due to the incapacity of the prince and the loss of a number of the commanders that had assured his earlier triumphs, such as Audley, a lack of co-ordination marked the English defence. The earl of Pembroke refused to follow Chandos' command since he was 'only' a banneret and when Sir John died after a skirmish at Lussac on 2 January 1370, the collapse was hastened, further encouraged by the loss of the earls of Warwick and Suffolk. The prince's own health had deteriorated steadily since his return from Castile and he was by now virtually incapable of leading troops. By the end of 1369 the French had reached Bazas. In the Rouergue, Thomas Wetenhale was killed, and Bigorre had also fallen to the duke of Anjou. With the help of Du Guesclin, Moissac and Agen were taken. In 1370, the attack turned towards the centre of English rule, Bordeaux.[41]

Walter Hewitt was dispatched from England with a retinue of 200 men-at-arms and 300 archers. Robert Knolles led a *chevauchée* from Calais; it was a retaliatory action following a co-ordinated attack led by the dukes of Berri and Anjou and the count of Armagnac, which may have been aimed at the prince himself, bedridden in Angoulême. Lancaster and Warwick tried to reconquer Ponthieu but failed to bring the French to battle. Warwick died of plague on the march. Louis of Anjou retook Porte-Saine-Marie, Montpezat, Tonneins and Aiguillon. In the Agenais, he took Villeneuve, Astafford and La Sauvetat. On 8 August, he was at Agen. Armagnac entered Bigorre on 1 September and took Tarbes.[42]

The speed with which the principality fell was startling and shaming and may explain the reaction of the prince and his commanders to the desertion of Limoges. The surrender of the town, commanded by Jean de Vinemur, to the duc de Berri resulted in the prince, accompanied by Lancaster, Cambridge and the captal de Buch, laying siege on 19 September 1370. At the time, the prince's headquarters were at Cognac. His forces numbered about 1,200 men-at-arms, 1,000 archers and 1,000 foot soldiers. The siege was brief, lasting only six days. The walls were mined and Froissart suggested that 3,000 were killed in the ensuing massacre. The order to respect all churches in the city seems to have been generally observed although there was damage to the cathedral. However, it is entirely possible that the massacre of civilians never took place, at least not on the scale that has been popularised. The event is not attested in any local chronicles and the extent of that retribution is questionable as is the culpability of the Black Prince. That military action took place and the city was sacked is not in doubt, but the scale of the slaughter may have been much exaggerated and it has been suggested that only 300 died. As for personal responsibility, at Limoges the prince is said to have directed operations from a litter and may only have been in nominal command. Under the strictures of the laws of war, the actions described by Froissart as taken at Limoges were entirely justifiable and it may be that 'What Froissart is depicting is the *expected* behaviour of a successful army after a siege;

he does not deny the Black Prince's right to carry out such deeds when he suggests that mercy would have been well-placed.'[43]

Nonetheless, it was certainly brutal but 'If one condemns the Black Prince, then one condemns virtually all medieval siege commanders.'[44] That Froissart saw fit to indict the prince for his actions at Limoges whilst lauding the slaughter and destruction of the 1355 *chevauchée* was a consequence of the author's condition and circumstances at the time of writing rather than great moral indignation. A French chronicle records that the English 'put many of the citizens to death because they had turned French'.[45] Attitudes to non-combatants were changing and affected by a variety of influences. In practical terms, the attitudes of besieging commanders had been altered by improvements to urban defences. As the 1346-7 siege of Calais demonstrated, it was a long and very expensive business to reduce the walls of a strongly fortified town and extreme penalties were imposed to discourage resistance. According to Honoré Bouvet no besieged city or fortress could make a truce or treaty to save itself from the consequences of an assault after its walls had been breached. If the inhabitants failed to make terms, they were at the besiegers' mercy. Attitudes to treason had also changed, at least in England by the 1352 Act and similar developments took place in France. One of the first examples of the use of quartering was in 1346 when a poor unfortunate named Simon Pouillet murmured too loudly that Edward III should be king rather than Philip of Valois. 'Like a slab of meat in a butcher's shop [he was] stretched and bound on a slab of wood . . . and was there beheaded and dismembered, first his arms, then his legs, and then his head; and finally [his corpse] was hanged on the gibbet.'[46] It would not be unlikely that the English considered the people of Limoges to have committed treason. In such a circumstance retribution was expected, even required.

The Hundred Years War is remembered for its battles but was characterised by its sieges. The *chevauchée* tactics, so successful in bringing the French to battle at Crécy and Poitiers and of great psychological and economic value, relied on a swiftly moving mounted force which was not prepared for a siege. Such an army could not transport all the necessary equipment and sieges were lengthy and expensive. The assault on Romorantin in 1355 was a rare example of a successful quick assault that delayed a raid by only a few days. In the engagement, surrender was encouraged by the use of Greek fire, which served to ignite thatched roofs and other flammables. The foundations may also have been mined. By contrast, the defences at Tours, still under construction in 1356, probably deterred the Black Prince from attacking. Control of territory depended on control of the major urban areas. In the main, before the wide-scale use of artillery, defensive architecture was superior to offensive weaponry and tactics; the siege of Calais had been a triumph of endurance, not ingenuity or superior military technology.[47]

While the prince was actively attacking French strongholds he was also concerned with the defence of his own lands and their centres of defence, government and administration. Anglo-Welsh defensive measures were features of all periods of military activity, and Cheshire and north Wales in 1355 and 1359-60 were protected against possible invasions or Welsh revolts. Repairs were made to the castles in Wales, Cornwall and Cheshire, supplies were gathered and their garrisons strengthened 'in view of the multitude of perils which might arise'.[48] For example, at this time, John Wogan was charged with the defence

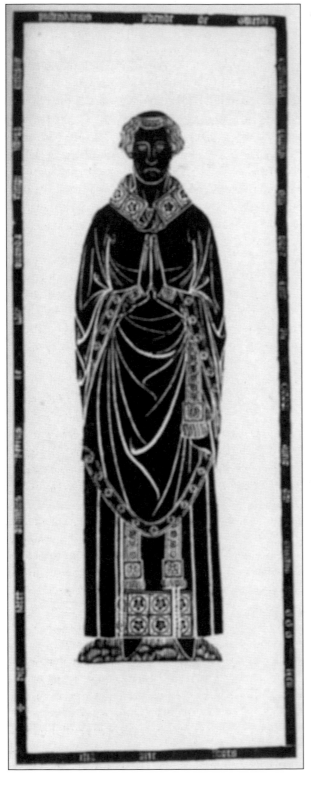

40 *Brass of Peter de Lacy, wearing alb, maniple, amice and stole. Norfleet, Kent. Peter Lacy entered the prince's service in 1344 and became receiver-general, member of the council and keeper of the great wardrobe. In 1367 he became keeper of Edward III's privy seal*

of the Welsh coast and a writ was sent to the prince by his father and passed on to officials in north and south Wales ordering defensive preparations in accordance with the Statute of Winchester.[49] In the course of the Reims campaign, responsibility for the 'safe-keeping' of the castles in Cornwall and Devon in 1359 was left in the hands of John Dabernon and John Kendale. In this instance, particular attention was to be given to the castle at Tintagel, which, at the time, was without a garrison and John Skirbeck, formerly butler of the prince's household and constable of Launceston and Tintagel castles, then keeper of the prince's fees in Cornwall, was to make similar preparations for the manning and victualling of Launceston. The maintenance of castle defences was a continual drain on the prince's purse. In February 1360, repairs were ordered to the Cornish castles, again under the supervision of Kendale and Dabernon.[50] Additional security was also required at Berkhamsted castle where the captured king of France was kept, although it appears that John Clay, the prince's receiver of Berkhamsted, handed over the buildings (and responsibility) for Jean's safe-keeping to his jailers.[51] Measures were also taken at that time at Wallingford and at Castle Rising, both for the building and the bridge so that it was 'safely guarded in these times so that no peril [would] befall it'.[52] Such measures were entirely in keeping with national procedure. In July 1355, all the port authorities from Dover to Fowey had been ordered to protect their shipping and make defensive preparations. The fears of an attack were realised in 1360 with the French raid on Winchelsea. The potential resumption of hostilities further galvanised defensive preparations. In 1367, Richard FitzAlan, earl of Arundel and lord of Bromfield and Yale, was commanded to prepare 'all fencible men' to defend the principality of Wales.[53]

Urban defences also contributed to the difficulties involved in governing Aquitaine and they were to facilitate its destruction. The principality contained a multiplicity of fortified locations. These added to the problems of feuding, particularly between the families of Foix and Armagnac. The possession of a number of these strongholds gave command of communications and supply routes, either by road or water.[54] When these sites turned to Valois allegiance there was little that could be done to retake them or maintain the integrity of the principality.

However, the importance of urban defences, the time it might take to break them and the general role of the fortified town or castle, was in the course of widespread revision at this time. There is no doubt that artillery was used and increasingly so by the prince throughout his career. By 1369, Chandos' troops were always accompanied by a cannon and this was not an entirely new innovation. Cannon had been used during the campaign of 1346 and possibly at Crécy as field artillery. At that time, the guns used 'were simple light weapons, almost as dangerous to those firing them as to those at whom they were fired'.[55] They were certainly used during the Calais siege as supplies of ammunition and firearms were sent for from England. Edward III had at least ten cannons and materials for over 5,000 lbs of gunpowder but they do not appear to have been highly influential in taking the town. By 1370, many towns and almost all the great powers in Western Europe came to possess their own arsenals. The receiver of Ponthieu in 1368-9 purchased for Edward III: twenty copper cannons, five iron cannons, 215 lbs of saltpetre, sulphur and amber for making powder, and 1,300 large quarrels/bolts for the cannons. Nonetheless, the period of rapid innovation in gunnery happened in the second and third decades of the fifteenth century. For much of the fourteenth century they did not replace the trebuchet or mangonel as siege weapons and on the battlefield did not influence tactical thinking to any great extent. They were used primarily for frightening horses.[56]

The Limoges expedition, in which he was present if not prominent, brought about a further deterioration in the prince's condition. The collapse of his health and authority was marked by the transfer of authority to Gaunt. La Roche-sur-Yon and the lordship of Bergerac passed to him on 8 October 1370, prior to his appointment as lieutenant of Aquitaine on 11 October 1370.[57] The death of his first son, Edward of Angoulême, underlined the prince's personal tragedy. He returned to England and, alongside Gaunt, the captal de Buch and Thomas Felton took over the government of Gascony in July 1371. Soon after, Owain Lawgoch, the Welsh *condottiere* allied to France, captured the captal at Soubise. It is said that he was tempted briefly to give his allegiance to France but remained loyal and unlike the Black Prince and Du Guesclin, Charles 'the Wise' refused to ransom him and he ended his days in prison, soon after hearing the news of the death of the Black Prince.

# 8 LAST YEARS AND LEGACY

The prince's last years were marked by a slow, inconsistent but inexorable decline. He was never again involved in military activity although he remained concerned with coastal defences and provision was made for munitioning a number of castles such as through the purchase of supplies in Ireland for Welsh fortifications in 1375.[1] He did set sail for Calais with his father in August 1372, following the news that Thouars, the last great English fortress, was under threat but the elements conspired against them and the fleet never reached France. On returning to England, the prince handed over all his rights in Aquitaine to his father giving a reason, which had always been true, but was now a mere technicality, that revenue was no longer sufficient to meet expenses.[2]

The prince's role and level of activity in these last years is not altogether certain and it seems that his condition varied considerably allowing more involvement in national affairs at some times than others. Further, it has been suggested that the prince's interest in politics at this time was not restricted to domestic matters. Relations with Castile, during both the brief rule of Pedro the Cruel and the early years of the Trastamaran regime had not been cordial following Pedro's failure to pay the prince after Nájera. However, Pedro did, it seems, have long-term ambitions that one or more of his daughters would marry sons of Edward III. That ambition was realised after Pedro's murder at Montiel in 1369 and 'the Prince of Wales . . . probably approved of the transfer to his younger brother of his own aspirations to the Castilian throne'. On 10 February 1372, the prince escorted his brother's bride to be, Constanza, into London, acknowledged by England as queen of Castile and rode with her to Gaunt's palace of the Savoy. Constanza had spent five years in exile in Gascony. Gaunt thereby became pretender to the Castilian throne although he did not claim lordship of Vizcaya out of deference to the prince's claims to the Basque country.[3]

The prince's final flourish, his last bow, has traditionally been seen as taking place not on the battlefield but in parliament. The Good Parliament of 1376 is one of the final myths of the prince's life that remains in popular memory. He is said to have formed the bulwark of the defence against the over-reaching political ambitions of his brother, John of Gaunt, duke of Lancaster.

The chief reason for the belief in the mutual antagonism of the prince and Gaunt is the account by Thomas Walsingham whose rabid anti-Lancastrian attitudes have coloured subsequent comment. There is no evidence of difficulties between the brothers prior to this. They both fought at Winchelsea and Gaunt lived in the prince's household in the early 1350s. In 1367, Gaunt supported the Spanish expedition and was so highly praised for his role in the expedition by Chandos Herald, an eyewitness, that it has been suggested

*41 Coin of Edward the Black Prince*

that his *Life of the Black Prince* was written for, or in support of, the Castilian ambitions of the duke of Lancaster. It has also been suggested that Edward resented being replaced by Gaunt in Aquitaine but again there is nothing to substantiate this and rather than bearing a grudge towards his brother it would seem likely that he handed over the reins of power willingly, although not with relief.

From the reopening of the war in 1369 (although hostilities in Aquitaine had begun in the previous year) until the Good Parliament in 1376 there was almost no English success. The *chevauchées* of Robert Knolles and John of Gaunt were expensive in men and money and achieved nothing of note. Defeats at sea and attacks on the south coast were testimony to the authority of the Castilian fleet. It has been argued that the new breed of commanders, weaned on tales of Crécy and Poitiers, were not the match of their predecessors who had been responsible for such victories and certainly many of the great commanders had died in war and of the plague or were, like the king and his eldest son, now old and ill. But circumstances were different also, and if personalities and people can be said to be representative of national success, then Charles V was a far more capable ruler than his father or grandfather. French domestic policy, leading to improved defences, military strategy and the ability to fund such action had created a formidable structure although these realities cut little ice in England. The source of the agitation is uncertain but complaints rained down on the government concerning the management of the war from certain sections of the Commons and these may have been encouraged in 'another place'.

The Commons was becoming increasingly important as the crown became increasingly dependent on parliament for financial support through taxation. As this developed so too did the interest of magnates in influencing the Commons and elections to it. Among the prince's retinue were a number of MPs, but there is little to suggest that the prince was following a deliberate policy comparable to that of which Gaunt was accused, namely trying to pack the Commons for certain votes. There were only six claiming the prince's support in the Good Parliament and this was the highest total apart from sessions in 1358, 1365 and 1369 in which seven members of the retinue sat in the Commons. It is true, although probably coincidental, that those sessions when he was best represented were tax-granting parliaments, but beyond this, membership of the Commons does not seem to have been a major factor in recruitment to the retinue. It may have been the case that the prince's authority and that of his friends and his father's adherents was sufficient to influence the Commons as they wished, without the need to secure the support of members of the house.[4]

The role of the prince was thus, at most vicarious and probably fictitious, the creation of Thomas Walsingham, and an early example of the myth of the prince, the broken knight, still struggling even on his death-bed for the good of his country, urging on his supporters in parliament to stand up to the wicked council and dark intentions of his brother.

> But [their] vigour dissolved away immediately after the untimely death of Prince Edward. For after that death the duke [Gaunt] could do whatever he desired and willed. . . . [T]he death of prince Edward filled the knights of the shire with despair. The duke entered the assembly of the knights. He urgently begged them . . . the knights, and the lords and barons associated with them, [to] deliberate as to who should inherit the kingdom of England after the death of the king and of the prince his son. He begged further that . . . they would decree a law that a woman should not become heir to the kingdom; for he considered the great age of the king, who was on the threshold of death, and he considered the youth of Prince Richard whom, so it was said, he thought of poisoning if he could not gain the kingdom in any other way.[5]

Gaunt's royal ambitions, if not involving murder, do at least bear some further consideration. Edward III took steps to clarify the order of succession, which was clouded by the issue of 'representation' (that Richard should have precedence over his uncle/s) by making an entail detailing the descent of the Crown. Michael Bennett has pointed out that Richard's coronation was by no means a foregone conclusion, noting remarks by Chandos Herald and others.[6] Interestingly, the problem lay, as it had and did in France, with whether the Crown might be inherited through the female line. It remains uncertain, although improbable, if Gaunt had deliberate intentions to try and seize the throne on his father's death. Edward wished to avoid possible strife in the event of an uncertain succession, particularly in the context of the declining English position in France and political opposition at home. It was such opposition that may account for Walsingham's version of events and it is not unlikely that he was guilty of a deliberate anachronism with regard to Gaunt's role in the Good Parliament. As the king's representative, Gaunt saw it necessary to reverse the steps it had taken in 1376 in the Hillary parliament of 1377. Charges brought by the Commons of mismanagement and corruption had resulted in the impeachment of the chamberlain, William Lord Latimer, the steward, John Lord Neville, a number of merchants, and the king's mistress, Alice Perrers. Gaunt engineered and oversaw a vindictive and deliberate reversal of the measures taken by the 1376 parliament, targeting those that had been most prominent in the demands for reform.

With the succession secure, any daydreams Gaunt may have had of assuming the throne of England were soon subsumed by his more realistic ambitions in Spain. There is certainly no doubting the appeal of a crown;

> To the mentality of a fourteenth-century English magnate . . . great wealth and power were of secondary significance when set against the prospect his attaining, in is own right, the supreme position in the medieval social order. If he [Gaunt] could not be king of England, it was perfectly natural to a mind such as his that he should wish to be king of Castile.[7]

The myth of the Black Prince, built on a reputation earned in battle, grew with his death. John of Reading's eulogy said that he followed wise council, never preferred secular affairs to divine office, that he was honourable, he endowed the church generously and kept his marriage vows.[8] It was not a terribly accurate portrayal but nor was it completely fanciful. Certainly in death, and it was a death for which he must have been preparing for some time, some surprising aspects of his character become apparent.

Edward the Black Prince was buried, as he wished, in Canterbury Cathedral but not where he wished. He had requested to be laid in the chapel of 'Our Lady Undercroft' ('so that the end of our tomb towards the feet be ten feet distant from the altar'[9]) but instead is to be found in a much more prominent position and one of even more significance than today, prior as it was to the removal and destruction of Becket's tomb. In death, the figure of the prince became once more that of the consummate warrior that he had not been for some nine years. That the tomb retained an aura many years after the prince's death is evident, as Shakespeare has the archbishop of Canterbury say to Henry V:

> Look back into your mighty ancestors:
> Go, my dread lord, to your great-grandsire's tomb,
> From whom you claim; invoke his warlike spirit,
> And your great-uncle's, Edward the Black Prince,
> Who on the French ground play'd a tragedy,
> Making defeat on the full power of France,
> While his most mighty father on a hill
> Stood smiling to behold his lion's whelp
> Forage in blood of French nobility.[10]

The tomb, Chandos Herald, Froissart and later writers compounded the image of a model prince and of a model knight that remained at least until the beginning of the twentieth century (see Leeds statue). The prince was extremely particular in his will regarding the disposition of his body. Details of the tomb, its placement and design, the use and display of his arms and mottoes (*houmout* and *ich diene*), the passage of the cortege through Canterbury, black pennons with ostrich feathers, two destriers trapped with his arms, requests for vigils, masses and divine office were made. Gifts were made for the altar of the chapel as well as vestments, candlesticks, basins and chamber-hangings and a cross fashioned from the wood of the Holy Cross.

*42 Coin of Edward
the Black Prince*

The prince's will, as well as the image on the 'tester' above his tomb show his dedication to the cult of the Trinity. He bequeathed his soul to God and his saints, most particularly the Trinity and the Virgin. The prince also gave to Canterbury cathedral an image of the Trinity, and chamber-hangings to be used for hanging in the choir-stalls to serve as a memorial for the prince on the feast of the Trinity and the other principal feasts of the year.

The Trinity was a cult which was by no means new in the fourteenth century although it seems to have regained some momentum at this time. In late Saxon times All Saints and Holy Trinity had become popular dedications: 'devotion to the Trinity — manifest still in innumerable paintings and sculptures — flourished greatly until and through the reformation. . .'.[11] Other Trinity images associated with the prince can be seen on the frontispiece of a Chandos Herald manuscript, a funerary lead badge, and another showing him worshipping the Trinity within the Garter. It is also evident from the document granting the prince custody of Aquitaine and his foundation of a chantry with two priests to say masses in the cathedral church of the Holy Trinity in Canterbury. The prince had been born within the quindene of Trinity Sunday and died on the feast itself, at three in the afternoon having been prince of Wales for 33 years. Joan was 33 when he married her. It is interesting that the guild of the Trinity was the pre-eminent guild of both Coventry, which the prince held, and Lynn where he had considerable interests.[12] Whether or not the prince influenced friends and associates in advocating the cult of the Trinity, many examples can be found of retinue members founding institutions and giving patronage to those with links to the Trinity. Miles Stapleton in *c.*1360 received a licence to found a perpetual chantry in honour of the Holy Trinity in the parochial church of Ingham, Norfolk. John Willoughby d'Eresby, who fought at Crécy and died three years later, founded a Trinity chapel in Spilsby church, Lincolnshire. John Wingfield, the prince's business manager, by the terms of his will, had a chapel built and similarly dedicated in 1362. Richard FitzAlan, a military companion, long-standing creditor and official in Wales and the border counties, began the building of a Trinity chapel at Arundel and left provision in his will for its completion. In Cheshire the sisters and fraternity of the Blessed Trinity were associated with Adam Wheteley, the mayor and escheator of Chester, in a petition requesting a licence from the prince to acquire and hold certain lands in perpetuity.[13]

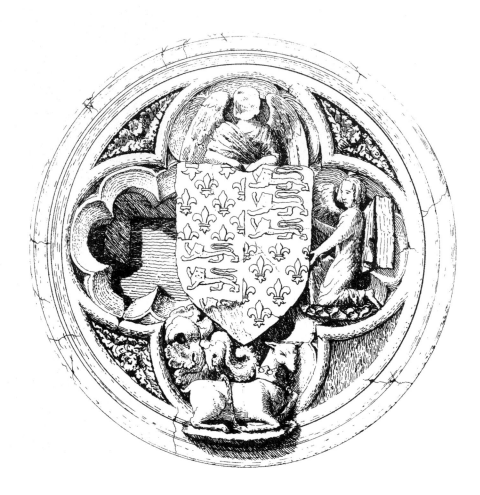

*43   The coat of arms of Richard II*

The prince's will also reveals other aspects of his personal religious beliefs and particular friendships. Grants were made to the house of the Bonhommes at Ashridge and to the chapel of St Nicholas at Wallingford. The former were an unusual order; the monastery or college of the Precious Blood at Ashridge had been founded for seven priests in 1283 by the prince's great-uncle, Edmund, earl of Cornwall. In 1376, the Black Prince augmented the endowments and the number of priests was increased to 20. He appears to have had little direct contact with this house of the order until this time when he became the 'second founder'. In 1346, a chantry had been founded in the conventual church for the soul of Bartholomew Burghersh, snr, after the appropriation of the church of Ambrosden. The foundation had been built on duchy land a short distance from Berkhamsted and endowed with Ashridge park and manor.[14]

The house at Ashridge was the first of the order but it was not the first house of Bonhommes with which the prince was connected. The order had expanded in the 1350s

*44 Badge of Richard II from MS Vincent 152 at the Heralds' College*

when two brothers from Ashridge were sent to Edington of which one, John Aylesbury (d. 25 March 1382), received a licence from the bishop of Lincoln in 1358 permitting him to take up office as the first rector. The Ashridge statutes were repeated at Edington and the unusual azure habit became uniform. However, after the transfer of brethren in 1358 there seems to be little evidence of any real enduring link between the two. There is little agreement as to the actual nature of the observance carried out at the houses. Certainly there was little obviously distinctive, apart from their habit, about them to attract patronage. They followed the Rule of St Augustine, or a very close variant, and normal monastic service was conducted according to the Use of Sarum. Despite the association of William Edington and the Black Prince, they had little or no political influence.[15]

The foundation at Edington was converted into a house of Bonhommes, not founded as such. It had been created as a college of the Blessed Virgin, St Katherine and All Saints by William Edington, bishop of Winchester, in 1351 as one of the last purely regular religious foundations. The conversion into a monastery of the Bonhommes in 1358 probably occurred at the insistence of the Black Prince, and served 'to free [the] priests from onerous parochial duties'.[16] A charter was given by Robert Wyvill, bishop of Salisbury, in March confirming that it was to become a house of 'fratres de ordine sancti

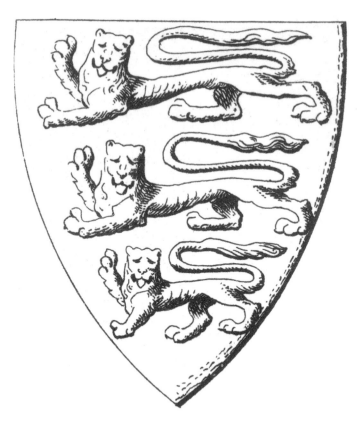

*45  The coat of arms of
Edward III*

Augustini, Boni Homines vulgariter nuncupati'.[17] A number of individuals with other connections to the prince can be found among records of the order as witnesses to charters and the like. It is surprising that with such luminaries as the prince of Wales and the bishop of Winchester as patrons, the order failed to gain a great deal of support. It was handsomely endowed by the prince who sought little material benefit and indeed handed over control over elections to the brethren. Edington Priory is also renowned for its glazing, which was built *c*.1358-61.[18]

To Richard (II), the prince bequeathed three beds, possibly including one with coverings showing a white hart encircled with the arms of Kent and Wake, and chamber-hangings embroidered with the arms of Saladin. To Roger Clarendon, his illegitimate son by Edith Willesford, he also bequeathed a bed, as he did to both Robert Walsham, his confessor, and his companion-in-arms, Alan Cheyne. The political iconography of the bed, especially a bed decorated with heraldic images, with their inherent statement of authority, made the gifts highly significant. The prince also requested that the grants and annuities he had given his knights, esquires and other servants should be confirmed. His executors were to be Gaunt (another indication that there was no 'bad blood' between them), Edington, John Harewell, bishop of Bath, William Spridlington, bishop of St Asaph, Robert Walsham, Hugh Seagrave, Alan Stokes and John Fordham. The will was witnessed by John, bishop of Hereford, Lewis Clifford, Nicholas Bonde, Nicholas Sarnesfield, and William Walsham.[19]

46 *The coat of arms of*
*Edward III*

The tomb itself, commissioned by Richard II in the mid-1380s, bears an epitaph at odds with the image and figure of the prince. The epitaph may have been indicative of the prince's own state of mind and religious concerns. It is certainly indicative of a changing attitude to death in the later fourteenth century and with that the search for a more 'personal relationship' with God. It includes the lines;

> . . . Mais je sui ore poevres et cheitifs
> Parfond en la terre gis
> Ma grande beauté est tut alée,
> Ma char est tut gasté . . .[20]

After the prince's death, Richard's childhood did not last long and little is known about it. Much of it was spent in Joan's household and in the guardianship of three *magistri*, chosen for him by the Black Prince, namely Guichard d'Angle, Richard Abberbury and Simon Burley.[21]

The political turbulence enveloping his father's household in his early years cannot have affected him greatly, and it is impossible to say if he was aware of the death of his brother, Edward. It is unlikely that he had many memories of Aquitaine and equally improbable that he remembered his father in his pomp. Perhaps this made the comparisons, when he acceded the throne, even more difficult to bear. John Gower in his *Vox Clamantis* wrote:

It is also your concern, O king, to be your people's defender in arms. And in order to defend justice with valour, remember your father's deed as a model for this . . . France felt the effects of him; and Spain . . . was fearful of him. Throwing his foes into disorder, he hurled his troops into the midst of his enemies and broke up their course of march like a lion.[22]

His childhood was brief and his time to prepare for the crown was similarly limited. He clearly had a number of common interests with his father. In the few months in which he was prince of Wales after the death of his father and before the demise of Edward III he made payments to two pipers called Henrico and Petirkyn as well as to numerous heralds and minstrels. From the duke of Lancaster, his uncle, and his grandfather he received presents of horses.[23]

Richard's education was in the care of those well versed in chivalric and martial pursuits. In these fields Burley, and particularly d'Angle, had impeccable credentials.[24] He had served both the kings of England and France loyally, as Philip of Valois' seneschal of Saintonge from 1346, at Poitiers, where he was gravely wounded, and in the prince's service in Aquitaine and at Nájera. In 1372 he was nominated a knight of the Garter and on Richard's coronation he became earl of Huntingdon.[25] It may have been a result of such tutors that the chivalric example was not lost on Richard and he endeavoured to use it for the political advantages it had given his father and grandfather. Unlike them, unfortunately, he lacked the military success by which a king and a knight were judged. The senility of Edward III and the political failures of the Black Prince were forgotten in a haze of military victories. Richard did not have a Poitiers or a Crécy on which to fall back. Indeed, it has been suggested that this had more debilitating consequences and that 'Richard's inability to meet the martial standards of his father . . . was a component of the king's psychological trauma.'[26] However, this is not to suggest that Richard was militarily incapable or certainly a coward, his actions at Mile End in 1381 gives the lie to such an accusation. But it might be argued that Richard's temperament and disposition and the consequent shape taken by his kingship, the pomp, the ceremony and indeed the chivalry, informed and shaped his conception of monarchy, in a manner which was by no means out of character with the nobility or the style adopted by his father and grandfather; he simply could not substantiate it militarily.

While Richard was burdened by the reputations of his father and grandfather their legacies to him were inversely although similarly problematic. Political instability was bequeathed by Edward III and insufficient institutional support by the Black Prince. In spite of its size and expense during his militarily active life, the prince did not bequeath a sizeable retinue to his son. The actions of Richard, particularly in the late 1380s and 1390s, reveal his lack of political support. There were a number of important individuals who went on to serve the Black Prince's son, and a significant number of those who sat on the continual councils during Richard's minority had begun their careers with the young king's father. The chamber knights in the first six or seven years of Richard's reign were mainly his father's former servants. They included Richard Abberbury, Baldwin Bereford, Nicholas Bonde, John and Simon Burley, Lewis Clifford, Peter Courtenay, John del Hay, Nicholas Sarnesfield, Aubrey Vere and Bernard van Zedeles. Among the former servants of Edward III who served as chamber knights to his successor, Nicholas Dagworth, Robert Roos and Richard Stury all had dealings with the Black Prince as did the new men William Beauchamp, John Holland and William Neville. Nine out of 19 of Richard's esquires of the chamber also formerly saw service with the Black Prince, namely John Breton, Roger Coghull, Lambert Fermer, Richard Hampton, John Peytevyn, Adam Ramsey, Philip Walweyn, snr, Richard Wiltshire and William Wyncelowe.[27] Indeed, it was many of these who were the focus of attack by the Appellants in 1388. Simon Burley suffered execution and a number of others were required to absent themselves from court including Abberbury, Bereford, Dagworth and Vere. Although they were prominent at court, the remnants of the Black Prince's retinue that went on to serve his son were neither popular nor powerful. It is probably unfair to suggest it, but the failure of the Black Prince may not only have been the loss of Aquitaine but also the failure to establish a secure retinue and a body of support for Richard. As Goodman has said, 'His [Richard's] affinity signally failed to provide effective military support against Henry of Lancaster's invasion in 1399, and few of his former retainers rallied to support the "Epiphany Plot" in 1400, intended to restore him to the throne.'[28] The prince cannot be held responsible for events nearly 25 years after his death but a retinue, household or affinity needed foundations from which to grow and a core around which it could develop. This was not something available to Richard and it was not something that he could fashion during the years of his minority; the 'blunt instrument' of his Cheshire archers and retainers was no more reliable than the mercenary forces recruited by Chandos and the Black Prince for the Spanish campaign.

The young king's close circle of knights also did not have the same military reputation as those of his father and grandfather. Thomas Walsingham called them knights of Venus rather than Mars, more suited to the bedchamber than the battlefield.

Such men have also been held responsible for the style of Richard's government and his own elevated conception of his kingship. The Gascon influence may have been important — Guichard d'Angle, Baldwin Raddington, John Devereux and David Craddock had all experienced the regime in Aquitaine, and Simon Burley in particular has been noted in context of his experiences of the Black Prince's court — and through literary influences such as that of Giles of Rome's *De Regimine Principum*. This emphasised a subject's obligation of obedience, claimed the greatest possible authority for a monarch, stated that all privilege and nobility came from the king and that as the supreme lawgiver he was himself above the law. Certainly both Burley and Michael de la Pole owned copies of Giles' work. Such concepts also compounded traditions of Roman and civil law more generally. The continuity of personnel may well have had some influence and it may not have been beneficial to a young English monarch thrust prematurely on the throne as their mutual experience was in south-west France and their common frame of reference was far from London.[29] However, to emphasise this link does raise questions about the nature of the prince's court in Bordeaux and/or the 'despotic' requirements of service with Richard and behaviour in his presence. If the collapse of the principality of Aquitaine was, if only in part, attributable to the appalling manner in which Edward treated his subjects then it does not seem likely that Burley or anyone else would encourage the young king to follow a pattern of behaviour that had such disastrous consequences. The most regularly cited example and comparison concerns court etiquette and Richard's demand that subjects should kneel if he so much as glanced at them. It should be noted, however, that this is only evidenced in a single source, as is the *Anonimalle Chronicle* account of the prince requiring his great magnates to wait for 15 minutes on their knees before addressing him.[30]

Caroline Barron described Richard's rule as 'arbitrary, uncustomary and bore heavily on certain individuals', but noted that this 'formed the normal small change of English medieval kingship' and it was unlikely that it was 'widely resented or so unpopular as seriously to undermine Richard's government'.[31] Similarly Nigel Saul has suggested that 'in character and style there was probably little to distinguish it [Richard's court] from the other main courts of the day'.[32]

One of the most striking and yet elusive images of Richard II is in the Wilton Diptych. It has been interpreted in many ways. 'At the most eccentric end of the scale is [the] suggestion that [the diptych] was commissioned by Richard's half-sister as a memorial to their mother, Joan of Kent — that the Virgin Mary is a portrait of Joan and the Christ Child is Edward of Angoulême, Richard's elder brother who died in infancy, handing over his inheritance to him.'[33] Portraits of Edward II, Edward III and the Black Prince have also been suggested as providing the models for the saints presenting Richard to Jesus.[34] The combination of secular and religious themes is also extremely significant and has engendered considerable debate. Yet, as Nigel Saul says, 'It is doubtful if Richard saw anything incongruous in this combination of religious and secular imagery. Throughout his reign he viewed kingship in essentially religious terms [and] [h]e was deeply conscious of [its] theocratic roots.' Furthermore, 'The fusion of religious and secular ideas, evident in the symbolism and subject-matter of the Diptych, also found expression in the king's commitment to the suppression of heresy.'[35] This is particularly interesting considering the household in which he was raised and the religious peccadilloes evident therein.

That household, and perhaps the centre of a circle around which those of less than orthodox religious attitude gathered was that of the king's mother. Joan of Kent has tended to be remembered for the intricacies of her marriages or misremembered for her role in the Order of the Garter. Yet, both she and members of her knights and associates played significant political roles in the last years of Edward III's reign and after his death in 1377. The construction of the household of the Fair Maid, 'la plus belle et plus amoreuse' in all the land, after the death of her second or third husband after 1376, is not merely a footnote to the career of the Black Prince but a worthy topic in itself. This is due to Joan's status, after 1377, as the king's mother in the minority, although fictionally majority, years of her son, as a study of the entourage of one of the great dowagers and for the careers and particular interests of those that comprised her following. With regard to such interests, it is well known that John Wyclif received the support and favour of John of Gaunt, certainly in February 1377 and again, through the intervention of Princess Joan, in March 1378. It has also been asserted that the Lollard knights, identified by the chroniclers Thomas Walsingham and Henry Knighton, formed a 'court circle' in the reign of Richard II that was active in parliament and may have received support or at least shared some views with Thomas of Woodstock, who may not have been the only son of Edward III to have harboured such attitudes. It has been suggested, although with little evidence, that the 'prince was a man of vaguely puritanical religion'.[36] If so, this may have chimed with Joan's own sympathies; among the executors of her will were the Lollard knights, John Clanvowe, William Beauchamp, Lewis Clifford, and Richard Stury, although they also included Robert Braybroke and William of Wickham, bishops of London and Winchester respectively.[37] Among the other Lollard knights, William Neville served in the household of Richard as prince of Wales and was associated with the family prior to that and Reginald Hilton may have been in the prince's service in the diocese of Lichfield and became controller of Richard's wardrobe. Thomas Latimer had some connections to the prince and served in the 1355 expedition and in Spain, but this may have been in a 'freelance' capacity, while John Montague, who maintained the Wyclifite preacher, Nicholas Hereford, in his house at Shenley, was a knight of the prince's household from 1354 and Richard's steward from 1381-6.[38]

However, for these and probably for Joan herself, there was a considerable 'grey area' on the margins between orthodoxy and Lollardy. Anti-papalism and what has been described as 'a certain brand of alehouse anticlericalism'[39] were not necessarily indicative of heretical attitudes to transubstantiation or other aspects of Wyclifite belief. Rather they may have been 'attracted to the pietistic and moralistic attitudes of the early Lollards rather than to their more specifically antisacramental, antihierarchical and pacifist teachings'.[40] In any case, the Lollard knights were almost all connected with either the short lived 'dynasty' of the prince of Wales, Edward himself, Joan of Kent, and Richard II or John of Gaunt, and they provided financial and political support allowing for the patronage of Wyclifite preachers and the 'Lollard library'. The extent to which they shared religious attitudes, except in a broad sense is more difficult to determine.[41]

One who was very much aware of the strains within the church and who wrote a great deal about its representatives was Geoffrey Chaucer. He had fought in the Reims campaign, possibly in the prince's division, during which he was captured and later ransomed by the king. He was closely associated with Sir John Clanvowe, one of the most interesting of the Wyclifite circle since he was an author and wrote a clear statement of his views in a work entitled *The Two Ways*.[42] The treatise was puritanical certainly, heretical probably, but not necessarily a direct statement of Lollard belief. In this he shared with a number of others, attitudes that were on or a little beyond the boundaries of orthodoxy in some 'no man's land' before Lollardy. Other knights of the group have been identified through the language of their wills although there are clearly problems with such an analysis and many strictly orthodox individuals made wills that might be described as Lollard in tone or character. Similarly, such men as Clanvowe and William Neville 'indulged' in such activities as crusading, and Lewis Clifford was a member of Philippe de Mézières' Order of the Passion. Thomas Latimer, before Wyclif's ideas became public, acquired a grant from the pope to have a portative altar, a personal confessor and have mass celebrated before daylight. While such attitudes clearly do not sit easily with Lollard anti-papalism they do show a search for a means of salvation not entirely within the commonplace structure of the church.[43] Latimer joined the prince in Aquitaine and may have seen service in Spain and in the rearguard action after 1369. In June 1385, he was one of a number of knights summoned to be in constant attendance on the king's mother. The group also included Clifford and Stury although his links to Joan may have been through his wife, Anne, who attended the princess at Richard's birth and brought news of the event to the prince.[44] Latimer was also associated with one Robert Lychlade, who was expelled from Oxford in 1395 for holding heretical opinions. He became, by 1401, rector of Kemerton, Gloucestershire, of which Sir William Beauchamp, the probably Wyclifite knight was patron and in the following year he acted as an executor of the will of Anne Latimer, widow of Thomas Braybroke, a noted Lollard sympathiser. Another of the prince's close associates, Gerard Braybroke, also had close links to the Lollard circle, but was never named as one himself. An overseer of the same will was Lewis Clifford. Clifford was forced in 1402 to recant his theological errors and offer public penance. Similarly, Richard Stury was ordered to abjure heresy or face execution.[45]

It was a confused, conflicting and contentious childhood for Richard II. His father, who he only knew as old and ill, was remembered in the collective consciousness and by posterity as young and vigorous and chivalrous and successful. His grandfather, similarly, all but senile was the hero of Crécy, who had dragged England out of the mire of the reign of Edward II and the despotism of Mortimer and Isabella. It is a fascinating aside, and perhaps more than that being indicative of his own conception of his kingship, that Richard was at the forefront of a movement seeking the canonisation of his great-grandfather. His mother's household and his own 'masters' revealed the dichotomies of (pseudo?) Lollardy and chivalry as the 'hawks' and 'doves' in the court and the country showed conflicting attitudes to the war and later to Richard's style of rule and eventually the king himself.

The legacy of the Black Prince was, characteristically, ambivalent, opaque, conflicting and, to an extent, self-destructive, and as such it was completely representative of the forces at work in the period that we have chosen to call late medieval. It was a period in England that harkened back to the triumphs of the Angevin Empire and forward via the Wars of the Roses to the Yorkist kings and the authoritarianism of the Tudor monarchs. It was a period of bureaucracy and administration and parliament and high finance that was founded on spectacle and chivalry even when those same qualities were becoming increasingly outmoded, not to say undesirable on the battlefield where the final analysis of success and kingship were made.

# NOTES

## PREFACE

1. Richard Barber, *Edward Prince of Wales and Aquitaine: A Biography of the Black Prince,* Woodbridge, 1978; Barbara Emerson, *The Black Prince*, London, 1976; J. Harvey, *The Black Prince and his Age*, London, 1976; H. Cole, *The Black Prince*, London, 1976; Micheline Dupuy, *Le Prince Noir. Edouard seigneur d'Aquitaine*, Paris, 1970.

## CHAPTER 1

1 The Hundred Years War has been seen by some as part of a much broader conflict lasting certainly from the treaty of Paris (1259) and probably with much deeper roots, perhaps stretching as far back as the Norman Conquest and not resolved until long after the fall of Bordeaux in 1453. See for example, Malcolm Vale, *The Origins of the Hundred Years War: the Angevin Legacy, 1250-1340*, Oxford, 1996.
2. *The Itinerary of John Leland in or about the Years 1535-1543*, iv, ed. L.T. Smith, London, 1909, 38.
3. Ellen C. Caldwell, 'The Hundred Years War and National Identity', *Inscribing the Hundred Years War in French and English Cultures*, ed. Denise N. Baker, Albany, 2000, 239-40.
4. *Henry V*, II. iv.
5. Michael Prestwich, *The Three Edwards: War and State in England, 1272-1377*, London, 1980, 96-9, 111-13.
6. For a discussion of Froissart's importance see for example Peter Ainsworth, 'Froissardian Perspectives on Late Fourteenth Century Society', *Orders and Hierarchies in Late Medieval and Renaissance Europe*, ed. Jeffrey Denton, Manchester, 1999, 56-73, esp. 58.
7. *Oeuvres* ed. Kervyn de Lettenhove, Brussels, 1867-77; *Chroniques*, ed. S. Luce, (SHF) Paris, 1869-; G. Brereton, *Chronicles, Froissart*, Harmondsworth, 1976. Richard Barber, *Life and Campaigns of the Black Prince*, Woodbridge, repr. 1986; Diana B. Tyson, *La Vie du Prince Noir*, Tübingen, 1975; M. Pope and E. Lodge, *Life of the Black Prince by the Herald of Sir John Chandos*, Oxford, 1910.
8. Chris Given-Wilson and Alice Curteis, *The Royal Bastards of Medieval England*, London, 1984, 143-6. Clarendon's coat of arms: Or, on a bend sable, *three ostrich feathers argent*, the quills transfixed through as many escrolls gold. Summer Ferris, 'Chronicle, Chivalric Biography and Family Tradition in Fourteenth Century England', *Chivalric Literature: Essays on Relations Between Literature and Life in the Later Middle Ages*, ed. L. Benson, Michigan, 1980, 33-4. On Joan see Karl P. Wentersdorf, 'The Clandestine Marriages of the Fair Maid of Kent', *Journal of Medieval History*, 5 (1979), 203-31; N. Careyron, 'De chronique en roman: l'étrange épopée amoureuse de la jolie fille de Kent', *Le Moyen Age*, 5th ser., 8 (1994), 185-204.
9. Chandos Herald, *Life of the Black Prince*, ed. Pope and Lodge, 135.
10. M.J. Bennett, 'Courtly Literature and Northwest England in the Later Middle Ages', *Court and Poet*, ed. Glyn S. Burgess, Liverpool, 1981, 72-3. See also T. Turville-Petre, *The Alliterative Revival*, Cambridge, 1977, 30, 38, 46-7.
11. The poem continues with references to the *fleur de lys* of France, the leopards of England and how he was loved by one of the loveliest of ladies.
*Bot that that hillede the helme byhynde in the nekke*
*Was casten full clenly in quarters foure:*
*Two with flowres of Fraunce before and behynde,*

> *And two out of Ynglonde with sex grym bestes,*
> *Thre leberdes one lofte and thre on lowe undir;*
> *At iche a cornere a knoppe of full clene perle,*
> *Tasselde of tuly silke, tuttynge out fayre.*
> *And by the cabane I knewe the knyghte that I see,*
> *And thoghte to wiete or I went wondres ynewe.*
> *And als I waytted withinn I was warre sone*
> *Of a comliche kynge crowned with golde,*
> *Sett one a silken bynche, with septure in honde,*
> *One of the lovelyeste ledis, whoso loveth hym in hert,*
> *That ever segge under sonn sawe with his eghne.*

12. Elizabeth Salter, 'The Timeliness of Wynnere and Wastoure', *Medium Aevum*, 43 (1977) 48-59.Thanks to Victoria Blashill for this reference.

13. Terry Jones, *Chaucer's Knight*, rev. ed., London, 1994 and for comparison M. Keen, 'Chaucer's Knight, the English Aristocracy and the Crusade', *English Court Culture in the Later Middle Ages*, ed. V.J. Scattergood and J.W. Sherborne, London, 1983, 45-60.

14. See *La guerre de Cent Ans. Textes: Les chroniques de Froissart, Journal des États généraux, Le traité de Brétigny, Complainte sur la bataille de Poitiers et Vues critiques sur la bataille de Poitiers*, ed. S. Luce, Paris, 1972.

15. J. Barnie, *War in Medieval Society: Social Values and the Hundred Years War, 1337-99*, London, 1974, 82.

## CHAPTER 2

1. *CPR, 1330-4*, 74.

2. *Vie du Prince Noir*, ed. Tyson, 50-1.

3. Rymer, II, ii, 880, 1049, 1125, 1212; May McKisack, *The Fourteenth Century: 1307-1399*, Oxford, 1959, 159-60; M. Packe, *King Edward III*, ed. L.C.B. Seaman, London, 1983, 91; Margaret Sharpe, 'The Administrative Chancery of the Black Prince Before 1362', *Essays in Medieval History Presented to T.F. Tout*, Manchester, 1925, 321.

4. Stretton may have been related to Robert Stratton, an auditor (*auditores sacri apostolici palacii*) and papal chaplain of the *Rota*, the central court of the papal curia from 1362-80. He died in the curia on 20 Oct. 1380, Margaret Harvey, *The English in Rome, 1362-1420. Portrait of an Expatriate Community*, Cambridge, 1999, 133-4 and n. 4.

5. She was rewarded with a £20 annuity by the king on 10 Mar. 1351, *CCR, 1349-54*, 299.

6. T.F. Tout, *Chapters in the Administrative History of Mediaeval England. The Wardrobe, the Chamber and the Small Seal*, Manchester, 1920-33, v, 319-20; Nicholas Orme, *From Childhood to Chivalry. The Education of the English Kings and Aristocracy, 1066-1530*, London, 1984, 20-1.

7. BL Cotton Galba E III f. 190; Barber, *Edward*, 19.

8. Gervase Wilford, Ambrose Newburgh and Hugh Colewick, auditors of the duchy, were regularly employed by the prince, PRO E101/369/13 (all mss references hereafter will be to the Public Record Office unless stated otherwise).

9. David S. Green, 'The Household and Military Retinue of Edward the Black Prince', Unpub. PhD thesis, University of Nottingham, 1998, Appendix.

10. Thomas Gray, *Scalachronica*, ed. and trans. Herbert Maxwell, Glasgow, 1907, 104.

11. Clifford J. Rogers, *The Wars of Edward III: Sources and Interpretations*, Woodbridge, 1999, 59-62; Jonathan Sumption, *The Hundred Years War, i: Trial by Battle*, London, 1990, 199, 241-2.

12. Barber, *Edward*, 31.

13. Jean Le Bel, *Chronique*, ed. J. Viard et E. Déprez, Paris, 1904, 168; trans. Rogers, *Wars of Edward III*, 79.

14. Elizabeth Danbury, 'English and French Propaganda During the Period of the Hundred Years War: Some Evidence from Royal Charters', *Power, Culture and Religion in France c.1350 – c.1550*, ed. C.T. Allmand, Woodbridge, 1989, 82, 94.

15. Clifford J. Rogers, *War Cruel and Sharp*, Woodbridge, 2000, 196.

16. Archives départementales de Lois-Atlantique, Natnes, E119 no. 5; Michael Jones, *Ducal Brittany, 1364-99*, Oxford, 1970, 18-19, 45 and nn. 2-4.

17. BL Harley 4304 ff 16v.-20.

# CHAPTER 3

1. Barber, *Edward*, 44-5.
2. J. Viard, 'La campagne de juillet-août 1346 et la bataille de Crécy', *Le Moyen Age*, 2nd ser., xxvii (1926)', 9; Léopold Delisle, *Histoire du château et des sires de Saint-Sauveur-le-Vicomte*, Valognes, 1867, 50-108.
3. Jean-Yves Marin, 'Geoffroy d'Harcourt: une 'conscience normande'', *La Normandie dans la guerre de Cent Ans, 1346-1450*, ed Jean-Yves Marin, Caen, 1999, 147-9.
4. *Knighton's Chronicle, 1337-1399*, ed. G. Martin, Oxford, 1995, 58, 59; Barber, *Edward*, 47; McKisack, *Fourteenth Century*, 130, 133; Sumption, *Hundred Years War*, i, 498-9, 494, 497. For Hastings' pay accounts see E371/191/49. For French preparations see Viard, 'La campagne de juillet-août', 3-4.
5. Emerson, *Black Prince*, 26-7. This figure includes 5,113 Welsh troops as well as one chaplain, one *medicus*, one *proclamator*, 5 standard-bearers and 25 vintners, G. Wrottesley, *Crécy and Calais* (William Salt Archæological Society, 18), 1880, 193. The Brut roll for Crécy and Calais calculates the Welsh contingent as 600 in addition to 480 footmen and 69 archers also on foot, *The Brut*, ii, ed. F.W.D. Brie (Early English Texts Society), 1906, 538. For a full discussion of the problems with sources for the 1346-7 expedition see Andrew Ayton, 'The English Army and the Normandy Campaign of 1346', *England and Normandy in the Middle Ages*, ed. David Bates and Anne Curry, London, 1994, 253-68.
6. *BPR*, i, 5. See Wrottesley, *Crécy and Calais*, 74-6 for directions to wardens of maritime land to defend ports and coastal areas against invasion.
7. *Knighton's Chronicle*, ed. Martin, 58, 59; G.L. Harriss, *King, Parliament and Public Finance in Medieval England to 1369*, Oxford, 1975, 315-6; H.J. Hewitt, *The Organisation of War under Edward III*, Manchester, 1966, 1-27.
8. Sumption, *Hundred Years War*, i, 495. On Dagworth's expedition see E101/25/17, 18, 19; Michael Jones, 'Sir Thomas Dagworth et la guerre civile en Bretagne au xive siècle: quelques documents inédits', *Annales de Bretagne*, lxxxviii (1980), 627-30; A.E. Prince 'The Strength of English Armies in the Reign of Edward III', *EHR*, xlvi (1931), 364-5. In Sept. 1348, Dagworth was assigned £4,900 by the king from a parliamentary subsidy. His squire, Colkyn Lovayn, received £2,166, for Charles de Blois who had been purchased from them, Harriss, *King, Parliament ands Public Finance*, 335.
9. Sumption, *Hundred Years War*, i, 497-8. Loryng received letters of protection on 24 May, Wrottesley, *Crécy and Calais*, 92; Viard, 'Campagne de juillet-août', 11-12. For the career of Godfrey de Harcourt see Delisle, *Histoire du château et des sires de Saint-Sauveur-le-Vicomte*, 50-108.
10. See Sumption, *Hundred Years War*, i, 532-3 and for a contrary view of Edward's intentions see Rogers, *War Cruel and Sharp*.
11. Adam Murimuth, *Continuatio Chronicarum*, ed. E.M. Thompson, London, (Rolls Ser.), 1889, 200-2, cited by Rogers, *War Cruel and Sharp*, 242-3 and n. 25.
12. 'Lanercost Chronicle', ed. and trans. H. Maxwell, *Scottish Historical Review*, vi-x, 327; Barber, *Edward*, 49.
13. Rogers, *War Cruel and Sharp*, 240.
14. André Plaisse, *À travers le Cotentin: la grande chevauchée guerrière d'Édouard III en 1346*, Cherbourg, 1994, 18.
15. *Knighton's Chronicle*, ed. Martin, 56-9; Barber, *Edward*, 52; Rogers, *War Sharp and Cruel*, 245-6 and n. 45.
16. Sumption, *Hundred Years War*, i, 520.
17. Barber, *Edward*, 57.
18. Chandos Herald, *Vie du Prince Noir*, ed. Tyson, ll. 215-18.
19. Rogers, *War Cruel and Sharp*, 258.
20. Barber, *Edward*, 60. The location of the ford was provided either by: Gobin Agace; a squire in the retinue of Oliver Ghistels; a prisoner of war; or a Yorkshireman, from Rushton near Nafferton, living in the area.
21. 25 Mar. 1348-27 Mar. 1350, G. Dupont-Ferrier, *Gallia Regia*, iii, Paris, 1947, i, 265.

22. M. Bennett, 'The Development of Battle Tactics in the Hundred Years War', *Arms, Armies and Fortifications in the Hundred Years War*, ed. Anne Curry and M. Hughes, Woodbridge, 1994, 6-7; Clifford Rogers, 'Edward III and the Dialectics of Strategy', *TRHS*, 6th ser., iv (1994), 90-9; Kenneth Fowler, 'Letters and Dispatches of the Fourteenth Century', *Guerre et societé en France en Angleterre et en Bourgogne XIVe-XVe siècles*, ed. Philippe Contamine, Charles Giry-Deloison et M. Keen, Lille, 199, 179; Barber, *Edward*, 62.

23. Barber, *Edward*, 71; Rogers, 'Edward III and the Dialectics of Strategy', 93, 95, 99. See also Harriss, *King, Parliament and Public Finance*, 320-1. Edward had borrowed considerable sums from the Bardi to mount the campaign. The renewal of the parliamentary subsidy in Sept. 1346 was used as security for further loans. For further discussion of the use and control of war taxation and finance see *ibid.*, 324-6.

24. *Knighton's Chronicle*, ed. Martin, 61, 63.

25. Viard, 'Le campagne de juillet-août', 67, 70-1; Barber, *Edward*, 65. There is no consensus of the disposition of the leaders of the 3 'battles', Viard states Northampton fought in the bishop of Durham's division (the second 'battle') while the king was at the rear. He includes Manny who was almost certainly with Lancaster. Other bannerets in the vanguard included James Audley of Stretton and Bartholomew Burghersh. Bachelors included Alexander Venables and Richard Baskerville and Emerson includes Oxford, Warwick, Stafford, Harcourt, Thomas Holland, Burghersh and Chandos, *Black Prince*, 40. Knighton indicates the prince led the vanguard, with Arundel and Northampton in the second with the bishop of Durham subordinate, and the king in command of the third. Knighton states that the prince, Northampton and Warwick were 'in the first line of battle', *Chronicle*, ed. Martin, 63. Murimuth placed the prince, Northampton and Warwick in the vanguard, Murimuth, *Chronicarum*, 246. Froissart believed that the vanguard included; the prince, Warwick, Kent, Harcourt, Cobham, Holland, Richard Stafford, Manny and de la Ware. Northampton and Arundel led the second division with Hereford, Roos, Percy and 'Noefville' [Robert Neufville]. The third battle was under the command of the king, *Oeuvres*, ed. Lettenhove, v, 33-4. See also Jean Le Bel, *Chronique*, ii, 105; Froissart, *Chroniques*, ed. Luce, iii, 169, 405, 407, 409.

26. He is also recorded as Sir Thomas 'Danyers' a Cheshire veteran of low birth, rewarded for retrieving the standard and for his deeds at Caen with a £20 land grant. This became the Lyme Handley estate and was bequeathed to his son-in-law, Peter Legh, in 1398, Philip Morgan, *War and Society in Medieval Cheshire, 1277-1403*, Manchester (Chetham Society), 1987, 182, 186. An annual grant of 40 marks to the prince's bachelor made on 26 Feb. 1347, to be taken from Frodsham manor, was made as a result of Daniel's good service in the capture of Tancarville and at Crécy, *BPR*, i, 45.

27. It was probably for this that he was granted a £20 annuity from Wallingford manor on 1 Sept. 1346, *BPR*, i, 14. Further deeds were rewarded with a gift of 100 marks, 10 Dec. 1346, *ibid.*, 40. There is an alternative tradition that the standard-bearer was one Richard Beaumont, Geoffrey Le Baker, *Chronicon Galfridi le Baker de Swynebroke, 1330-56*, ed. E.M. Thompson, Oxford, 1889, 261. He was said to have covered the prince with the great banner of Wales and defended him when he fell, Bibliothèque Nationale (Paris), Tramecourt MS, cited by Emerson, *Black Prince*, 45.

28. Reinforcements may have been sent led by the bishop of Durham and the earls of Huntingdon and Suffolk, *Anonimalle Chronicle, 1333-1381*, ed. V.H. Galbriath, Manchester, 1927, 22. Thomas of Norwich supposedly delivered the message to the king, Froissart, *Chroniques*, ed. Luce, iii, 183; Brereton, *Chronicles*, 92.

29. Jean le Bel, *Chronique*, ii, 99ff.; Baker, *Chronicon*, 82-5; Froissart, *Oeuvres*, ed. Lettenhove, v, 37-8. On the *Oriflamme* see, Philippe Contamine, *L'oriflamme de Saint-Denis aux xive et xve siècles*, Nancy, 1975.

30. Barber, *Edward*, 68. The prince is not mentioned as participating in the morning attack by Knighton, Baker or the Anonimalle Chronicler, Sumption, *Hundred Years War, i*, 530.

31. Murimuth, *Chronicarum*, 247. The Hundred Years War was generally fought as a *bellum hostile*, i.e. declared under the authority of a prince and allowing the ransom of prisoners, E. Porter, 'Chaucer's Knight, the Alliterative *Morte Arthure* and the Medieval Laws of War: A Reconsideration', *NMS*, xxvii (1983), 67. A *guerre mortelle*, as demanded by Edward III at Crécy and indicated by the presence of the *Oriflamme*, was a war to the death with no surrender or ransoming of captives.

32. According to Knighton, the prince himself slew the kings of Bohemia and Mallorca, the latter did not die at Crécy, *Knighton's Chronicle*, ed. Martin, 198, 199. For a list of the fallen see: *ibid.*, 62, 63; *Lanercost Chronicle*, ed. and trans. Maxwell, 329 which differs from the casualty list given in *Anonimalle Chronicle*, ed. Galbraith, 23, 160.

33. Andrew Ayton, 'English Armies in the Fourteenth Century', *Arms, Armies and Fortifications in the Hundred Years War*, ed. A. Curry and M. Hughes, Woodbridge, 1994, 33-4; Andrew Ayton, *Knights and Warhorses: Military Service and the English Aristocracy under Edward III*, Woodbridge, 1994, 19.

34. Plaisse, *À travers le Cotentin*, 31.

35. Bennett, 'Development of Battle Tactics', 9-10.

36. 'et Franci xvi uicibus dederunt eis insultam antequam dies illucesceret', *Knighton's Chronicle*, ed. Martin, 62. Baker, refers to 16 attacks, *Chronicon*, 85. Jim Bradbury, *The Medieval Archer*, New York, 1985, 108, states there were 15.

37. Ayton, 'English Army and the Normandy Campaign', 253-68, indicates problems associated with previous estimates of the 1346-7 armies. With regard to the specific size of individual retinues, he states, '...numbers of retinue personnel cannot be ascertained from these records. All they can do is offer confirmation of the general order of magnitude — and the order of precedence — of those retinues that appear on the Calais roll.'

38. *A History of Carmarthenshire*, ed. John E. Lloyd, Cardiff, 1935, i, 249. See also D.L. Evans, 'Some Notes on the History of the Principality of Wales in the Time of the Black Prince, 1343-1376', *Transactions of the Honourable Society of Cymrodorion* (1925-6), 80.

| | North Wales | South Wales |
|---|---|---|
| Knights | 3 | - |
| Esquires | 3 | - |
| Leaders | 4 | 2 |
| Constables | 24 | 30 |
| Chaplains | 1 | 1 |
| Surgeons | 1 | 1 |
| Proclamator | 1 | 1 |
| Standard Bearers | 9 | 29 |
| Vinteners | 112 | 108 |
| Footmen | 2252 | 1990 |
| Total | 2410 | 2162 |

39. Peter Coss, *The Knight in Medieval England, 1100-1400*, Stroud, 1993, 91, 100; Hugh E.L. Collins, *The Order of the Garter, 1348-1461. Chivalry and Politics in Late Medieval England*, Oxford, 2000, 12.

40. For discussion of the Round Table see Collins, *Order of the Garter*, 6-10. Froissart confused this with the foundation of the Garter.

41. The whereabouts of d'Aubrechicourt and Henry Eam in 1346 are uncertain. The captal de Buch and Lancaster were involved in subsidiary action elsewhere in France, D'A.J.D. Boulton, *The Knights of the Crown. The Monarchical Orders of Knighthood in Later Medieval Europe, 1325-1520*, Woodbridge, 1987, 127-8. For biographical details see Green, 'Household and Military Retinue', Appendix.

42. *CPR*, 1377-81, 197. John Burley was granted an annuity for his service in the prince's bodyguard at Nájera; J.L. Gillespie, 'Richard II's Knights: Chivalry and Patronage', *Journal of Medieval History*, 13 (1987), 154; See also Green, 'Household and Military Retinue', Appendix.

43. Bodleian MS Ashmole 1128, fos. 1-8, 41-116; Collins, *Order of the Garter*, 22-3.

44. In 1334, Edward III had fought incognito as *Mons Lionel* under the banner of Stephen Cosington and Thomas Bradeston at the Dunstable tournament, and at Dartford he competed under William Clinton's banner, J. Vale, *Edward III and Chivalry. Chivalrous Society and its Context, 1270-1350*, Woodbridge, 1982, 68; R. Barber and J. Barker, *Tournaments. Jousts, Chivalry and Pageants in the Middle Ages*, Woodbridge, 1989, 32.

45. *BPR*, iv, 73; Vale, *Edward III and Chivalry*, 86.

46. The gifts for Chandos and Audley cost £6 13s. 4d., the prince's own expenses were 20s., *BPR*, iv, 123. See also, *ibid.*, 252, 284, 323-4.

47. Cuvelier, *Chronicle de Bertrand Du Guesclin*, ed. E. Chariere, Paris, 1839, i, ll. 11070*ff*; R. Barber, *The Knight and Chivalry*, rev. ed., Woodbridge, 1995, 225.

•

48. John Taylor, *The Universal Chronicle of Ranulph Higden*, Oxford, 1966, 146.
49. Thomas Walsingham, *Historia Anglicana*, ii, ed. H.T. Riley, London (Rolls Ser.), 1863, 239; T.A. Sandquist, 'The Holy Oil of St Thomas of Canterbury', *Essays in Medieval History Presented to Bertie Wilkinson*, ed. T.A. Sandquist and M.R. Powicke, Toronto, 1969, 337.
50. Those that suffered the 'Plague of Justinian' in the 6th century might disagree.
51. W.C. Sellar and R.J. Yeatman, *1066 and All That. A Memorable History of England, Comprising all the Parts you can Remember, Including 103 good things, 5 bad Kings and 2 genuine dates*, London, 1930.
52. Juliet and Malcolm Vale, 'Knightly Codes and Piety', *History Today*, 37 (1987), 13, see also M.G.A. Vale, *Piety, Charity and Literacy among the Yorkshire Gentry, 1370-1480*, (Borthwick Papers, 50), York, 1976, 11-14.
53. Harvey, *English in Rome*, 60-1 and see nn. 40-5.
54. Northburgh left £2,000 to the London Carthusians in his will of 1361, William F. Taylor, *The Charterhouse of London*, London, 1912, 3, 17.
55. W. Hope St. John, *History of the London Charterhouse*, London, 1925, 6. A papal bull of Clement VI, 14 Mar. 1350-1 authorized the foundation of the chapel.
56. *DNB*, xvi, 49-50. His mother, Katherine (d. 1381) was buried in the Hull charterhouse although his father, William, rested in the Trinity Chapel, Hull, *Testamenta Eboracensia*, i, ed. J. Raine (Surtees Society, 4), 1836, 76-7, 119.
57. Nigel Saul, *Richard II*, New Haven and London, 1997, 298 n. 13.
58. 3 Mar. 1362, 19 Feb. 1363, *BPR*, iv, 423, 462, 488.
59. Baker, *Chronicon*, 103-6; Sumption, *Hundred Years War, ii*, 61-2.
60. *Chroniques*, ed. Luce, iv, 88-98; Packe, *Edward III*, 200-1; Sumption, *Hundred Years War, ii*, 66-7.
61. Graham J. Dawson, 'The Black Prince's Palace at Kennington, Surrey', *British Archaeological Reports*, 26, 1976; John Harvey, *English Mediaeval Architects*, rev. ed., Gloucester, 1984, 358-66.
62. For the text of the treaty of Guîines see F. Bock, 'Some New Documents Illustrating the Early Years of the Hundred Years War (1353-1356)', *Bulletin of the John Rylands Library*, xv (1931), 34-6.
63. P.H.W. Booth, 'Taxation and Public Order: Cheshire in 1353', *Northern History*, xii (1976), 19, 21-2, 28-9
64. R.R. Davies, *Lordship and Society in the March of Wales, 1282-1400*, Oxford, 1978, 271-2.

## CHAPTER 4

1. Armagnac had served as lieutenant in Languedoc, 1346-7 and was re-appointed 1352-7, Dupont-Ferrier, *Gallia Regia*, iii, 472, no. 13675; J. Moisant, *Le Prince Noir en Aquitaine, 1355-6, 1362-70*, Paris, 1894, 29.
2. Labarge, *Gascony*, 135-6. For a contrary view of the Gascons' reasons for wanting the participation of the prince see J.M. Tourneur-Aumont, *La Bataille de Poitiers (1356) et la construction de la France*, Paris, 1940.
3. C61/67/29; 8 Mar. 1355, *CCR, 1354-60*, 256; Rymer, III, i, 298-9, 302, 307, 309-10, 323, 325. Similar warrants were issued to the sheriffs of Devon and Southampton
4. 1 Dec. 1354, *BPR*, iv, 158, 160; 16 June 1355; *ibid.*, 166. Henry Keverell presumably was a merchant or supplier for ships and boats. He also supplied items to the prince's barge, *ibid.*, 160. Rymer, III, i, 308; Thomas Carte, *Catalogue des rôles Gascons, Normans et Français dans les archives de la Tour de Londres*, 2 vols, London and Paris, 1746, i, 134.
5. C61/67/5; Kenneth Fowler, *The King's Lieutenant: Henry of Grosmont, First Duke of Lancaster*, London, 1969, 147. For a tentative list of the ships arrested for the prince's use see H.J. Hewitt, *The Black Prince's Expedition of 1355-57*, Manchester, 1958, 40-2. This excludes the *Saint Mary* cog of Winchelsea which, at 200 tons, was the largest ship in the fleet, E61/76/4; T.J. Runyan, 'Ships and Mariners in Later Medieval England', *Journal of British Studies*, 16:2 (1977), 2 n. 3. The prince himself sailed on his father's ship, the *Christophre*, Emerson, *Black Prince*, 90.
6. *BPR*, ii, 80-8; *ibid.*, iii, 212-6; *ibid.*, iv, 78, 158, 161; Hewitt, *Black Prince's Expedition*, 26. Tiderik was also involved in delivering money to the prince's chamber and received a gift of £10.
7. Pierre Capra, 'Le séjour du Prince Noir, lieutenant du Roi, à l'Archévêché de Bordeaux (20 septembre 1355 - 11 avril 1357)', *Revue historique du Bordeaux et du département Gironde*, NS 7

(1958), 246-7; Labarge, *Gascony*, 136-7; Hewitt, *Black Prince's Expedition*, 37. Ships were arrested for Warwick's departure from 10 Mar. 1355, C61/67/14. By 8 May, 44 ships were at Southampton for the prince's use, E101/26/37. For the account of Thomas Hoggeshawe, admiral of the fleet and for William Wenlock's account of mariners' wages see E101/26/34. For text of the oath and a list of witnesses see *Livre de Coutumes*, ed. Henri Barckhausen (Archives Municipales de Bordeaux), 1890, 439-44, see also the *resumé*, 487.

8.  *BPR*, ii, 77; iv, 143-5; Rogers, *War Cruel and Sharp*, 295 and n. 48; Harriss, *King, Parliament and Public Finance*, 344-5. For the prince's appointment and duties as lieutenant see Rymer, III, i, 307, 312. Gray in *Scalacronica* considered the combined attacks in 1355-6 part of a coherent strategy, Barnie, *War in Medieval* Society, 93.

9.  Sumption, *Hundred Years War, ii*, 175-6.

10. *CIPM*, x, no. 258; *GEC*, viii, 73-6.

11. Emerson, *Black Prince*, 94; Barber, *Edward*, 119.

12. Sumption, *Hundred Years War, ii*, 181.

13. A.H. Burne, *The Crécy War: A Military History of the Hundred Years War from 1337 to the Peace of Brétigny, 1360*, London, 1955, 252-8; Sumption, *Hundred Years War, ii*, 183-4.

14. Rogers, 'Edward III and the Dialectics of Strategy', 100-1.

15. Robert of Avesbury, *De gestis mirabilis regis Edwardi tertii*, ed. E.M. Thompson, 1889, 445-7; *Life and Campaigns*, ed. Barber, 53.

16. Françoise Lehoux, *Jean de France, duc de Berri. Sa vie. Son action politique (1340-1416)*, Paris, 1966, i, 57; Pierre-Clément Timbal, *La Guerre de Cent Ans vue à travers les registres du Parlement, 1337-1369*, Paris, 1961, 108-9. At Béziers a tax was instituted for the repair of the fortifications, *ibid.*, 240.

17. Burne, *Crécy War*, 252. '...c'étatit plutot l'invasion d'une forte armée de brigands pillant le pays sans défense, faisant le plus butin possible...', Henri Denifle, *La guerre de cent ans et la désolation des églises, monasteres et hospitaux en France*, Paris, 1902, ii, 86. For further discussion of the damage to ecclesiastical buildings, see, *ibid.*, 86-95. See also Pierre Tucoo-Chala, *Gaston Fébus et la vicomté de Béarn (1343-1391)*, Bordeaux, 1959, 70. If not before, the prince and Gaston met on 17 Nov., Baker, *Chronicon*, 128, 135, 138; Hewitt, *Black Prince's Expedition*, 45; R. Delachenal, *Histoire de Charles V*, i, Paris, 5 vols, 1909-31, 128 n.1.

18. Emerson, *Black Prince*, 97-8; Hewitt, *Black Prince's Expedition*, 69, 76.

19. 'La France loyaliste deviendra 'armagnaque'', Touneur-Aumont, *La bataille de Poitiers*, 65. Delachenal, *Charles V*, i, 127-8.

20. Sumption, *Hundred Years War, ii*, 190.

21. The accounts of the raids are summarized by Fowler, 'Letters and Dispatches', 77-8, 80, nn. 69-76.

22. John of Reading, *Chronica Johannis de Reading et Anonymi Cantuarensis 1346-1367*, ed. James Tait, Manchester, 1914, 120; Avesbury, 437, 439.

23. The prince's clerk, Robert Brampton, prepared the ships for Stafford's return journey to Gascony in 1356, C61/68/4; C66/68/4. Brampton received £3 6s. 8d. as a gift from the prince for this, 24 Oct. 1356, *BPR*, iv, 192.

24. *Register of John de Trillek, Bishop of Hereford (A.D. 1344-1361)* ed. Joseph H. Parry, Hereford, 1910-12, 242; Froissart, *Oeuvres*, ed. Lettenhove, xviii, 389-92; *Chronicle of London from 1089 to 1483*, ed. E. Tyrrell and N.H. Nicolas, London, 1827, 204-8; Delachenal, *Charles V*, ii, 381-4; *Life and Campaigns*, ed. Barber, 57-9.

25. Froissart, *Oeuvres*, ed. Lettenhove, v, 528-9; *Chartulary of Winchester Cathedral*, ed. A.W. Goodman, Winchester, 1927, 159-61, no. 370, 162-4, no. 371; Fowler, 'Letters and Dispatches', 77-8; Delachenal, *Charles V*, i, 205-6; Hewitt, *Black Prince's Expedition*, 79.

26. 7 Feb. 1356, Rymer, III, i, 322. The mayor and people received letters of protection on the same day, Henxteworth ff. 13, 21, 25.

27. Burne, *Crécy War*, 276; Barber, *Edward*, 129-30; Emerson, *Black Prince*, 102. Durfort's lordship of Blanquefort had been confiscated on 21 Mar. 1355 and given to Auger de Mussidan as a result of his Valois sympathies. In 1356, he returned to favour and with it received Blanquefort. Mussidan was compensated with the chateau of Blaye, 3 offices in Bordeaux and revenue from the *grande coutume* on 600 tons of wine. Durfort also received rights in Saint-Foy, elsewhere and 4 bastides, C61/70/4; 71/7; Capra, 'Le séjour du Prince Noir', 245.

28. Work was carried out there by Chandos' order, for which payment was made in March, Henxteworth, 68.

29. Sumption, *Hundred Years War, ii*, 193.

30. Rymer, III, i, 325. For a description of the route from Bergerac see *Eulogium Historiarum,* iii, 215-22.

31. This authority was given at the pope's request, 15 Dec. 1355 and repeated 1 Aug. 1356, Rymer, III, i, 333.

32. Fowler stated a definite strategic plan had been formulated in 1355, by which Lancaster was to join the prince (although he failed to cross the Loire) and the earls of March, Northampton and Stafford were obliged to provide assistance, *King's Lieutenant*, 153-5; E36/278/88; *BPR*, iv, 145.

33. Barber, *Edward*, 131-2; Hewitt, *Black Prince's Expedition*, 102.

34. For the composition of the army see Delachenal, *Charles V*, i, 192-7. From Jan. to May the main Cheshire archer companies declined in number from around 180 to little over 50. This was due to their division along the Gascon march, withdrawal and desertion. Letters to the lieutenant-justice of Cheshire were written regarding 43 deserters and a further 20 or so were given leave of absence such as William Jodrell who received the famous Jodrell deed. His brother, John, fought at Poitiers as part of a company of bowmen raised from among the burgesses and inhabitants of Llantrisant, Robert Hardy, 'The Longbow', *Arms, Armies and Fortifications*, ed. Curry and Hughes, 163; Morgan, *War and Society*, 111, 113.

35. Delachenal, *Charles V*, i, 190; Denifle, *La désolation*, ii, 112-21; Hewitt, *Black Prince's Expedition*, 104; Fowler, *King's Lieutenant*, 154; Emerson, *Black Prince*, 108-9.

36. Letter to the mayor, aldermen and commons of London, 22 October, *Life and Campaigns*, ed. Barber, 57.

37. Froissart, *Chroniques*, ed. Luce, v, 414-16; Delachenal, *Charles V*, i, 225-6; Barber, *Edward*, 134, 136-7; Burne, *Crécy War*, 276-8; Hewitt, *Black Prince's Expedition*, 107-9; Labarge, *Gascony*, 139-41.

38. Burne, *Crécy War*, 292-7; Labarge, *Gascony*, 141. Regarding the previous day, 'Des ordres avaient du être donnés, le matin par le prince de Galles, soit pour une marche offensive, soit, ce qui est beaucoup plus probable pour une retraite', Delachenal, *Charles V*, i, 210-1.

39. Letter to the mayor, aldermen and commons of London, *Life and Campaigns*, ed. Barber, 58.

40. Hewitt, *Black Prince's Expedition*, 118-19; Packe, *Edward*, 217.

41. Hewitt, *Black Prince's Expedition*, 121; Delachenal, *Charles V*, i, 222 and n. 3.

42. Bennett, 'Development of Battle Tactics', 12-13; Burne, *Crécy War*, 300-6.

43. T.F. Tout, 'Some Neglected Fights Between Crécy and Poitiers', *EHR*, xx (1905), 726-30. For the royal ordinance of Apr. 1351 see *Ordonnances de Roys de France de la Troisième Race,* ed. D.F. Secousse, iv, 67-70, partly translated by Allmand, *Society at War*, 45-8. See also Delachenal, *Charles V*, i, 221, 224.

44. Hewitt, *Black Prince's Expedition*, 115. The French also received advice from the Scottish knight, William Douglas.

45. *Anonimalle Chronicle*, ed. Galbraith, contains unique details of the battle, see 36-9, 165n. Baker, *Chronicon*, 140*ff.* also provides a full account and includes an exhortation made by the prince to his men before the battle. Chandos Herald details the pre-battle negotiations, *Life of the Black Prince*, ed. Pope and Lodge, 193, ll. 881. See also Burne, *Crécy War*, 296-7; Delachenal, *Charles V*, i, 212-4, 228-33; Bennett, 'Development of Battle Tactics', 11-12.

46. Bradbury, *Medieval Archer*, 109, 111, 113; Barber, *Edward*, 139; Hewitt, *Black Prince's Expedition*, 114. Burne asserts that 'The English army was about 6,000 strong and the French over 20,000', *Crécy War*, 298. See also Delachenal, *Charles V*, i, 215-18.

47. Philippe Contamine, *Guerre, État et Société à la fin du Moyen Âge. Etudes sur les Armées des Rois de France, 1337-1494*, Paris, 1972, 45, 175. It was not the only such attack on the French aristocracy, see BL Cotton Caligula D III f. 33; Froissart, *Oeuvres*, ed. Lettenhove, xviii, 388.

48. Delachenal, *Charles V*, i, 220. N.B. according to Baker, *Chronicon*, 151, French crossbows at Poitiers did considerable damage.

49. Stephen Turnbull, *The Book of the Medieval Knight*, London, 1985, 54-5.

50. Much of the argument concerning the weapons stems from archaeological evidence concerning the Mary Rose bows that showed an effective range of 300 yards or more. The wooden or composite crossbows of the time could shoot about 200 yards and for every 2 quarrels, a bowmen might fire 20 arrows. The proportion of longbowmen to other troops in armies were regularly 3, 4 or 5:1 and sometimes reached as high as 20:1, Hardy, 'The Longbow', 161-3, 180. See also Rogers, 'Military Revolutions', 249-51 and nn. 36-41. The 'invincibility' of the longbow has been questioned in recent years. It is argued that, rather than causing a great number of

casualties, archer fire caused the enemy to become very disorganised which made them easy targets for the Anglo-Gascon infantry, Claude Gaier, 'L'invincibilité anglaise et le grande arc après la guerre de cents ans: un mythe tenace', *Tijdschrift voor geschedenis*, 91 (1978), 378-85; John Keegan, *Face of Battle: A Study of Agincourt, Waterloo and the Somme*, Harmondsworth, 1978, 78-116. For a counter-argument see Clifford J. Rogers, 'The Efficacy of the English Longbow: A Reply to Kelly DeVries, *War in History*, 5:2 (1998), 233-42. The formation and disposition of the archer corps was described by Froissart, 'a la maniere d'une herse' which, according to Oman and Burne, was a triangular formation with the apex facing the enemy placed between divisions of dismounted men-at-arms. This is based on the translation of *herce* as 'harrow'. Alternatively, they may have been placed on the flanks. Bradbury provides a number of possibilities: a candleabrum; a horn-shaped projection on the wings of the army; a hedgehog or something with spikes possibly using stakes or pikemen for protection, *Medieval Archer*, 99.

51. See Ayton, 'English Armies', 34; Bradbury, *Medieval Archer*, 93, 95-101.
52. Bennett, 'Development of Battle Tactics', 8-9; Sumption, *Hundred Years War, i*, 527; Hardy, 'The Longbow', 180; Bradbury, *Medieval Archer*, 111, 113.
53. *Froissart's Chronicles*, ed. J. Jolliffe, London, 1968, 175; Froissart, *Oeuvres*, ed. Lettenhove, v, 461, 463.

# CHAPTER 5

1. Rymer, III, ii, 348-51; Delachenal, *Charles V*, ii, 52.
2. *BPR*, ii, 98.
3. BL Add. 40510 ff. 340, 342. Froissart says 'that day he never took prisoner but always fought and went on after his enemies.' *The Chronicles of Froissart*, trans. Berners, ed. Macaulay, 125; *Oeuvres*, ed. Lettenhove, v, 456-7. However, Audley, with Chandos and Robert Neville sold an unnamed prisoner to the Black Prince for £565 12s. 6d., *BPR*, iv, 252.
4. These were; Philip, son of King Jean, the count of Sancerre and the lord of Craon, *CPR*, 1358-61, 300. A payment of £3,333 was made in 1362, F. Devon, ed., *Issues of the Exchequer [Henry III – Henry VI]*, London, 1847, 177.
5. John Palmer, 'The War Aims of the Protagonists and the Negotiations for Peace', *The Hundred Years War*, ed. K. Fowler, London, 1971, 59.
6. Fowler, *King's Lieutenant*, 201. Craon had been bishop of Reims since 1355 and was apparently friendly to the English royal family, Delachenal, *Charles V*, ii, 155.
7. Delachenal, *Charles V*, ii, 144; Barber, *Edward*, 159.
8. On the course of the campaign, see also *Anonimalle Chronicle*, 49-50; Delachenal, *Charles V*, ii, chs. iv-v and the sources cited there.
9. A. Bricknell, *The History of Edward Prince of Wales, Commonly termed the Black Prince*, London, 1776, 212; *Scalacronica*, 146-7; Burne, *Crécy War*, 334. For an itinerary of the route see Delachenal, *Charles V*, ii, 151-3.
10. Fowler, *King's Lieutenant*, 200; Delachenal, *Charles V*, ii, 146 and n. 1, 154; see Timbal, *La Guerre de Cent Ans*, 170 n. 190 and the references given.
11. Bradbury, *Medieval Siege*, 156; Michael Wolfe, 'Siege Warfare and the *Bonnes Villes* of France During the Hundred Years War', *The Medieval City Under Siege*, ed. Ivy A. Corfis and Michael Wolfe, Woodbridge, 1995, 52.
12. *Archives administratives de la ville de Reims*, ed. Pierre Varin, Paris, 1848, iii, 81-2, 93, 96-7, 119, 136-41, 150-1; Pierre Desportes, *Reims et les Remois aux xiii^e et xiv^e siècles*, Paris, 1979, 550-3, 560-1.
13. In one of his early raids at Attigny, d'Aubrechicourt captured supplies that included 3,000 tuns of wine, Delachenal, *Charles V*, ii, 159 and n. 7.
14. Burghersh fought a duel outside the walls of the city, *à outrance*, killing one opponent and wounding 2 others. He was stated incorrectly by Gray to have been in Lancaster's retinue, *Scalacronica*, 148. He is noted as going 'beyond seas with the prince for the furtherance of the war', *BPR*, iii, 371.
15. *Knighton's Chronicle*, ed. Martin, 170-3. Burne stated that Mortimer, Burghersh and Gaunt alone were involved in the capture, *Crécy War*, 339. Audley joined the prince's force after this, having travelled from his castle of Ferte in Brie with the captal de Buch, *Scalacronica*, 149; Fowler, *King's Lieutenant*, 203; Barber, *Edward*, 162.

16. *Scalacronica*, 150.
17. On the Burgundian alliance and the terms of the treaty see Delachenal, *Charles V*, ii, 166-70, 169 n. 3. King Jean took over responsibility for the payment in 1361, Tout, *Chapters,* iii, 243-4; Burne, *Crécy War*, 342.
18. *Scalacronica*, 153, 157, 159. Gray recounted an incident when the prince used siege engines to capture a fortified country house and with it Jacques de Greville, Hagenay de Bouille and 60 men-at-arms plus 100 others.
19. BL Stowe 140.
20. Léon Mirot et E. Déprez, *Les ambassades Anglaises pendant la guerre de cent ans*, Paris, 1900, 27-9; J. le Patourel, 'The Treaty of Brétigny, 1360', *TRHS*, 5th ser., 10 (1960), 24-5, 28-31.
21. Curry, *Hundred Years War*, 152-5
22. Denise N. Baker, 'Meed and the Economics of Chivalry in *Piers Ploughman*', *Inscribing the Hundred Years War in French and English Cultures*, ed. Denise N. Baker, Albany, 2000, 55-9 and n. 2.
23. For further discussion see Clifford J. Rogers ed., *The Military Revolution Debate. Readings on the Military Transformation of Early Modern Europe*, Colorado and Oxford, 1995. Rogers describes the military developments of the war as a 'punctuated equilibrium evolution', *ibid.*, 76-7.
24. R.F. Green, 'The *Familia Regis* and the *Familia Cupidinis*', *English Court Culture*, ed. Scattergood and Sherborne, 90-1; Barnie, *War in Medieval Society*, 57-8; Gervase Mathew, 'Ideals of Knighthood in Late Fourteenth Century England', *Studies in Medieval History Presented to F.M. Powicke*, ed. R.W. Hunt, W.A. Pantin and R.W. Southern, Oxford, 1948, 358-62; John Taylor, *English Historical Literature in the Fourteenth Century*, Oxford, 1987, 168.
25. Chandos Herald, *Vie du Prince* Noir, ed. Tyson, ll. 2729-80, 2740, 'Raoul de Hastynges, Qi la mort ne counte a deux gynges.' [Felton] 'Comme homme sans sens et sans avis'.
26. Barber, *Knight and Chivalry*, rev. ed., 43. See also Ayton, 'War and the English Gentry', 34-40.
27. Ayton, *Knights and Warhorses*, 121-5; C. Given-Wilson, *The English Nobility in the Late Middle Ages*, London, 1987, 56.
28. Hugh Collins, 'The Order of the Garter, 1348-1461: Chivalry and Politics in Later Medieval England', *Courts, Counties and the Capital in the Later Middle Ages*, ed. Diana E.S. Dunn, Far Thrupp, 1996, 156.
29. Aldo Scaglione, *Knights at Court. Courtliness, Chivalry and Courtesy From Ottonian Germany to the Italian Renaissance*, Berkeley and Los Angeles, 1991, 28.
30. M. Keen, *The Laws of War in the Late Middle Ages*, London, 1965, 3.
31. Jean de Bueil, *Le Jouvencel*, ii, ed. C. Favre et L. Lecestre, Paris, 1887-9, 20 cited by Nicholas Wright, *Knights and Peasants, The Hundred Years War in the French Countryside*, Woodbridge, 1998, 26.
32. R. Kaeuper and E. Kennedy, *The Book of Chivalry of Geoffroi de Charny. Text, Context and Translation*, Philadelphia, 1996, 37-8, 44-7; Keen, *Chivalry*, 14.
33. Barnie, *War in Medieval Society*, 60-1, 65. Collins also refers to the 'growing secularisation of the chivalric ethos', 'Order of the Garter', 156.
34. Barber, *Edward*, 49.
35. *Froissart's Chronicles*, ed. and trans, Jolliffe, 136.
36. Froissart, *Oeuvres*, ed. Lettenhove, iv, 430; Hewitt, *Black Prince's Expedition*, 72; Denifle, *La désolation*, 88-9.
37. Noel Denholm-Young, 'The Tournament in the Thirteenth Century', *Studies in Medieval History Presented to F.M. Powicke*, ed. R.W. Hunt, W.A. Pantin and R.W. Southern, Oxford 1948, 240.
38. Anna Comnena, *The Alexiad*, trans. Elizabeth A.S. Dawson, London, 1967, 122-3, 342.
39. Ayton, 'English Armies', 1-13; 21-36; M. Prestwich, *Armies and Warfare in the Middle Ages: The English Experience*, New Haven and London, 1996, 231-43.
40. Clifford J. Rogers, 'The Military Revolutions of the Hundred Years' War', *Journal of Military History*, 57 (1993), 247-52; idem., 'Edward III and the Dialectics of Strategy', 83-102; Hardy, 'Longbow', 161-80; Philippe Contamine, *War in the Middle Ages*, trans. M. Jones, Oxford, 1984, 132-3.
41. At Crécy, as at Poitiers, the deployment of the *Oriflamme* was seen by the English as a sign of *guerre mortelle*, see Murimuth, *Chronicon*, 247 and *Knighton's Chronicle*, ed. Martin, 142 who states that 'Dominus Galfridus Charneys baiulauit uexillum rubium quod erat mortis signiferum. Rex Francie edidit preceptum ne quis Anglicus uite reseruaretur, solo principe excepto.'

42. *The Chronicles of Froissart*, trans. Berners, ed. Macaulay, 120; Froissart, *Oeuvres*, ed. Lettenhove, v, 403-4; Sumption, *Hundred Years War, i*, 515.

43. Contamine, *War in the Middle Ages*, 126; Ayton, 'English Armies', 34-5.

44. Prestwich, *Armies and Warfare*, 117-18; Ayton, *Knights and Warhorses*, 26.

45. Bradbury, *Medieval Archer*, 91; Edouard Perroy, *The Hundred Years War*, trans. W.B. Wells, London, 1951, 119.

46. Rogers, 'Military Revolutions', 247-8.

47. See Prestwich, *Armies and Warfare*, 319-21 for a discussion of the possible formations used at Crécy.

48. Prestwich, *Three Edwards*, 199.

49. Andre Corvisier et Philippe Contamine, *Histoire militaire de la France*, Paris, 1992, i, 133-4.

## CHAPTER 6

1. SC 7/22/17.

2. *Chronique des quatre premiers Valois (1327-1393)*, ed. S. Luce (SHF), Paris, 1862, 123; Montagu Burrows, *The Family of Brocas of Beaurepaire and Roche Court*, London, 1886, 53, 55. Burrows' account of the life of Bernard, which was very similar to that in *DNB*, ii, 1273, has been questioned, particularly with regard to his relationship with the Black Prince in Roskell *et al.*, *History of Parliament*, ii, 359-62.

3. Dupuy, *Prince Noir*, 300.

4. *DNB*, x, 829-30.

5. For his appointment and powers as prince of Aquitaine see BL Stowe 140 ff. 50v-56; Add. 32097 f. 108v.

6. See A. Bardonnet, *Procès-verbal de deliverance a Jean Chandos commissaire du roi d'Angleterre des places Françaises abandonees par le traite de Brétigny*, Niort, 1866; Lodge, *Gascony Under English Rule*, 93-4; Delachenal, *Charles V*, iv, 33-6, 44-50.

7. Delachenal, *Charles V*, iv, 62-3; Charles Higounet, ed., *Histoire de l'Aquitaine*, Toulouse, 1971, 217.

8. Delachenal, *Charles V*, iv, 16. It has been suggested that the creation of the principality could have been as banishment resulting from the prince's marriage to Joan of Kent, *Chronique de quartre premiers Valois*, 122ff.

9. For example, the Ombrière, Fronsac, Bourg, Blaye, Bayonne, Dax, Saint Sever, Malcolm Vale, 'The War in Aquitaine', *Arms, Armies and Fortifications*, ed. Curry and Hughes, 69, 74, 77.

10. Pierre Capra, 'L'Administration Anglo-Gasconne au temps de la lieutenance du Prince Noir, 1354-62', Unpub. Thesis, Paris, 1972, ix.

11. Robert Favreau, 'Le cession de La Rochelle à l'Angleterre en 1360', *La France Anglaise au Moyen Age*, Paris, 1988, 217-31; Capra, 'L'administration Anglo-Gasconne', 770, 835-50.

12. E101/176/4, 13, 20.

13. Capra, 'L'Administration Anglo-Gasconne', 811-24, 828, 836, 844 n. 12, 885-6, 890 n. 12. For Loryng's accounts see E372/206/10 m. 2; E403/408/31-2; 411/34; 413/15. Hoghton arrived at Rabastens on 28 Jan. 1362, took oaths from nobles, churchmen and urban authorities and occupied 4 castles. Like Chandos he used many Gascon officers.

14. Harewell received £17,476 from the English exchequer but there were no further receipts before 1370, Harriss, *King, Parliament and Public Finance*, 476 n. 3. Gascon revenues never covered the pay of the chief officials, some £750 a year, Frank Musgrove, *The North of England. A History*, Oxford, 1990, 160.

15. Lodge, *Gascony Under English Rule*, 138-41, 147-50. The court was a permanent tribunal in Bordeaux held by the seneschal or his lieutenant, the judge of Aquitaine. It was superior to other courts and could hear appeals from municipal courts and deal with disputes between secular and ecclesiastical jurisdictions, for which, in 1365, Edward III handed over responsibility. In 1370, a *curia superioritatis*, largely composed of Gascons was established.

16. Capra, 'L'administration Anglo-Gasconne', 826, 838-40; 843 n. 3; C76/44/6; E361/5/3 r.-v.

17. Françoise Bériac, 'Une principauté sans chambre des comptes ni échiquier: L'Aquitaine (1362-1370)', *La France des principautés. Les chambre des comptes xiv^e et xv^e siècles*, ed. Philippe Contamine et Olivier Mattéoni, Paris, 1996, 109-10, 113-15. He was commissioned at La Rochelle on 25

Apr. 1372. His duties were those of treasurer of Aquitaine. In 1362 he had served Nicholas Loveigne and was receiver of La Rochelle from 26 Oct. 1364, Timothy Runyan, 'The Constabulary of Bordeaux: The Accounts of John Ludham (1372-3) and Robert de Wykford (1373-5)', *Mediaeval Studies*, xxxvi, (1974), i, 221-4, 239 n. 1. The Ombrière housed the court of Gascony, the council, the chancery of the seneschal and perhaps the court of sovereignty. It served as the local prison and was topped by 2 large towers; the *tour du roi* and the *tour Arbalesteyre*.

18. Capra, 'L'administration Anglo-Gasconne', 741-2.

19. *Life and Campaigns*, ed. Barber, 105.

20. For details of the transportation of horses see C61/75/10. Thomas Dautre, John Ellerton and others provided ships for the prince and de Montfort, Rymer, III, ii, 666. Further supplies, forage and litter were levied in Devon, Cornwall and bows and arrows from London, Rymer, III, ii, 671, 720; Labarge, *Gascony*, 151.

21. For Stafford's and Chivereston's ships see C61/74/3; 75/27. Adam Hoghton received letters of protection 15 July 1361, Carte, *Rôles Gascons*, i, 149.

22. Barber, *Edward*, 178-9. Ships were 'arrested' on 4 June 1362 and 16 Feb. 1363 for this purpose, C61/75/25; *CPR, 1361-4*, 317, also see C61/75/6, 8, 16-18; 76/5, 7; Carte, *Rôles Gascons*, i, 151-2. On 3 and 4 June 1363, payments were made to the masters of the ships *Christophre* of Fowey and *Katerine* of Hull, presumably in connection with the transfer to Aquitaine, *BPR*, iv, 497; Rymer, III, ii, 652. For payments to the masters of ships in 1363-4 see E101/29/1 (Ralph Kesteven's account); 36/20 and payments to mariners, 1362-3 see E101/28/26 (Robert Crull's account).

23. The captal de Buch fought at Cocherel and Chandos led de Montfort's forces at Auray.

24. Charles T. Wood, *The Age of Chivalry. Manners and Morals, 1000-1450*, London, 1970, 148.

25. By contrast, poems of social protest were circulating stressing knightly pride and vanity and demanding a return to the religious devotion thought of as the norm in some earlier age. Later writers such as Philippe de Mézieres, Honoré Bouvet and Christine de Pizan described the pillaging of the Companies and their maltreatment of churchmen and civilians in terms of abandoning the laws of true chivalry, M.H. Keen, 'War and Peace in the Middle Ages', *Nobles, Knights and Men-at-Arms in the Middle Ages*, ed. B.P. McGuire, London and Rio Grande, 1996, 8-9.

26. Russell, *Intervention*, 79*ff*; M. Keen, 'Brotherhood-in-Arms', *History*, 47 (1962), 1-16; K.B. McFarlane, 'An Indenture of Agreement Between Two English Knights for Mutual Aid and Counsel in War and Peace', *BIHR*, xxxviii (1965), 200-10.

27. Linda M. Paterson, *The World of the Troubadours. Medieval Occitan Society c.1100-c.1300*, Cambridge, 1993, 68.

28. Froissart, *Chroniques*, ed. Luce, vi, 81, 275-6.

29. *Anominalle Chronicle*, 56; Paterson, *World of the Troubadours*, 68-71, 88, 101-4, 108-10.

30. V.J. Scattergood, 'Literary Culture at the Court of Richard II', *English Court Culture*, ed. Scattergood and Sherborne, London, 1983, 35-6. After his execution, 40 books were recorded as formerly belonging to Simon Burley; 8 Nov. 1387, BL Add. 25459, f. 206.

31. D'A.J.D. Boulton, 'Insignia of Power: The Use of Heraldic and Paraheraldic Devices by Italian Princes, c.1350 - c.1500', *Art and Politics in Late Medieval and Early Renaissance Italy, 1250-1500*, ed. Charles M. Rosenburg, Indiana, 1990, 113.

32. See Pierre Tucoo-Chala, *Gaston Fébus: un grand prince d'Occident au XIVᵉ siècle*, Pau, 1976, 164-93.

33. *BPR*, iv, 484; *Sir Gawain and the Green Knight*, trans. Brian Stone, 2ⁿᵈ ed., Harmondsworth, 1975, 64-5, 71-2, 74-6, 79-81, 92; See Orme, *Childhood to Chivalry*, 191-8.

34. 1 Sept. 1362, *BPR*, iv, 467; Labarge, *Gascony*, 149.

35. Emerson, *Black Prince*, 171. For the nature of garments worn and other related comments see Stella M. Newton, *Fashion in the Age of the Black Prince. A Study of the Years 1340-1365*, Woodbridge, 1988; Sherborne, 'Aspects of English Court Culture in the Later Fourteenth Century', *English Court Culture*, ed. Scattergood and Sherborne, 14-16. See for comparison Baker, *Chronicon*, 122.

36. His mother's violist, Richard Merlin, visited the prince in 1338-9. In the following year he was entertained by a minstrel with a portative organ and by John 'the fool' of Eltham, Barber, *Edward*, 22, 30, 37. There were musicians with Queen Philippa and the prince at Waltham in 1358, *BPR*, iv, 251.

37. *BPR*, iv, 73. Instruments were also made for the prince. A pipe was made by Jakelyn costing the exorbitant sum of £6 13s. 4d., and a 'hakeney' was made by Zeulyn the piper at a cost of 66s. 8d., *ibid.*, 251.

38. At the Garter feast of 1358 the prince paid £100 to heralds and minstrels, Barber, *Edward*, 154-5. Other gifts included a destrier to a minstrel at a tournament in Bury St Edmunds, a drum for John 'the prince's minstrel', 40s. to minstrels of Bartholomew Burghersh, the younger, 40s. to 2 of the prince's minstrels, Ulyn the piper received £13 6s. 8d., and 7 of the prince's minstrels were given £9 6s. 8d., *BPR*, iv, 67, 72, 87, 167, 283, 388-9. Money was also paid to minstrels to settle debts, presumably these were in the prince's employ, Jakelyn received £16 13s. 4d. and 72s. 10d. and Tolle of Almain, 56s., *ibid.*, 89, 388. John Cokard received 20s. towards the costs of his stay in London, *ibid.*, 304; Nigel Wilkins, 'Music and Poetry at Court: England and France in the Late Middle Ages', *English Court Culture*, ed. Scattergood and Sherborne, 195. Hanz and Soz were provided with 3 quarters of a rayed cloth for making robes for themselves and 2 habergeons, *BPR*, iv, 71.

39. John Southworth, *The English Medieval Minstrel*, Woodbridge, 1980, 106-7. Gilbert Stakford, a trumpeter, was one of the minstrels left behind who may have been wounded on the Poitiers campaign, an alternative living was found for him in the household of the prior of St Michael's Mount. Stakford recovered from his injuries and later served Richard II who gave him with a pension of 6d. a day 'for service to the king's father and to the king'.

40. Froissart, *Chronicles*, ed. Berners, 91.

41. Froissart, *Oeuvres*, ed. Lettenhove, vi, 393-4; *CPR*, 1364-7, 180.

42. Froissart, *Chroniques*, ed. Luce, vi, 93, 285; 'A Fourteenth Century Chronicle of the Grey Friars of Lynn', ed. Antonia Gransden, *EHR*, lxxii (1957), 271.

43. The *chevauchées* of 1355-6 established taxation as a regular feature of southern French life. There had been opposition to the demands of the count of Armagnac and later Jean, count of Poitiers acting as Jean II's lieutenants in Languedoc, John Bell Henneman, *Royal Taxation in Fourteenth Century France*, Princeton, 1971, 272-82.

44. Wood, *Age of Chivalry*, 141. For further details on the Free Companies see Norman Housley, 'The Mercenary Companies, the Papacy and the Crusades, 1356-1378', *Traditio*, xxxvii (1982), 253-80; Kenneth Fowler, *Medieval Mercenaries. Volume 1 The Great Companies*, Oxford, 2001.

45. Housley, 'Mercenary Companies', 254; Fowler, *Medieval Mercenaries*, 51, 75; Delachenal, *Charles V*, ii, 319, 20; P.S. Lewis, *Later Medieval France: The Polity*, London, 1968, 51; Keen, 'Chivalry, Nobility and the Man-at-Arms', 38.

46. Russell, *Intervention*, 62.

47. Froissart, *Oeuvres*, ed. Lettenhove, vii, 96-9.

48. *Knighton's Chronicle*, ed. Martin, 194, 195; A. Mackay, *Spain in the Middle Age: From Frontier to Empire, 1000-1500*, London, 1977, 134-5.

49. E30/191. The alliance required any English military assistance to be paid by the Castilian treasury, Russell, *Intervention*, 59.

50. Clara Elstow, *Pedro the Cruel of Castile, 1350-1369*, Leiden, New York and Köln, 1995, 223-4.

51. Mackay, *Spain in the Middle Ages*, 125.

52. Elstow, *Pedro the Cruel*, 236.

53. Froissart, *Oeuvres*, ed. Lettenhove, vii, 98.

54. Fowler, *Medieval Mercenaries*, 192-3.

55. Rymer, iii, 805-6; Russell, *Intervention*, 65-6.

56. Fowler, *Medieval Mercenaries*, 194; Rymer, III, ii, 800 (23 Sept. 1366).

57. C61/79/13-15; Russell, *Intervention*, 75-7; Sumption, *Hundred Years War*, ii, 544.

58. 10 Feb. 1367, *CCR, 1364-8*, 371; Robert Boutruche, *La crise d'une société: seigneurs et paysans du Bordelais pendant la Guerre de Cent Ans*, new ed., Paris, 1963, 169-70, Fowler, *Medieval Mercenaries*, 200.

59. Fowler, *Medieval Mercenaries*, 197-8; Prince, 'Strength of English Armies', 369; J.J.N. Palmer, 'Froissart et le héraut Chandos', *Le Moyen Age*, 88 (1982), 271ff.; Diana B. Tyson, 'Authors, Patrons and Soldiers – Some Thoughts on Four Old French Soldiers' Lives', *NMS*, xlii (1998), 110.

60. BL Cotton, Caligula D III, f.141; Delachenal, *Charles V*, iii, 554 and Russell, *Intervention*, 93-4.

61. Barber, *Edward*, 198. According to Chandos Herald, 160 lancers and 300 archers made up the party.

62. Russell, *Intervention*, 87, 91 and n. 3; Fowler, *Medieval Mercenaries*, 206-7.

63. Fernao Lopes, *The English in Portugal, 1367-87*, ed. and trans. Derek W. Lomax and R.J. Oakley, Warminster, 1988, 9. This advice may have been given just prior to the battle or somewhat earlier, Russell, *Intervention*, 89.
64. Chandos Herald, *Life of the Black Prince*, ed. Pope and Lodge, ll. 2572-4.
65. Russell, *Intervention*, 94-6 and nn. 1-2. On the exchange of letters see Lopes, *English in Portugal*, 12-17; Delachenal, *Charles V*, iii, 398 and n. 1, 399 and nn. 1-2.
66. Delachenal, *Charles V*, iii, 402, 404; Russell, *Intervention*, 97-8, estimated 4,000-5,000 troops plus a number of *jinetes* on Trastamara's side.
67. Russell, *Intervention*, 101.
68. Chandos Herald, *Life of the Black Prince*, ed. Pope and Lodge, 163, ll. 3258, 3277-8.
69. E. Déprez, 'La bataille de Nájera: le communiqué du prince noir' *Revue Historique*, cxxxvi (1921), 37-59; A.E. Prince, 'A Letter of Edward the Black Prince describing the Battle of Nájera in 1367', *EHR*, xli (1926), 415-18; *Life and Campaigns* ed. Barber, 83.
70. For further discussion see Michael Jones, 'Edward III's Captains in Brittany', *England in the Fourteenth Century. Proceedings of 1985 Harlaxton Symposium*, ed. W.M. Ormrod, Woodbridge, 1986, 104; Rogers, 'Dialectics of Strategy', 83-102; Bennett, 'Development of Battle Tactics', 2, 5.
71. Case taken from Keen, *Laws of War*, 50-6.
72. Fowler, *Medieval Mercenaries*, 218-23.
73. P.E. Russell, 'The War in Spain and Portugal', *Froissart: Historian*, ed. J.J.N. Palmer, Woodbridge, 1981, 91.

## CHAPTER 7

1. For further comments see Green, 'Household and Military Retinue', esp. 279-95; 'The Later Retinue of Edward the Black Prince', *NMS*, xliv (2000), 141-51; 'The Military Personnel of Edward the Black Prince', *Medieval Prosopography*, 21 (2000), 133-52; 'Politics and Service with Edward the Black Prince', 53-68; *The Age of Edward III*, ed. J. Bothwell, Woodbridge, 2001.
2. Rising and the Lynn tollbooth were valued at only £116 13s. 4d. in 1376, C47/9/57. After his marriage to Joan, the prince acquired additional property in Norfolk, such as Ormsby manor. Members of the retinue with Norfolk connections included Thomas Felton, William Elmham, William Kerdeston, Stephen Hales, Thomas Gissing, Nicholas Dagworth, Robert Ufford and Robert Knolles.
3. Hewitt, *Black Prince's Expedition*, 80-1.
4. Hewitt, *Black Prince's Expedition*, 52.
5. Letter of the prince to the bishop of Winchester, *Life and Campaigns* ed. Barber, 54.
6. Barber, *Edward*, 146.
7. £2,000 was advanced by Arundel on the security of a crown and a jewelled star taken from the king of France at Poitiers, 24 July 1359, *BPR*, iv, 302, 333. The chamberlain of Chester was ordered to levy funds on 20 May 1360 to repay FitzAlan, *ibid.*, iii, 381. On 21 May, John Delves, lieutenant of the justices of north Wales and Cheshire, was notified that he was to receive £1,000 and then deliver it to the prince. Delves was also to inform the chamberlains of Chester (John Brunham) and north Wales that they also to bring/send all available funds to London, *ibid.*, 354. See also 27 July, *ibid.*, 355. Delves received £3 expenses in connection with this transaction at Holt castle and the transportation costs, *ibid.*, 364.
8. Antony 'Maubaille', merchant of Ast and Hugh Provane, merchant of Carignano, loaned 1,000 marks, *BPR*, iii, 319.
9. 500 marks were provided by Humphrey Bohun, earl of Hereford and Essex, 30 July 1359, *BPR*, iv, 304. Ralph Nevill and the bishop of Lincoln each loaned 500 marks and the bishop of Winchester, 1,000 marks, *ibid.*, 319, 327.
10. John Peche borrowed £1,000 from various London merchants on the prince's behalf and repaid 250 marks to William de la Pole for him. Peche was appointed the prince's attorney for the transfer of certain jewels from the sire de Lesparre and Sir Petiton de Curton and also received the crown which had been pledged as security for Arundel's loan, *BPR*, iv, 321, 327, 333. £100 was borrowed from both Henry Pickard and Adam Franceys, *ibid.*, 327.

11. *BPR*, iv, 326. Wingfield, another East Anglian in the retinue, held this office until his death in 1360 in addition to being the prince's attorney, steward of his lands and chief of the council. He received wages of 10s. a day. Delves replaced him until his own death in 1369, Sharpe, 'Administrative Chancery of the Black Prince', 331.

12. For comparison, 14 of the MPs sitting for Westmoreland between 1386 and 1421 were associated with the Clifford family and 14 members of Richard, earl of Worcester's affinity represented that county between 1404 and 1421, Linda Clark, 'Magnates and their Affinities in the Parliaments of 1386-1421' *The McFarlane Legacy. Studies in Late Medieval Politics and Society*, ed. R.H. Britnell and A.J. Pollard, Stroud, 1995, 139; W.M. Ormrod, *The Reign of Edward III: Crown and Political Society in England, 1327-1377*, New Haven, 1990, 129-30.

13. Green, 'Politics and Service', 67.

14. Sumption, *Hundred Years War, ii*, 540-2. See also Delpit, *Documents français*, 136-7 9 (no. 48), 175 (nos. 19, 22), 134-68 (nos. 4, 9, 12, 14, 19, etc), 176 (nos. 53, 55, 56).

15. E101/38/15, 17-18; Delpit, *Documents Français*, 176; Green, 'Household and Military Retinue', 143-4, 160-1; Bériac, 'Une principauté sans chambre de comptes ni échiquier', 120-1; Barber, *Edward*, 209.

16. C. de Vic et J. Vaisette, ed., *Histoire générale de Languedoc avec des notes et les pieces justicatives*, re-ed. A. Molinier, 16 vols, Toulouse, 1872-1904, x, 1211-55, 1264-73, 1273-8. In 1364, the *fouage* was levied at 1 *guyennois d'or*; in 1365 at a half *guyennois d'or*; in 1366 at a minimum of 4 *sous*, Boutruche, *La crise d'une société*, 202; Delachenal, *Charles V*, iv, 56-7, 66. For French taxation policy in the Languedoc in the years before Brétigny see John Bell Henneman, *Royal Taxation in Fourteenth Century France. The Captivity and Ransom of John II, 1356-1370*, Philadelphia, 1976, 123-47.

17. The tax was not to be levied again for 5 years, grievances of clergy were addressed and certain trade concessions were made. Complaints were also heard about the encroachment of seneschals and other officials on siegneurial rights including violations of ancient privileges, Delachenal, *Charles V*, iv, 58-9.

18. He was constable of Bordeaux from 11 Nov. 1362 until his appointment as chancellor in Michaelmas 1364. As bishop of Bath and Wells he was an executor of the prince's will, Pierre Chaplais, 'The Chancery of Guienne, 1289-1453', *Studies Presented to Sir Hillary Jenkinson*, ed. J.Conway Davies, London, 1957, 85-6 and n. 7.

19. Malcolm Vale, *The Angevin Legacy and the Hundred Years War, 1250-1340*, 82-4, 124-39; Delachenal, *Charles V*, iv, 65; Maurice Rey, *Les finances royales sous Charles VI. Les causes du déficit, 1388-1413*, Paris, 1965, 447.

20. *Histoire générale de Languedoc*, x, 1347-8 ; Delachenal, *Charles V*, iv, 67-9; Henneman, *Royal Taxation*, 250.

21. See *Anonimalle Chronicle*, 55-6; also Cuvelier, *Chronique de Bertrand du Guesclin*, I, 236-9, 325, 348, 368, 435, 459; II, 15, 245, 249; Froissart, *Oeuvres*, ed. Lettenhove, vi, 82; vii, 92.

22. Totesham had succeeded Bernard de Montferrand as governor of La Rochelle in Dec. 1360and in Oct. 1361 he received the captaincy of the castle of St-Jean-d'Angély with annual wages of 100 *livres*. He had been a French prisoner and fought a duel during his captivity, *Chronique Normande du xiv^e siècle*, ed. E. et A. Molinier (SHF), Paris, 1882, 104-5; Robert Favreau, 'Comptes de la sénéchausée de Saintonge, 1360-2' *BEC*, 117 (1959), 74-5.

23. For example in Périgord, see Arlette Higounet-Nadal, *Perigeux au xiv^e et xv^e siècles*, Bordeaux, 1978, 148.

24. Favreau, 'Comptes', 76. Seris was a royal counsellor receiving wages of 500 *écus* yearly. However, the 2 seals with which he was to authorize his actions were never used as in 1367 he returned them, no case of *ressort* having been brought before him. Rymer, III, i, 548; Pierre Chaplais, 'Some Documents Regarding the Fulfilment and Interpretation of the Treaty of Brétigny', *Camden* 3^rd ser., xix (1952) 52-3 and nn. 1, 2.

25. For further examples including William Boulard and Renoul Bouchard (*procureurs*) of the king in Saintonge, Boulard was also mayor of La Rochelle, 1361-2; Macé d'Aiguechaude (royal advocate in Saintonge); Pierre Bernard (receiver of Saintonge); Pierre de Vergny (receiver of a number of *prévôtés* and other revenues later including La Rochelle 1374-6 and of Saintonge and Angoumois in 1376 as well as Andilly, the 'baillie' of Chagnolet, the customs on wine passing through the port of Périgny, revenues of the royal seal of La Rochelle and of the great fief of Aunis), see Favreau, 'Comptes', 78.

26. Davies, *Lordship and Society*, 203, 207.

27. A.D. Carr, 'Rhys ap Roppert', *Transactions of the Denbighshire Historical Society*, 25 (1976), 155-70.

28. Fowler, *Medieval Mercenaries*, 69*ff*, 98-100 and n. 33, 149, 151, 153-4; Delachenal, *Charles V*, iv, 16, 20 and n. 1.

29. Emerson, *Black Prince*, 215.

30. Corvisier et Contamine, *Histoire militaire*, 145-9; Contamine, *War in the Middle Ages*, 153-6; Sumption. *Hundred Years War, ii*, 579. For the prince's letter to the lord of Séverac who had refused to allow levying of the *fouage* and regarding the appeal of Castelbon see *Histoire générale de Languedoc*, x, 1337-8, 1420-1. See also *Documents sur la ville de Millau*, nos., 316, 318, 319, 322-5.

31. *CCR, 1364-8*, 371; Sumption, *Hundred Years War, ii*, 579. See *CPR, 1367-70*, 56, 58 (11, 13, 20 Nov. 1367); 22 Nov. 1367, Rymer, III, ii, 837.

32. *Histoire générale de Languedoc*, x, 1404-6.

33. Froissart, *Chroniques*, ed. Luce, vii, 95-9; Chandos Herald, *Vie du Prince Noir*, ed. Tyson, ll. 3889-96; Barber, *Edward*, 219-20; James Sherborne, 'John of Gaunt, Edward III's Retinue and the French Campaign of 1369', *Kings and Nobles in the Later Middle Ages*, ed. Ralph A. Griffiths and James Sherborne, Gloucester, 1986, 41. For the payments for reinforcements made to Peter Lacy see E403/436 mm. 25-6; 438 m. 24.

34. BL Harleian MS. 2074 f. 230v. For further discussion of this document and some of the inherent problems see Green, 'Later Retinue of the Black Prince', 142, 144-5.

35. E101/29/24. Wetenhale was paid £54 for men-at-arms and archers, SC6/772/5 m. 2d.; P.J. Morgan, 'Cheshire and the Defence of the Principality of Aquitaine', *Transactions of the Historical Society of Lancashire and Cheshire*, 128 (1978), 147-9, 158 n. 41.

36. C61/81/4; *CPR, 1367-70*, 228.

37. For a description of the castle see Kelly DeVries, *Medieval Military Technology*, Ontario, 1992, 240-1.

38. Archives Nationales, *Trésor des Chartes*, JJ 100, no. 778 and J 655 n. 18.

39. Sumption, *Hundred Years War, ii*, 581-2.

40. Emerson, *Black Prince*, 232. Thanks to Jonathan Burr for this reference.

41. Froissart, *Chroniques*, ed. Luce, vii, 199-204; Barber, *Edward*, 222-3; Corvisier et Contamine, *Histoire militaire*, 142-3.

42. Charles Higounet ed., *Histoire de l'Aquitaine*, , Toulouse, 1971, 214; Louis Pérouas, *Histoire de Limoges*, Toulouse, 1989, 106; Stéphane Baumont ed., *Histoire d'Agen*, Toulouse, 1991, 80; Packe, *Edward III*, 277.

43. Porter, 'Chaucer's Knight', 65, 68-9; Barber, *Edward*, 225-6. On the severity of siege warfare see Keen, *Laws of War*, 121-2; Barber, *Knight and Chivalry*, rev. ed., 239-40; Barnie, *War in Medieval Society*, 77.

44. Bradbury, *Medieval Siege*, 161; Froissart, *Oeuvres*, ed. Lettenhove, xvii, 501-2.

45. *Chronique de quartre premiers Valois*, 210; *Wars of Edward III*, ed. Rogers, 193; Barber, *Edward*, 224-6 and n. 23; Paul Ducourtieux, *Histoire de Limoges*, Limoges, 1925, repr. Marseille, 1975, 53-7, 59.

46. S.H. Cuttler, *The Law of Treason and Treason Trials in Later Medieval France*, Cambridge, 1981, 117.

47. *Eulogium Historiarum*, iii, 219-20; Baker, *Chronicon*, 141; Ayton, 'English Armies', 36.

48. 3 Dec. 1355, *BPR*, iii, 220-1.

49. *BPR*, iii, 375-9; 16 Feb. 1360, *CCR, 1360-4*, 6.

50. *BPR*, ii, 14, 24, 66, 166, 169.

51. 20 Mar. 1360, *BPR*, iv, 345-6.

52. 14 Feb. and 26 Mar. 1360, *BPR*, iv, 344, 346.

53. *CCR, 1354-60*, 214, 215; *1364-8*, 371; D. Pratt, 'Wrexham Militia in the Fourteenth Century', *Transactions of the Denbighshire Historical Society*, (1963), 38-9.

54. Vale, 'Seigneurial Fortification', 74-5.

55. Prestwich, *Armies and Warfare*, 293; T.F. Tout, 'Firearms in England in the Fourteenth Century', *EHR*, xxvi (1911), 670-4, 676.

56. Froissart, *Chroniques*, ed. Luce, iv, 11; Jim Bradbury, *The Medieval Siege*, Woodbridge, 1992, 159; Contamine, *War in the Middle Ages*, 140; S. Storey-Challenger, *L'administration anglaise du Ponthieu apres le traité de Brétigny, 1361-1369*, Abbeville, 1975, 286; Robert D. Smith, 'Artillery and the Hundred Years War: Myth and Interpretation', *Arms, Armies and Fortifications*, ed. Curry and Hughes, 153-5.

57. Delpit, *Documents français*, 130-1.

## CHAPTER 8

1.  4 Feb. 1375, *CPR, 1374-7*, 70.
2.  Emerson, *Black Prince*, 249.
3.  Russell, *Intervention*, 174-5, 176 n. 3.
4.  Green, 'Politics and Service', 64-7. MPs in Gaunt's affinity were concentrated in a handful of counties, whereas those in the prince's retinue represented at least 21 of the 36 counties that returned members. Gaunt had as few as 3 and as many as 13 MPs in every parliament from 1372 to 1397 (5 or 6 in the 1370s, 7 or 8 in the 1380s and ten to 12 in the 1390s), Walker, *Lancastrian Affinity*, 238-9. Clark suggests that in the 11 parliaments from 1386 to 1397 Gaunt's representatives in the Commons averaged a dozen and rose on occasion to 17, 'Magnates and their Affinities'; Ormrod, *Reign of Edward III*, 208-9.
5.  Walsingham, *Chronicon Angliae*, trans. E. M. Thompson, London (Rolls Ser.), 1874, 68-101. At least part of Walsingham's account of the prince's death was taken from a continuation of Higden's *Polychronicon*, Taylor, *Universal Chronicle of Ranulph Higden*, 120.
6.  Michael Bennett, 'Edward III's Entail and the Succession to the Crown, 1376-1471', *EHR*, cxiii (1998), 580-607.
7.  Russell, *Intervention*, 185.
8.  Antonia Gransden, *Historical Writing in England, ii, c.1307 to the Early Sixteenth Century*, London, 1982, 108.
9.  Harvey, *Black Prince and his Age*, 160.
10. *Henry V*, 1, ii.
11. Christopher Brooke, 'Reflections on Late Medieval Cults and Devotions', *Essays in Honor of Edward B. King*, Tennessee, 1991, 38-9.
12. J.J.G. Alexander and P. Binski, ed., *Age of Chivalry: Art in Plantagenet England 1200-1400*, London, 1987, 222, 478-9; Patrick Collinson, Nigel Ramsay and Margaret Sparks, ed., *A History of Canterbury Cathedral*, Oxford, 1995, 495 n. 192; Patricia Cullum and Jeremy Goldberg, 'How Margaret Blackburn Taught her Daughters: Reading Devotional Instruction in a Book of Hours', *Medieval Women: Texts and Contexts in Late Medieval Britain*, ed. J. Wogan-Browne *et al.*, Turnhout, Belgium, 2000, 222.
13. Husting Roll 89 (183); Lincoln Archives Office Reg. xii, fo. 170; *BPR*, iii, 408-9; Arthur Mee, *Lincolnshire*, London, repr. 1992, 349.
14. H.F. Chettle, 'The Boni Homines of Ashridge and Edington', *Downside Review*, 62 (1944), 47; *VCH*, Bucks, 387; G.E. Chambers, *The Bonhommes of the Order of St. Augustine at Ashridge and Edington*, 2nd ed., pamphlet, 1979, 4.
15. Janet H. Stevenson, *The Edington Cartulary* (Wiltshire Record Society), 1986, xv-xvii; Chettle, 'Boni Homines', 43-4.
16. Stevenson, *Edington Cartulary.*, xiv.
17. William Dugdale, *Monasticon Anglicanum*, London, 1655-73, vi, 536. See Stevenson, *Edington Cartulary.*, 9-14 for letters patent dated 29 Mar. 1358.
18. Stevenson, *Edington Cartulary*, 36, 108, 119-20, 128; Harvey, *Black Prince and his Age*, 160-5; *Age of Chivalry*, ed. Alexander and Binski, 145.
19. Eleanor Scheifele, 'Richard II and the Visual Arts', *Richard II: The Art of Kingship*, ed. A. Goodman and J. Gillespie, Oxford, 1999, 258; Harvey, *Black Prince and his Age*, 160-5; W.M. Ormrod, 'In Bed with Joan of Kent: The King's Mother and the Peasants' Revolt', *Medieval Women*, ed. Wogan-Browne, 281-2.
20. *But now a caitiff poor am I, Deep in the ground, lo here I lie. My beauty great is all quite gone, My flesh is wasted to the bone.* For a discussion of the source and 3 different versions of the epitaph, the earliest being the *Disciplina Clericalis* by Petrus Alphonsi, see D.B. Tyson, 'The Epitaph of the Black Prince', *Medium Aevum*, 46 (1977), 98-104.
21. E101/400/4 m. 20; Orme, *From Childhood to Chivalry*, 122.
22. Eric W. Stockton, *The Major Latin Works of John Gower*, Seattle, 1962, 242.
23. BL Add. Mss 24511 f. 69, household expenses, 1 Jan. -16 July 1377.
24. James L. Gillespie, 'Richard II: Chivalry and Kingship', *The Age of Richard II*, ed. James L. Gillespie, Stroud, 1997, 115-16.
25. *GEC*, i, 650-3.

26. James L. Gillespie, 'Richard II: King of Battles?', *Age of Richard II*, ed. Gillespie, 139; A.B. Steel, *Richard II*, Cambridge, 1941, 41.

27. E101/398/8; Given-Wilson, *Royal Household*, 161-2, 306 n. 128; Green, 'Politics and Service'.

28. A. Goodman, 'Introduction', *Richard II: The Art of Kingship*, ed. A. Goodman and J. Gillespie, Oxford, 1999, 4-5.

29. Michael J. Bennett, 'Richard III and the Wider Realm', *Richard II*, ed. Goodman and Gillespie, 189-90.

30. John Taylor, 'Richard II in the Chronicles', *Richard II*, ed. Goodman and Gillespie, 21-2.

31. C.M. Barron, 'The Deposition of Richard II', *Politics and Crisis in Fourteenth Century England*, ed. J. Taylor and W. Childs, Gloucester, 1990, 145.

32. Nigel Saul, 'The Kingship of Richard II', *Richard II*, ed. Goodman and Gillespie, 40.

33. Dillian Gordon, 'The Wilton Diptych: An Introduction', *The Regal Image of Richard II and the Wilton Diptych*, ed. Dillian Gordon, Lisa Monnas and Caroline Elam, London, 1997, 21; M. Galway, 'The Wilton Diptych: A Postscript', *Archaeological Journal*, cvii (1952 for 1950), 9-14.

34. Scheifele, 'Richard II and the Visual Arts', 269 and n. 57.

35. Nigel Saul, 'Richard II's Ideas of Kingship', *Regal Image of Richard II*, ed. Gordon *et al.*, 27-8. For discussions of Richard's own depiction as Christ-like, especially in the context of the 1381 revolt, by Froissart and others see Ormrod 'In Bed with Joan of Kent', 286-7 and n. 33.

36. Saul, *Richard II*, 9; Walsingham, *Chronicon Anglie*, 183; *Historia Anglicana*, ed. H.T. Riley (Rolls Ser.), London, 1863-4, i, 356; Anne Hudson, *The Premature Reformation: Wycliffite Texts and Lollard History*, Oxford, 1988, 110, 112, nn 310-12.

37. N.H. Nicolas, ed., *Testamenta Vetusta*, 2 vols, London, 1826, i, 14-15; J.I. Catto, 'Sir William Beauchamp between Chivalry and Lollardy', *The Ideals and Practices of Medieval Knighthood*, ed. C. Harper-Bill and R. Harvey, Woodbridge, 1990, 39-48; W.T. Waugh, 'The Lollard Knights', *Scottish Historical Review*, xi (1913-14), 58, 64, 75-6; K.B. McFarlane, *Lancastrian Kings and Lollard Knights*, Oxford, 1972, 207-26.

38. Green, 'Household and Military Retinue', 241-4.

39. M. Keen, 'The Influence of Wyclif', *Wyclif in his Times*, ed. Anthony Kenny, Oxford, 1986, 129.

40. J.A. Tuck, 'Carthusian Monks and Lollard Knights: Religious Attitudes at the Court of Richard II', *Studies in the Age of Chaucer, Proceedings I: Reconstructing Chaucer*, ed. P. Strohm and T.J. Heffernan, 1984, 153.

41. Jeremy Catto, 'Fellows and Helpers: The Religious Identity of the Followers of Wyclif', *The Medieval Church: Universities, Heresy and the Religious Life*, ed. Peter Biller and Barry Dobson (*SCH* Susidia 11), Woodbridge, 1999, 145, 154*ff.* and n. 35.

42. See V.J. Scattergood ed., *The Works of Sir John Clanvowe*, Cambridge, 1975.

43. J.A.F. Thomson, 'Orthodox Religion and the Origins of Lollardy', *History*, 74 (1989), 44-8.

44. Green, 'Household and Military Retinue', Appendix.

45. E403/551; *Annales Ricardi Secundi et Henrici Quarti*, in J. de Trokelowe ed., *Chronica et Annales*, ed. H.T. Riley (Rolls Ser.), London, 1866, 183; Hudson, *Premature Reformation*, 89-90. On Clifford see *ibid.*, 291-2 and Margaret Aston, *Lollards and Reformers: Images and Literacy in Late Medieval Religion*, Hambledon, 1984, 98 n. 117.

# SELECT BIBLIOGRAPHY

## PRIMARY SOURCES

*British Library*
Additional Charters
Additional MSS
Cotton Julius
Cotton Nero
Cotton Charters
Harley MSS

*Public Record Office*
C47 Miscellanea
C61 Gascon Rolls
C76 Treaty Rolls
E30 Diplomatic Documents
E36 Exchequer Books
E101 King's Remembrancer, Accounts Various
E361 Wardrobe and Household Accounts
SC1 Ancient Correspondence
SC6 Ministers' and Receivers' Accounts
SC8 Ancient Petitions
CHES Palatinate of Chester
DL  Duchy of Lancaster

*Lincoln Archives Office*
Episcopal Register xii  Register of John Buckingham (Memoranda)

*Guildhall Library (London), Court of Hustings*
Husting Roll 89, 104

*Duchy of Cornwall Office (London)*
*Journale* or 'day book' of John Henxteworth, 1355-6

*University of Nottingham*
Middleton Deeds, Mi F 10/8

*Chronicles*
*Anonimalle Chronicle, 1333-1381*, ed. V.H. Galbriath, Manchester, 1927.
Avesbury, Robert of *De gestis mirabilis regis Edwardi tertii*, ed. E.M. Thompson, 1889.
Baker, Geoffrey Le *Chronicon Galfridi le Baker de Swynebroke, 1330-56*, ed. E.M. Thompson, Oxford, 1889.
Brie, F.W.D. ed. *The Brut*, ii, (Early English Texts Society), 1906.
Chandos Herald – editions, *Life of the Black Prince by the Herald of Sir John Chandos*, ed. M. Pope and E Lodge, Oxford, 1910; *La Vie du Prince Noir*, ed. Diana B. Tyson, Tübingen, 1975.
*Chronica Johannis de Reading et Anonymi Cantuarensis 1346-1367*, ed. James Tait, Manchester, 1914.

*Chronicle of London from 1089 to 1483*, ed. E. Tyrrell and N.H. Nicolas, London, 1827.

*Chronique des quatre premiers Valois (1327-1393)*, ed. S. Luce (SHF), New York, repr., 1965.

Cuvelier *Chronicle de Bertrand Du Guesclin*, ed. E. Chariere, 2 vols, Paris, 1839.

*Eulogium Historiarum,* ed. F.S. Haydon, 3 vols, London, 1858-63.

Froissart, Jean – editions, *The Chronicles of Froissart*, trans. John Bouchier Lord Berners, ed. G.C. Macaulay, London, 1895; *Froissart's Chronicles*, ed. John Jolliffe, London, 1968; *Chronicles, Froissart*, ed. G. Brerton, Harmondsworth, 1976; *Oeuvres*, ed. Kervyn de Lettenhove, Brussels, 1867-77; *Chroniques*, ed. S. Luce, (SHF) Paris, 1869.

Gransden, Antonia, ed. 'A Fourteenth Century Chronicle of the Grey Friars of Lynn', *EHR*, lxxii (1957), 270-8.

Gray, Thomas, *Scalachronica*, ed. and trans. Herbert Maxwell, Glasgow, 1907.

*Knighton's Chronicle, 1337-1399*, ed. G. Martin, Oxford, 1995.

*La guerre de Cent Ans. Textes: Les chroniques de Froissart, Journal des États généraux, Le traité de Brétigny, Complainte sur la bataille de Poitiers et Vues critiques sur la bataille de Poitiers*, ed. S. Luce, Paris, 1972.

'Lanercost Chronicle', ed. and trans. H. Maxwell, *Scottish Historical Review*, vi-x, (1910-14).

Le Bel, Jean *Chronique*, ed. J. Viard et E. Déprez, Paris, 1904.

Murimuth, Adam *Continuatio Chronicarum*, ed. E.M. Thompson, London, (Rolls Ser.), 1889.

Walsingham, Thomas *Chronicon Angliae*, trans. E.M. Thompson, London (Rolls Ser.), 1874.

Walsingham, Thomas *Historia Anglicana*, ii, ed. H.T. Riley, London (Rolls Ser.), 1863.

## SECONDARY SOURCES

Ainsworth, Peter 'Froissardian Perspectives on Late Fourteenth Century Society', *Orders and Hierarchies in Late Medieval and Renaissance Europe*, ed. Jeffrey Denton, Manchester, 1999, 56-73.

Aston, Margaret, *Lollards and Reformers: Images and Literacy in Late Medieval Religion*, London, 1984.

Ayton, Andrew, *Knights and Warhorses: Military Service and the English Aristocracy under Edward III*, Woodbridge, 1994.

——————— 'The English Army and the Normandy Campaign of 1346', *England and Normandy in the Middle Ages*, ed. David Bates and Anne Curry, London, 1994, 253-68.

——————— 'English Armies in the Fourteenth Century', *Arms, Armies and Fortifications in the Hundred Years War*, ed. A. Curry and M. Hughes, Woodbridge, 1994, 21-38.

Baker, Denise N. 'Meed and the Economics of Chivalry in *Piers Ploughman*', *Inscribing the Hundred Years War in French and English Cultures*, ed. Denise N. Baker, Albany, 2000.

Barber, Richard *Edward Prince of Wales and Aquitaine: A Biography of the Black Prince,* Woodbridge, 1978.

——————— *Life and Campaigns of the Black Prince*, Woodbridge, repr. 1986.

——————— and Barker, Juliet *Tournaments. Jousts, Chivalry and Pageants in the Middle Ages*, Woodbridge, 1989.

——————— *The Knight and Chivalry*, rev. ed., Woodbridge, 1995.

Bardonnet, A. *Procès-verbal de deliverance a Jean Chandos commissaire du roi d'Angleterre des places Françaises abandonees par le traite de Brétigny*, Niort, 1867.

Barnie, J. *War in Medieval Society: Social Values and the Hundred Years War, 1337-99*, London, 1974.

Barron, C.M. 'The Deposition of Richard II', *Politics and Crisis in Fourteenth Century England*, ed. John Taylor and Wendy Childs, Gloucester, 1990, 132-49.

Baumont, Stéphane, ed. *Histoire d'Agen*, Toulouse, 1991.

Bennett, M. 'The Development of Battle Tactics in the Hundred Years War', *Arms, Armies and Fortifications in the Hundred Years War*, ed. Anne Curry and M. Hughes, Woodbridge, 1994, 1-20.

Bennett, M.J. 'Courtly Literature and Northwest England in the Later Middle Ages', *Court and Poet*, ed. Glyn S. Burgess, Liverpool, 1981, 69-78.

——————— 'Edward III's Entail and the Succession to the Crown, 1376-1471', *EHR*, cxiii (1998), 580-607.

Bock, F. 'Some New Documents Illustrating the Early Years of the Hundred Years War (1353-1356)', *Bulletin of the John Rylands Library*, xv (1931), 60-99.

Boulton, D'A.J.D. *The Knights of the Crown. The Monarchical Orders of Knighthood in Later Medieval Europe, 1325-1520,* Woodbridge, 1987.

———————— 'Insignia of Power: The Use of Heraldic and Paraheraldic Devices by Italian Princes, c.1350 - c.1500', *Art and Politics in Late Medieval and Early Renaissance Italy, 1250-1500*, ed. Charles M. Rosenburg, Indiana, 1990, 103-27.

Boutruche, Robert *La crise d'une société: seigneurs et paysans du Bordelais pendant la Guerre de Cent Ans*, new ed., Paris, 1963.

Bradbury, Jim *The Medieval Archer*, New York, 1985.

———————— *The Medieval Siege*, Woodbridge, 1992.

Bueil, Jean de *Le Jouvencel*, ii, ed. C. Favre et L. Lecestre, Paris, 1887-9.

Burrows, Montagu *The Family of Brocas of Beaurepaire and Roche Court*, London, 1886.

Capra, Pierre 'Le séjour du Prince Noir, lieutenant du Roi, à l'Archévêché de Bordeaux (20 Septembre 1355 – 11 Avril 1357)', *Revue historique du Bordeaux et du département Gironde*, NS 7 (1958), 241-52.

———————— 'L'Administration Anglo-Gasconne au temps de la lieutenance du Prince Noir, 1354-62', Unpub. Thesis, Paris, 1972.

Carte, Thomas *Catalogue des rôles Gascons, Normans et Français dans les archives de la Tour de Londres*, 2 vols, London and Paris, 1746.

Catto, Jeremy 'Fellows and Helpers: The Religious Identity of the Followers of Wyclif', *The Medieval Church: Universities, Heresy and the Religious Life*, ed. Peter Biller and Barry Dobson (*SCH* Susidia 11), Woodbridge, 1999, 141-62.

Chaplais, Pierre 'The Chancery of Guienne, 1289-1453', *Studies Presented to Sir Hillary Jenkinson*, ed. J. Conway-Davies, London, 1957, 61-96.

———————— 'Some Documents Regarding the Fulfilment and Interpretation of the Treaty of Brétigny', *Camden Miscellany*, 3rd ser., xix (1952), 5-84.

Chareyron, N. 'De chronique en roman: l'étrange épopée amoreuse de la jolie fille de Kent', *Le Moyen Age*, 5th ser., 8 (1994), 185-204.

Cokayne, George Edward *The Complete Peerage of England, Scotland, Ireland, Great Britain and the United Kingdom*, 14 vols, London, 1910-59.

Cole, H. *The Black Prince*, London, 1976.

Collins, Hugh 'The Order of the Garter, 1348-1461: Chivalry and Politics in Later Medieval England', *Courts, Counties and the Capital in the Later Middle Ages*, ed. Diana E.S. Dunn, Far Thrupp, 1996, 155-80.

———————— *The Order of the Garter, 1348-1461. Chivalry and Politics in Late Medieval England*, Oxford, 2000.

Contamine, Philippe *Guerre, État et Société à la fin du Moyen Âge. Etudes sur les Armées des Rois de France, 1337-1494*, Paris, 1972.

———————— *L'oriflamme de Saint-Denis aux xive et xve siècles*, Nancy, 1975.

———————— *War in the Middle Ages*, trans. M. Jones, Oxford, 1984.

Coss, Peter *The Knight in Medieval England, 1100-1400*, Stroud, 1993.

Cuttler, S.H. *The Law of Treason and Treason Trials in Later Medieval France*, Cambridge, 1981.

Danbury, Elizabeth 'English and French Propaganda During the Period of the Hundred Years War: Some Evidence from Royal Charters', *Power, Culture and Religion in France c.1350 – c.1550*, ed. C.T. Allmand, Woodbridge, 1989, 75-97.

Davies, R.R. *Lordship and Society in the March of Wales, 1282-1400*, Oxford, 1978.

Delisle, Léopold *Histoire du château et des sires de Saint-Sauveur-le-Vicomte*, Valognes, 1867.

Delpit, J. *Collection générale des documents Français qui se trouvent en Angleterre*, Paris, 1847.

Denholm-Young, Noel 'The Tournament in the Thirteenth Century', *Studies in Medieval History Presented to F.M. Powicke*, ed. R.W. Hunt, W.A. Pantin and R.W. Southern, Oxford, 1948, 240-68.

Denifle, Henri *La guerre de cent ans et la désolation des églises, monasteres et hospitaux en France*, Paris, 1902.

Déprez, E. 'La bataille de Nájera: le comuniqué de la Prince Noir', *Revue Historique*, cxxxvi (1921), 37-59.

Desportes, Pierre *Reims et les Remois aux xiiie et xive siècles*, Paris, 1979.

DeVries, Kelly *Medieval Military Technology*, Ontario, 1992.

Duby, Georges *The Chivalrous Society*, trans. Cynthia Postan, London, 1977.

Ducourtieux, Paul *Histoire de Limoges*, Limoges, 1925, repr. Marseille, 1975.

Dupont-Ferrier, G. *Gallia Regia ou état des officiers royaux des bailliages et des sénéchausées de 1328 à 1515*, Paris, 1942.

Dupuy, Micheline *Le Prince Noir. Edouard seigneur d'Aquitaine*, Paris, 1970.

Elstow, Clara *Pedro the Cruel of Castile, 1350-1369*, Leiden, New York and Köln, 1995.

Emerson, Barbara *The Black Prince*, London, 1976.

Evans, D.L. 'Some Notes on the History of the Principality of Wales in the Time of the Black Prince, 1343-1376', *Transactions of the Honourable Society of Cymrodorion* (1925-6), 25-107.

Favreau, Robert 'Le cession de La Rochelle à l'Angleterre en 1360', *La France Anglaise au Moyen Age*, Paris, 1988, 217-31.

Fowler, Kenneth *The King's Lieutenant: Henry of Grosmont, First Duke of Lancaster*, London, 1969.

———————— 'Letters and Dispatches of the Fourteenth Century', *Guerre et societé en France en Angleterre et en Bourgogne XIV^e-XV^e siècles*, ed. Philippe Contamine, Charles Giry-Deloison et M. Keen, Lille, 1991, 63-92.

———————— *Medieval Mercenaries. Volume 1 The Great Companies*, Oxford, 2001.

Galway, M. 'The Wilton Diptych: A Postscript', *Archaeological Journal*, cvii, 1952 (for 1950), 9-14.

Gillespie, J.L. 'Richard II's Knights: Chivalry and Patronage', *Journal of Medieval History*, 13 (1987), 143-59.

———————— 'Richard II: Chivalry and Kingship', *The Age of Richard II*, ed. James L. Gillespie, Stroud, 1997, 115-38.

———————— 'Richard II: King of Battles?', *The Age of Richard II*, ed. James L. Gillespie, Stroud, 1997, 139-64.

Given-Wilson, C. and Curteis, Alice *The Royal Bastards of Medieval England*, London, 1984.

———————— *The Royal Household and the King's Affinity: Service, Politics and Finance in England, 1360-1413*, New Haven, 1986.

———————— *The English Nobility in the Late Middle Ages: the Fourteenth Century Political Community*, London, 1987.

Goodman, A.W., ed. *Chartulary of Winchester Cathedral*, Winchester, 1927.

Gordon, Dillian 'The Wilton Diptych: An Introduction', *The Regal Image of Richard II and the Wilton Diptych*, ed. Dillian Gordon, Lisa Monnas and Caroline Elam, London, 1997, 19-26.

Gransden, Antonia *Historical Writing in England, ii, c.1307 to the Early Sixteenth Century*, London, 1982.

Green, David S. 'The Household and Military Retinue of Edward the Black Prince', 2 vols, Unpub. PhD thesis, University of Nottingham, 1998.

———————— 'The Later Retinue of Edward the Black Prince', *Nottingham Medieval Studies*, xliv (2000), 141-51.

———————— 'The Military Personnel of Edward the Black Prince', *Medieval Prosopography*, 21 (2000), 133-52.

———————— 'Politics and Service with Edward the Black Prince', *The Age of Edward III*, ed. J. Bothwell, Woodbridge, 2001, 53-68.

Green, R.F. 'The *Familia Regis* and the *Familia Cupidinis*', *English Court Culture*, ed. Scattergood and Sherborne, 87-108.

Hardy, Robert 'The Longbow', *Arms, Armies and Fortifications in the Hundred Years War*, ed. Anne Curry and Michael Hughes, Woodbridge, 1994, 161-82.

Harriss, G.L. *King, Parliament and Public Finance in Medieval England to 1369*, Oxford, 1975.

Harvey, J. *The Black Prince and his Age*, London, 1976.

Harvey, Margaret *The English in Rome, 1362-1420.Portrait of an Expatriate Community*, Cambridge, 1999.

Henneman, John Bell *Royal Taxation in Fourteenth Century France*, Princeton, 1971.

———————— *Royal Taxation in Fourteenth Century France. The Captivity and Ransom of John II, 1356-1370*, Philadelphia, 1976.

Hewitt, H.J. *The Black Prince's Expedition of 1355-57*, Manchester, 1958.

———————— *The Organisation of War under Edward III*, Manchester, 1966.

Higounet, Charles, ed. *Histoire de l'Aquitaine*, Toulouse, 1971.

Higounet-Nadal, Arlette *Perigeux au xiv^e et xv^e siècles*, Bordeaux, 1978.

*Histoire générale de Languedoc*, ed. C. Devic et J. Vaissete *et al.*, 16 vols, Osnabrück, 1973.

Housley, Norman 'The Mercenary Companies, the Papacy and the Crusades, 1356-1378', *Traditio*, xxxvii (1982), 253-80.

Hudson, Anne *The Premature Reformation: Wycliffite Texts and Lollard History*, Oxford, 1988.

Jones, Michael *Ducal Brittany, 1364-99*, Oxford, 1970.

——————— 'Sir Thomas Dagworth et la guerre civile en Bretagne au xiv<sup>e</sup> siècle: quelques documents inédits', *Annales de Bretagne*, lxxxviii (1980), 621-39.

——————— 'Edward III's Captains in Brittany', *England in the Fourteenth Century. Proceedings of 1985 Harlaxton Symposium*, ed. W.M. Ormrod, Woodbridge, 1986, 99-118.

——————— and Walker, S. 'Private Indentures for Life Service in Peace and War', *Camden Miscellany*, xxxii (1994), 1-190;

Jones, Terry *Chaucer's Knight*, rev. ed., London, 1994.

Kaeuper, Richard W. and Kennedy, Elspeth *The Book of Chivalry of Geoffroi de Charny: Text, Context and Translation*, Philadelphia, 1996.

Keen, M. *The Laws of War in the Late Middle Ages*, London, 1965.

——————— 'Chivalry, Nobility and the Man-at-Arms', *War, Literature and Politics in the Late Middle Ages*, ed. C.T. Allmand, Liverpool, 1976, 32-45.

——————— 'Chaucer's Knight, the English Aristocracy and the Crusade', *English Court Culture in the Later Middle Ages*, ed. V.J. Scattergood and J.W. Sherborne, London, 1983, 45-60.

——————— *Chivalry*, New Haven, 1984.

——————— 'The Influence of Wyclif', *Wyclif in his Times*, ed. Anthony Kenny, Oxford, 1986, 127-46.

——————— 'War and Peace in the Middle Ages', *Nobles, Knights and Men-at-Arms in the Middle Ages*, ed. B.P. McGuire, London and Rio Grande, 1996, 1-20.

Lehoux, Françoise *Jean de France, duc de Berri. Sa vie. Son action politique (1340-1416)*, i, Paris, 1966.

Lewis, N.B. 'The Organisation of Indentured Retinues in Fourteenth Century England', *TRHS*, 4<sup>th</sup> ser., xxvii (1945), 29-39.

*Livre de Coutumes*, ed. Henri Barckhausen (Archives Municipales de Bordeaux), 1890.

Lloyd, John E. ed. *A History of Carmarthenshire*, Cardiff, 1935.

Lopes, Fernao *The English in Portugal, 1367-87*, ed. and trans. Derek W. Lomax and R.J. Oakley, Warminster, 1988.

Mackay, A. *Spain in the Middle Age: From Frontier to Empire, 1000-1500*, London, 1977.

Marin, Jean-Yves 'Geoffroy d'Harcourt: une 'conscience normande'', *La Normandie dans la guerre de Cent Ans, 1346-1450*, ed. Jean-Yves Marin, Caen, 1999.

Mathew, Gervase 'Ideals of Knighthood in Late Fourteenth Century England', *Studies in Medieval History Presented to F.M. Powicke*, ed. R.W. Hunt, W.A. Pantin and R.W. Southern, Oxford, 1948, 354-62.

McFarlane, K.B. 'An Indenture of Agreement Between Two English Knights for Mutual Aid and Counsel in War and Peace', *BIHR*, xxxviii (1965), 200-10.

McGlynn, Sean 'The Myths of Medieval Warfare', *History Today*, 46 (1994), 28-34.

McKisack, May *The Fourteenth Century: 1307-1399*, Oxford, 1959.

Moisant, J. *Le Prince Noir en Aquitaine, 1355-6, 1362-70*, Paris, 1894.

Morgan, Philip 'Cheshire and the Defence of the Principality of Aquitaine', *Transactions of the Historical Society of Lancashire and Cheshire*, 128 (1978), 139-60.

——————— *War and Society in Medieval Cheshire, 1277-1403*, Manchester (Chetham Society), 1987.

Musgrove, Frank *The North of England. A History*, Oxford, 1990.

Newton, Stella M. *Fashion in the Age of the Black Prince: A Study of the Years 1340-1365*, Woodbridge, 1988.

Orme, N. *From Childhood to Chivalry: The Education of the English Kings and Aristocracy, 1066-1530*, London, 1984.

Packe, M. *King Edward III*, ed. L.C.B. Seaman, London, 1983.

Palmer, J.J.N. 'The War Aims of the Protagonists and the Negotiations for Peace', *The Hundred Years War*, ed. K. Fowler, London, 1971, 51-74.

——————— 'Froissart et le héraut Chandos', *Le Moyen Age*, 88 (1982), 271-92.

Paterson, Linda M. *The World of the Troubadours. Medieval Occitan Society c.1100-c.1300*, Cambridge, 1993.

Pérouas, Louis *Histoire de Limoges*, Toulouse, 1989.

Perroy, Edouard *The Hundred Years War*, trans. W.B. Wells, London, 1951.

Plaisse, André *À travers le Cotentin: la grande chevauchée guerrière d'Édouard III en 1346*, Cherbourg, 1994.

Porter, E. 'Chaucer's Knight, the Alliterative *Morte Arthure* and the Medieval Laws of War: A Reconsideration', *NMS*, xxvii (1983), 56-78.

Pratt, D. 'Wrexham Militia in the Fourteenth Century', *Transactions of the Denbighshire Historical Society*, (1963), 26-40.

Prestwich, Michael *The Three Edwards: War and State in England 1272-1377*, London, 1980.

———————— *Armies and Warfare in the Middle Ages: The English Experience*, New Haven, 1996.

Prince, A.E. 'A Letter of Edward the Black Prince Describing the Battle of Nájera in 1367', *EHR*, xli (1926), 415-18.

———————— 'The Strength of English Armies in the Reign of Edward III', *EHR*, xlvi (1931), 353-71.

*Register of John de Trillek, Bishop of Hereford (A.D. 1344-1361)* ed. Joseph H. Parry, Hereford, 1910-12.

Rey, Maurice *Les finances royales sous Charles VI. Les causes du déficit, 1388-1413*, Paris, 1965, 447.

Rogers, Clifford J. 'The Military Revolutions of the Hundred Years' War', *Journal of Military History*, 57 (1993), 241-78.

———————— 'Edward III and the Dialectics of Strategy', *TRHS*, 6th ser., iv (1994), 83-102.

———————— ed. *The Military Revolution Debate. Readings on the Military Transformation of Early Modern Europe*, Colorado and Oxford, 1995.

———————— 'The Efficacy of the English Longbow: A Reply to Kelly DeVries, *War in History*, 5:2 (1998), 233-42.

———————— *The Wars of Edward III: Sources and Interpretations*, Woodbridge, 1999.

———————— *War Cruel and Sharp*, Woodbridge, 2000.

Roskell, J.S., Clarke, L., Rawcliffe, C., ed. *History of Parliament, 1386-1421*, 4 vols, Stroud, 1993.

Runyan, Timothy J. 'The Constabulary of Bordeaux: The Accounts of John Ludham (1372-3) and Robert de Wykford (1373-5)', *Mediaeval Studies*, xxxvi (1974), i, 215-58; ii, xxxvii (1975), 42-84.

———————— 'Ships and Mariners in Later Medieval England', *Journal of British Studies*, 16:2 (1977), 1-17.

Russell, P.E. *The English Intervention in Spain and Portugal in the Time of Edward III and Richard II*, Oxford, 1955.

———————— 'The War in Spain and Portugal', *Froissart: Historian*, ed. J.J.N. Palmer, Woodbridge, 1981.

Salter, Elizabeth 'The Timeliness of Wynnere and Wastoure', *Medium Aevum*, 43 (1977), 48-59.

Sandquist, T.A. 'The Holy Oil of St Thomas of Canterbury', *Essays in Medieval History Presented to Bertie Wilkinson*, 330-44.

Saul, Nigel *Richard II*, New Haven, 1997.

———————— 'Richard II's Ideas of Kingship', *Regal Image of Richard II*, ed. Gordon *et al.*, 27-32.

Scaglione, Aldo *Knights at Court. Courtliness, Chivalry and Courtesy From Ottonian Germany to the Italian Renaissance*, Berkeley and Los Angeles, 1991.

Scattergood, V.J. ed. *The Works of Sir John Clanvowe*, Cambridge, 1975.

———————— 'Literary Culture at the Court of Richard II', *English Court Culture in the Later Middle Ages*, ed. V.J. Scattergood and J.W. Sherborne, London, 1983, 29-44.

Secousse, D.F., ed. *Ordonnances des roys de France de la troisie´me race, recueillies par ordre chronologique, etc.*, 23 vols, 1723-1849, repr. Farnborough, 1967.

Sharpe, Margaret 'The Administrative Chancery of the Black Prince Before 1362', *Essays in Medieval History Presented to T.F. Tout*, Manchester, 1925, 321-33.

Sherborne, James 'Aspects of English Court Culture in the Later Fourteenth Century', *English Court Culture*, ed. Scattergood and Sherborne, 1-28.

Sherborne, James 'John of Gaunt, Edward III's Retinue and the French Campaign of 1369', *Kings and Nobles in the Later Middle Ages*, ed. Ralph A. Griffiths and James Sherborne, Gloucester, 1986, 41-61.

*Sir Gawain and the Green Knight*, trans. Brian Stone, 2nd ed., Harmondsworth, 1975.

Smith, Robert D. 'Artillery and the Hundred Years War: Myth and Interpretation', *Arms, Armies and Fortifications*, ed. Curry and Hughes, 151-60.

Southworth, John *The English Medieval Minstrel*, Woodbridge, 1980.

Steel, A.B. *Richard II*, Cambridge, 1941.

Stockton, Eric W. *The Major Latin Works of John Gower*, Seattle, 1962.

Storey-Challenger, S. *L'administration anglaise du Ponthieu apres le traité de Brétigny, 1361-1369*, Abbeville, 1975.

Sumption, Jonathan *The Hundred Years War, i: Trial by Battle*, London, 1990.

———————— *The Hundred Years War ii: Trial by Fire*, London, 1999.

Taylor, John *English Historical Literature in the Fourteenth Century*, Oxford, 1987.

———————— *The Universal Chronicle of Ranulph Higden*, Oxford, 1966.

Thomson, J.A.F. 'Orthodox Religion and the Origins of Lollardy', *History*, 74 (1989), 39-55.

Timbal, Pierre-Clément *La Guerre de Cent Ans vue à travers les registres du Parlement, 1337-1369*, Paris, 1961.

Tourneur-Aumont, J.M. *La Bataille de Poitiers (1356) et la construction de la France*, Paris, 1940.

Tout, T.F. 'Some Neglected Fights Between Crécy and Poitiers', *EHR*, xx (1905), 726-30.

———— 'Firearms in England in the Fourteenth Century', *EHR*, xxvi (1911), 666-702.

———— *Chapters in the Administrative History of Mediaeval England. The Wardrobe, the Chamber and the Small Seal*, 6 vols, Manchester, 1920-33.

Tucoo-Chala, Pierre *Gaston Fébus et la vicomté de Béarn (1343-1391)*, Bordeaux, 1959.

———— *Gaston Fébus: un grand prince d'Occident au XIV^e siècle*, Pau, 1976.

Turnbull, Stephen *The Book of the Medieval Knight*, London, 1985.

Turville-Petre, T. *The Alliterative Revival*, Cambridge, 1977.

Vale, J. *Edward III and Chivalry. Chivalrous Society and its Context, 1270-1350*, Woodbridge, 1982.

Vale, Malcolm *The Angevin Legacy and the Hundred Years War, 1250-1340*, Oxford, 1990.

———— 'The War in Aquitaine', *Arms, Armies and Fortifications*, ed. Curry and Hughes, 69-82.

———— *The Origins of the Hundred Years War: the Angevin Legacy, 1250-1340*, Oxford, 1996.

Varin, Pierre ed. *Archives administratives de la ville de Reims*, Paris, 1848.

Verbruggen, J.F. *The Art of Warfare in Western Europe During the Middle Ages: From the Eighth Century to 1340*, trans. Sumner Willard and Mrs R.W. Southern, 2^nd ed. Woodbridge, 1997.

Viard, J. 'La campagne de juillet-août 1346 et la bataille de Crécy', *Le Moyen Age*, 2^nd ser., xxvii (1926), 1-84.

Wentersdorf, Karl P. 'The Clandestine Marriages of the Fair Maid of Kent', *Journal of Medieval History*, 5 (1979), 203-31.

Wilkins, Nigel 'Music and Poetry at Court: England and France in the Late Middle Ages', *English Court Culture*, ed. Scattergood and Sherborne, 183-204.

J. Wogan-Browne ed. *Medieval Women: Texts and Contexts in Late Medieval Britain*, Turnhout, Belgium, 2000.

Wolfe, Michael 'Siege Warfare and the *Bonnes Villes* of France During the Hundred Years War', *The Medieval City Under Siege*, ed. Ivy A. Corfis and Michael Wolfe, Woodbridge, 1995, 49-66.

Wood, Charles T. *The Age of Chivalry. Manners and Morals, 1000-1450*, London, 1970.

Wright, Nicholas *Knights and Peasants, The Hundred Years War in the French Countryside*, Woodbridge, 1998.

Wrottesley, G. *Crécy and Calais* (William Salt Archæological Society, 18), 1880.

# List of Abbreviations

| | |
|---|---|
| *BIHR* | Bulletin of the Institute of Historical Research |
| BL | British Library |
| *BPR* | *The Register of Edward the Black Prince preserved in the Public Record Office*, ed. M.C.B Dawes, 4 vols, London, 1930-33 |
| *CCR* | Calendar of Close Rolls |
| *C.Inq.Misc.* | Calendar of Inquistions Miscellaneous |
| *CIPM* | Calendar of Inquisitions Post Mortem |
| *CPR* | Calendar of Patent Rolls |
| *DNB* | Dictionary of National Biography |
| *EHR* | English Historical Review |
| *GEC* | G.E. Cokayne, *The Complete Peerage*, 13 vols, London, 1910-59 |
| Henxteworth | The day-book or *journale* of Sir John Henxteworth, Duchy of Cornwall Office |
| *NMS* | Nottingham Medieval Studies |
| PRO | Public Record Office, London |
| Rymer | Thomas Rymer, *Feodera, conventiones, literæ, et cujuscunque generis acta publica, inter reges Angliæ* etc, (2 editions, 1704-35; 1816-69.) |
| *TRHS* | Transactions of the Royal Historical Society |
| *VCH* | Victoria County History |

# INDEX